Lead to Succeed

The Only Leadership Book You Need

Mach 2 leadership in the 'new world of work' –
how to maximise your own, your people's and your
organisation's performance

Chris Roebuck

Lead to Succeed: the only leadership book you need

First published in 2014 by:

Wordscapes Ltd
Second Floor, Elevator Studios
27 Parliament Street
Liverpool, L8 5RN
England

www.wordscape.org.uk

ISBN: 978-0-9576945-6-9

A CIP Catalogue record for this book is available from the British Library.

Publisher: Fiona Shaw
Editor: Deborah Mulhearn
Design, typesetting and production: Ken Ashcroft
Editorial assistant: Thomas Jones

Contents

	Page

Introduction   v

Chapter 1:   1
The 'new world of work':
Why leadership matters so much more to your people and organisation

Chapter 2:   29
Moving to Mach 1 for individual leaders:
How to maximise efforts from your team

Chapter 3:   71
Step-by-step to Mach 1:
A toolkit for individual leaders

Chapter 4:   113
Moving to Mach 1 for teams and organisations:
How to maximise the effort from all your people

Chapter 5:   151
Moving to Mach 2 for individual leaders:
How to focus team effort onto what really matters and delivers success

Chapter 6:   175
Moving to Mach 2 for teams and organisations:
How to align everyone's effort into what matters and delivers success

Chapter 7:   203
UBS:
A 'real world' example of Mach 1 and Mach 2
delivering individual and organisational success

Chapter 8:   219
Mach 2 – the holistic catalyst for success in the 21st century –
The alignment of effort and collaboration

Introduction

WHY DID I WRITE THIS BOOK?

Over nearly 40 years I have seen great, good, indifferent and poor leadership across the world. The benefits that good leaders bring to the people they lead are significant – whether for a nation or a workplace team. I think there are too many people who are not inspired, or even worse, who hate going to work. That's literally billions of people across the world who aren't engaged at work[1]. And that not only means that their organisations don't perform well, it also makes their lives unfulfilled and affects their families. One survey showed that, out of all the bosses people had experienced, they would only willingly work again for 38% of them[2].

So I decided to go on a mission – a personal mission to make the world a better place! I would love to bring peace and harmony to the world, but even the United Nations (UN) can't do that, so sadly I have no chance. But I do believe that many, many people could have a more fulfilled life if I could help their leaders improve. I believe that good leaders enable their people to lead more fulfilled lives, be they leaders of nations, leaders of organisations or leaders of teams.

The simple, practical ideas in this book are drawn from my own experience and the leadership success I have seen across the world. From the Red Cross in Myanmar, major government organisations in China, top investment banks in the US to small organisations with only 10 employees, and the 1.4m employees of the UK National Health Service, better leadership can become a reality. I know it can because I've worked with them all.

This, then, is why I wrote this book: to launch my mission for fulfilment at work, to enable all individuals, teams and organisations to perform at their best. And to have many more happy individuals and families around the world who benefit from a genuinely inspiring work life and economic growth driven by slick, efficient, effective customer-focused organisations that care about their employees, the environment and society. Many will say that there isn't an issue but the figures show otherwise. 54% of people who are not being led well at work admit that the stress caused by this led them to behave badly to friends or family members, and the same percentage said that this negatively affected their health[3].

'The fault, dear Brutus, is not in our stars, But in ourselves, that we are underlings.'
Cassius in William Shakespeare's *Julius Caesar*, British playwright (d. 1616)

The ideas in this book are simple, practical and can be implemented quickly, and most importantly have been tested out in practice in the workplace. They apply not only to individual leaders, but also to leaders of leaders and organisations. It's no good just one or two leaders doing this as individuals – everyone has to join the mission to make it work. So welcome to the global mission for fulfilment at work, which gets leaders to the leading edge faster by way of Mach 2 leadership, to borrow an aeronautical term. All of this had to be delivered in one book – the only leadership book anyone should need to buy.

And you can take control and do it, starting now.

WHY IS THIS THE ONLY LEADERSHIP BOOK YOU WILL NEED TO BUY?

Simple: because it aims to help you become a Mach 2 leader irrespective of whether you are in a large corporation, a public body, a not-for-profit or a small or medium enterprise. This book explains in a simple way the critical, practical actions you need to take:

1. As an individual to be effective in your own work
2. As a leader to get maximum effort from your team
3. As an organisation or senior leader to get maximum effort from all your people
4. As a leader to then focus that maximum effort onto what is critical for the success of your organisation
5. As an organisation to align the effort of all your leaders and people onto maximising the organisation's performance
6. As a leader who can deliver all the above in the new world of work.

As you move through your career these are the six key goals that you have to achieve as an individual leader and, once you become one, as a senior leader responsible for other leaders or leading an organisation as a whole. This book also explains the systems that need to be in place that will help your organisation maximise the performance of people in a co-ordinated way and thus maximise the performance of the whole organisation. Much of this will need to be facilitated by the human resources (HR) function, and so this book is a good guide for those in HR as well.

This is not marketing hype; if you take the actions suggested in this book, which are proven to enable personal, professional, team and organisational success, then you will get a significant return on the time you invested in reading it, have a more rewarding work life, and on top of that get the associated benefits in your personal and family life – making you an example for others to also take up the Mach 2 mission. That's why there is no section on marketing yourself or career development in this book. If you implement what's in this book, what you achieve will lead to natural advancement at a much faster rate than your colleagues who haven't read it.

THE EVIDENCE

Everything said in this book is backed by evidence from a range of sources, personal observation over many years in working with leaders and organisations round the world together with published evidence from practitioners and academics. You will see that there are many references to support the statements made in the text. Please note that in most cases these are only one or two of the significant number of additional references that could also have been quoted but had to be omitted because of lack of space. So the evidence you see both in text and references is not exhaustive, but rather the tip of the iceberg.

SO WHAT'S THE BIG IDEA ?

The basis of the book – as founded in a massive volume of research studies and real world observations on what bring success – is really simple. It's applying what we do everyday for ourselves to achieve success in our personal lives to achieve success at work. We put in maximum effort to do what we want done and apply that effort onto exactly that and nothing else – be that decorating a room, learning to play a musical instrument, running a marathon or climbing Mount Everest. Maximum effort applied to what matters. The book just takes that idea and transfers it to work and gets everyone to do it together. So:

    Mach 1 – maximise the effort
    Mach 2 – apply it to what needs to be done and nothing else

WHY CALL IT MACH 2 LEADERSHIP?

Because it's leadership that maximises employee effort and collaboration and focuses it on what really matters for success. The term Mach 2 leadership is used in the book to describe leaders and organisations that are going further, moving faster and are at the leading edge of performance. Mach 1 is travelling at the speed of sound; Mach 2 is twice that. It describes aircraft at the leading edge of what is possible.

One example of such world-beating performance is Concorde, the only supersonic passenger aircraft. It went higher, faster, further than other aircraft, and still inspires people today. Concorde cruised at 60,000ft at Mach 2, twice the speed of sound, while every other plane, including many military jets, couldn't keep up. All other passenger aircraft were below Mach 1 and flying half as high, as they still are. Concorde, at a stroke, halved the travel time between Europe and the US, reducing it to three and a half hours. And it was a product of a group of individuals determined to go to the leading edge of what was possible in terms of the technology of the time.

So Mach 2 is a simple approach to leadership that seeks to help determined individuals and organisations get to the leading edge of what is possible in leadership and be the best: Mach 2 leaders creating a Mach 2 organisation. This book takes you through Mach 1, the speed of sound in terms of leadership, and onto Mach 2, the leading edge of what's possible.

THE NEW WORLD OF WORK

Why do we need to get to Mach 2? Because we are facing a more and more challenging world within which we are expected to perform better and better. People are feeling pushed to their limits and need help to understand that they can get even better, and this book will help you meet that challenge, in a way that is sustainable and effective, by bringing your people with you rather than pushing them to the point where they break or leave.

Mach 2 isn't an untested idea; it's based on actions that have already worked for successful people and organisations. Unlike most leadership books, this one provides ideas not only for you as an individual but also for you as an organisational leader, to help you to develop the performance of your team, your department or even the whole organisation. Mach 2 will work in all types of organisations from SMEs to large global corporations, from highly competitive commercial business to not-for-profits, from the US to China.

Even in the 21st century too many leaders in our organisations are still leading in an outdated 20th century way – and some are even using 19th century-style command and control. Mach 2 leadership is what's needed for the 21st century and the new world of work emerging.

Power and position are no longer enough; you cannot demand respect, you have to earn it. The way we now work, and how people expect to be treated, means that leaders have to build collaborative relationships, rather than use coersion, to be effective. But too many leaders lack the key skills to meet this challenge individually, and also the wider challenges that their organisations face in the 21st century.

Leadership is therefore, more than ever, a two way process: without willing followers you cannot lead; without collaboration you cannot succeed; without your people giving you their best you cannot deliver. Mach 2 is designed to take you and your organisation beyond the old 20th century leadership styles to those needed in the 21st century to be the best through simple, practical and proven steps to success. The world has moved on; the old approach no longer works. It only leads to a slow decline into failure.

As an individual, Mach 2 is designed to provide some really simple and practical ways to help you reach your full potential. But it is not just about you. If you are at Mach 2 then as you progress on your path to success you will help others do the same by your example. Furthermore, it will impact positively on your life outside work as you become more effective in work, enabling you to have a better personal life as well.

Sadly, too often, I have seen people who don't enjoy going to work, whose potential is wasted and whose organisations are often performing badly; both individual and organisation failing to reach the potential they have. This is a tragic waste of potential for success – organisations failing to satisfy their customers and maximise their performance, individuals feeling unfulfilled and this often having negative impact on family and friends as a result. Not only that but it restricts economic growth within the country concerned, every increase in engagement increasing GDP, such that for example UK could produce £59.5bn in additional GDP if people were more engaged at work[4]. Similar comparators apply to other economies globally.

IT'S THE SAME THE WHOLE WORLD OVER

People seem to assume that the challenges faced by organisations are different around the world. I have not found this to be the case at all in over 20 years of talking to leaders and groups of leaders from all types of organisations. I always ask leaders or groups of leaders what they want to achieve. The list is always the same, that is, to:

1. Try to get better all the time
2. Be more customer focused
3. Deliver a better quality product or service
4. Run a more efficient process
5. Innovate where we can
6. Keep costs down more effectively
7. Get more effort from our people
8. Make sure every employee understands what we are trying to achieve.

The order of priority, description and how they are delivered vary depending on type of organisation, culture and other factors, but the list seems to be consistent. As an indication of the consistency here are a few examples of organisations where leaders have identified these: HSBC, UK National Health Service, China Aviation Industry Corporation, Red Cross, GE Healthcare, Prudential, Eurostar, international law firms, British Airways, BP, UBS, Microsoft, and China Aeronautical & Scientific Corporation (the Chinese space programme).

IS LEADERSHIP DIFFERENT DEPENDING ON WHERE YOU ARE?

This book is designed to help leaders, or those wishing to be leaders anywhere in the world, so the commonality, or otherwise, of effective leadership across the globe is key. There has been much research work done, and much ongoing, for example the Global Leadership and Organisational Behaviour Effectiveness Research Project (GLOBE[5]), started in 1993 and covering over 800 organisations in 62 countries, and work by Hofstede[6] and Trompenaars[7]. To make this mass of information simple and practical for the purposes of this book, I take the following view based on a combination of the main research and my own experience. There are two key areas:

Core Common Leadership – human beings want the same core things out of work – or their boss and organisation – the world over. This conclusion is based on my own 'testing' using the 'best boss' list over 20 years across the globe, explained later and other[8] research.

Culturally Variable Leadership – but the way this is delivered must be adapted in a way that matches the society within which the organisation operates, for example, Anglo Saxon, Scandinavian or Asian, and the business model that it uses, for example is it essentially transactional or relationship based in its business? This again reflects both research studies and my own experience.

A further factor is that global organisations tend to reflect their 'base' location in their internal culture and systems. A Chinese or US-based organisation will to some degree reflect that national culture in the way it works globally. So a leader within a global organisation has to make sure they deliver the core common elements of leadership, but adapt it where required to the 'local' environment. Leaders leading in a single country often have a much less complex experience than those working across multiple cultures and time zones.

Here I would advise that the one thing likely to doom any leader when they work with others from a different culture is when they take an attitude of cultural superiority. As we will see, humility, the ability to learn from and listen to others is a crucial part of the effective leader's behaviour. There will be more discussion of this cultural element in Chapter 2.

IN THE REAL WORLD WITH REAL PEOPLE IN REAL ORGANISATIONS

This book isn't an academic review of leadership theories. I may be a visiting professor but we don't need a theoretical debate; what matters is doing things day-to-day in the real world that improve performance and make a difference. That's what leadership is about: the clue is in the word 'lead', which suggests movement from one place to another. And it's about positive transformation; hopefully you don't want to move to a worse place than you are currently in, but a better one.

Over the past 30 years much academic leadership theory has become more and more complex in an attempt to find the 'right' answer. This is laudable but the problem is that in so doing the leadership models often used are so complex they have ceased to be of practical use to those who lead day by day in real organisations. Also, this is not a quick fix; changing people and organisations takes time and effort. But if you use Mach 2 it minimises the time it takes and maximises your chances of success.

This book will help you understand the challenge that you and your organisation face and give you simple, practical ways to make it work. If you can get this right it will make a significant difference to you, your team and, if all leaders in the organisation can do it, your organisation.

BENEFITS OF GETTING TO MACH 2

You, and your organisation, based on evidence from elsewhere, could:

1. Get up to 57% more effort and 20% more performance from your people[9]
2. Improve the performance of new team members by 25%[9] in the first year
3. Deliver better customer service[10]
4. Get you within the top 8% of your peers so you have a 75% chance of being a top performer at the next level – thus increasing your chances of promotion.[11]
5. Improve your organisation's operating income by 52%[12]
6. Be significantly more effective financially[13] overall than competitors
7. Increase total shareholder return by 9.6% over 3 years[14]
8. Reduce the chances of your talent being taken by competitors by 87%[9]
9. Increase willingness to innovate from 3% to 59% of employees[15]
10. Increase profits by 5.8% year-on-year more than comparable business units[16]
11. More than halve sickness absence[17]

And you will see many, many more benefits accrue as you read the book.

References

1. *Driving performance and retention through employee engagement*; Corporate Leadership Council, 2004 and *Working life: employee attitudes and engagement*, K. Truss, E. Soane, C. Edwards, K. Wisdom, A. Croll and J. Burnett; Chartered Institute of Personnel and Development, London, 2006

2. Dr Gordy test results: www.leadershipkeynote.net

3. *Feeling good matters in the workplace*; Gallup Management Journal, 2005 and *Engagement keeps the doctor away*; Gallup Management Journal, 2005

4. *Engage for Success: Enhancing performance through employee engagement*, MacLeod & Clarke; Department of Innovation and Skills, London, July 2009

5. *Culture, Leadership, and Organisations*: The GLOBE Study of 62 Societies, Robert J House et al; Sage Publications, 2004

6. *Cultures and Organisations: Software of the Mind*, Hofstede & Geert: Administrative Science Quarterly (Johnson Graduate School of Management, Cornell University) 38 (1), March 1993 (p132–134) and *The GLOBE debate: Back to relevance*, Hofstede & Geert: Journal of International Business Studies (Sage Publications) 41 (8), 2010 (p1339–46)

7. *Riding the Waves of Culture: Understanding Cultural Diversity in Business*, Fons Trompenaars & Charles Hampden-Turner; Nicholas Brealey Publishing Limited, 2012

8. *Creating the Best Workplace on Earth*, Goffee & Jones; Harvard Business Review, May 2013

9. *Employee engagement framework and survey*; Corporate Leadership Council, 2004

10. *Positive gain spirals at work: From job resources to work engagement, personal initiative and work-unit innovativeness*, J.J. Hakanen, R. Perhoniemi et al; Journal of Vocational Behavior 73(1), 2008 and *The Employee – customer profit chain at Sears*, Rucci, Kirn & Quin; Harvard Business Review, Jan 1998 and *From people to profits*, Hayday & Bevan; Institute for Employment Studies, 1999

11. *Realising the full potential of rising talent*; Corporate Leadership Council, 2005 (p19)

12. *ISR Employee Engagement Report*; Towers Perrin, 2006

13. *Manage your human sigma*, Coffman & Harter; Harvard Business Review, 2005 and *Q12 Meta Analysis*, Harter; Gallup, 2006

14. *Realising the full potential of rising talent*; Corporate Leadership Council, 2005 (p6)

15. *The innovation equation*, Kuger & Killham; Gallup Management Journal 2007

16. Gallup, 2008

17. *Q10 Meta Analysis*, Harter; Gallup, 2006

1

The 'new world of work':
why leadership matters
so much more to your people
and organisation

1

The 'new world of work':
why leadership matters
so much more to your people
and organisation

MANY 'LEADERS' AREN'T LEADERS

First let's smash the myth that someone in a leadership role is automatically a leader. Many aren't. They may be in a role that anticipates effective leadership, but for reasons we will see later this often does not happen. They may be a maintainer – someone who keeps the *status quo* ticking over and who resists change. They may be a self-obsessed climber – someone who is prepared to do anything to make sure they achieve their personal ambitions despite the cost to anyone else. Or they may be out of their depth – promoted to a level where their skills and capabilities do not meet the needs of the role. All of these people could occupy positions classified as leadership roles. That does not mean they are leaders.

Leadership is about what you *do*, not what role you have or which chair you sit in. Just because someone is a CEO does not mean they are a leader: whether they are a leader and how good a leader they are is something only others can judge, because their own opinion may be slightly biased!

This potential bias is clearly demonstrated in a number of self-assessment studies[1] over many years. For example, in the UK in 2010 the Chartered Management Institute (CMI), the UK's main management professional body, surveyed more than 2,000 managers, including those from international organisations working in the UK[2]. They were asked which aspects of management they thought they were best at, while a further 6,000 completed a diagnostic tool to identify their real strengths and weaknesses.

Did self-perception match reality? Just over one-fifth said they were good at getting results compared with 41% that actually were; 20% believed they were strongest at managing themselves, but only 8% were; 44% said they excelled at managing people compared with 37% who were, and 14% felt they were born to lead – an interesting self perception which sounds like a watered down version of the divine right of kings!

Even those defined as delivering high performance from their teams may not be effective leaders, but just good at pressuring people to work very hard. They are not the same, and pressure is not a sustainable approach and causes loss of service quality and higher risks.

Also – no matter what level a leader – what is also clear is that while we know good leaders deliver better organisational performance, as this book shows, exactly what the characteristics of a good leader are is more open to dispute, especially from the psychological perspective. Strangely[3], there is more agreement on what they are for a bad leader [4] and the significant organisational and personal damage they cause. This personal damage impacts on societies as well via increased stress and subsequent medical costs[5].

Perhaps one reason for these shortfalls might have been that the CMI also revealed that a horrifying 63% had no management or leadership training prior to taking up their senior posts and so, potentially, could never have been fully effective in those roles. While this is a UK survey, similar issues are reflected across the world. Thus one key message to anyone reading this book is that, sadly, you may not be quite as good as you think you are – hence the importance of feedback and humility.

Remember that getting your first 'leadership' role leading people does not mean you are a leader. It's what you do in that role that defines whether you are truly a leader. Furthermore, to be effective, much of this capability needs to be developed. The purpose of this book is to help you be that leader, to reach your full potential and hopefully be as good a leader as you can be.

THE NEW REALITY OF ORGANISATIONS AND LEADERSHIP CHALLENGES

We need to understand that as well as the traditional challenges that leaders have always faced, for example motivating people, setting out clear action plans, and making things happen, the changes in the world and society in the past few years have added to those challenges. Twenty-first century challenges demand new and different ways of thinking and acting from leaders and organisations. So what are the challenges that our organisations now face? And what does that mean for you as a leader?

THE NEW ECONOMIC REALITY

The economic downturn at the start of the 21st century forced a reshaping of the economic landscape. The long-established markets in Europe and the US, already slowing in their growth rates, went into recession and even the high growth emerging markets of Asia slowed significantly. In a market that seemed to be constantly growing, organisations that had been structured and run for operation in a growing economy were left struggling in a sharply reduced one.

During this period top lines were dramatically squeezed and the income organisations were receiving from customers was significantly reduced. To counter this, organisations had two simple options: to do less, but in the same way, by cutting back on staff and other costs in the hope that the organisation remained profitable; or to meet its challenges by reviewing how everything was done, how staff were motivated and customers served to find a new way of working to fit the new market conditions.

The first option might have been viable had the downturn continued for a year or two, but as it reached three, four and then five years this became self-defeating, as this mode of operation often could not remain profitable or even viable. As the downturn continued what was needed to meet the challenge was much more than cutbacks, and the latter option, a new way of working, became the only real solution.

As funding from banks and markets tightened there was little room for error. Many organisations were forced to make deeper and deeper cuts in costs as the downturn continued, and this started to restrict their ability to deliver even basic levels of customer service. In the end many organisations failed and this in turn caused further loss of confidence in the economic prospects. This was a global problem, although worse in Europe and the US. So if simply making cuts was not enough, and a new way of working was needed, how did organisations start to adjust?

Not only were markets tougher due to the downturn, but also customers were increasingly careful and demanding, given their own individual income had often reduced as well. The expansion of the Internet also allowed customers wider access to more suppliers and provided them with a greater knowledge of markets. Thus the level of competition rose. This also allowed easier market access for new competitors in many areas, or a new way of delivering products and services, often with technology, that disrupted existing markets.

So the challenge for organisations was effectively: do more with less! But this wasn't enough. The environment that had been created was effectively the economic and organisational version of a perfect storm, where only the strongest would survive.

Yes, organisations needed to do more with less, but they had to do it better in a new way! The doing less is easy, but doing more with less is difficult, and doing more with less but better requires a significant change in the way the organisation works to optimise performance. This applies to all organisations, be they private sector or public; the economic downturn and other factors, such as government funding cuts due to their own falling tax revenues and debt, affected the public as well as the private sector.

The ideas in this book are effective in all sectors, be they private, public or not-for-profit. Falling tax revenues have forced the public sector across the globe to become more effective and efficient to deliver everything from healthcare to infrastructure, and in local and national government and emergency services. As suggested by many reports globally and by international organisations such as the OECD and the UN[6], there is scope for this to be achieved in particular by the public sector adapting approaches used in the private sector, such as efficiency, innovation and a customer-focused mindset that has been embedded in the private sector for years. Not only this but a change to leadership is key. An OECD report[7] *Improving Public Sector Efficiency*

– *Challenges & Opportunities* states clearly: 'Human resource management practices also matter a great deal. The soft aspects of human resource management, such as employee satisfaction and morale, are considered to be the most important drivers of performance.' Thus Mach 2 provides a vital set of tools for the public sector as well as the private sector globally.

The challenge applies even more to the not-for-profit sector, which is faced with an almost unlimited demand on its services but with more limited resources.

> **Challenges for the Red Cross in Myanmar**
>
> This was brought home to me when I was asked by the CEO of the Myanmar Red Cross Society to go to his country to deliver a masterclass on Mach 2 leadership. He introduced me to his leaders with the following words: 'Can you please come to speak to our leaders, as these are the people who make the Red Cross work? If you can tell them about delivering more with less to those in need, that would be a great advantage for us.' The humbling week I spent with the Red Cross in Myanmar confirmed to me that getting leadership right in their world is even more important than in the business world because so many lives depend upon it.

WHAT IS THE IMPACT ON PEOPLE?

As you would expect with reduced headcounts and cost pressures, there are fewer people in organisations to deliver the work. And headcounts have often been reduced more than workloads. As a result, employees are under more and more pressure. Research[8] by the Corporate Executive Board (CEB) and supported by other studies shows that between 2009 and 2012 88% of employees had experienced an increase in workload, 56% had increased hours of work and 78% had experienced an increase in the team workload.

The percentage of employees who said that they did not have sufficient time to complete the work they were expected to do increased from 32% to 55% over the same period, and the proportion of time spent multitasking increased by 15%. Furthermore, everyone is now having to deal with more information, with 76% of employees saying that they are spending more time either finding or dealing with data. This is probably distracting them from higher priorities.

UK-based data from Hay Group paints a similar picture – and is probably reflected elsewhere – where around 60% of employees globally are keen to give their best, but then 33% on average, rising to 42% in Europe and Middle East, feel that their organisation obstructs them from delivering it![9]

From a practical perspective having 55% of employees saying they don't have enough time to deliver what they have been asked to deliver poses very significant questions about the quality of existing leadership. How can you be a competent leader if you give people more work than they can do in the time you have allowed? However, this does not mean that employees could not still improve performance. It is likely that some of this is caused by ineffective prioritisation, with work that is not critical to the organisation's success taking up too much time. Unless Mach 1 leadership engages employees, they will not be delivering maximum effort anyway. Bureaucracy also compounds the problem by removing focus from key priorities. So it is probably false to assume that these figures mean that people have no capability to add more value to the organisation.

HAVE ORGANISATIONS CHANGED?

There are also increasing issues about frequent change and the impact on employees' ability to focus on what needs to be delivered. For example between 2009 and 2012, 63% of employees said that the frequency of change in organisational objectives had increased[8]. Such changes, unless communicated effectively, would cause increased confusion. The economic and organisational drivers have forced organisations to change more than most people realise. Objectives are changed faster to respond to customer and market needs. Organisational structures have had to become more matrixed to deal with the lower headcount, 50% of employees say that they have to deal with more stakeholders to get decisions in 2012 than in 2009. Other trends continue with global dispersion increasing – 57% of employees increasingly have to work with others in different locations. Generation X now makes up 62% of the workforce and these demographic changes also bring different attitudes and approaches to organisations and work/life balance.

SO WHAT ARE THE CURRENT AND FUTURE ORGANISATIONAL CHALLENGES?

The key to continued viability in this new world is to:

1. Maximise the top line by making sure you attract the right customers by offering them the right services or products and then getting them to use them.
2. Maximise the bottom line by finding the most efficient and effective way to deliver those services or products to the customers.

That essentially depends on two critical elements:

1. The right process – to attract customers and deliver
2. People who maximise their effort for you to make the process work

In reality, the success of (1) is dependent on (2).

At the most basic level then, to survive and succeed in the 21st century, an organisation has to get the best from its people. But people already have to work longer and harder to deliver what their organisations want. All of the above suggests that employees are now being pushed to, and perhaps beyond, the limit of what is viable with current leadership and ways of operating.

BUT IT'S LIKELY TO GET EVEN MORE CHALLENGING!

Despite all the *current* challenges about workloads, complexity, demanding customers and limited resources discussed above, organisations, CEOs and investors are expecting better and better performance. The annual objectives set by many organisations demand constant improvements year-on-year. Research by CEB [8] shows that in general terms most CEOs and senior executives say they need a 20% increase in performance to achieve their targets. Set that against the current environment where people are already close to, or at, their limits, then something has to change to make this possible.

As suggested there is likely to be scope for some improvement, but this will only occur if Mach 2 leadership is implemented to ensure that:

• Work critical to organisational success is prioritised

• Mach 1 leadership is achieving maximum effort from employees through engagement.

DON'T LET PROFIT THROUGH COST REDUCTION BECOME THE ONLY FOCUS!

This comment will sound like total madness for anyone in a profit-driven organisation. However, all my experience and a number of studies[13], (see below) show that organisations that focus purely on maximising profit via minimising costs tend to underperform. Customers realise that profits come before service, employees realise that profit comes before their getting fair remuneration and development, and suppliers realise that the relationship is not the 'partnership' they anticipated. This focus on profit often drives leadership behaviour that can have negative effects as we shall see later in Chapter 2.

A total focus on profit through cost cutting will potentially bring a short-term burst of additional financial benefit, but in the longer term, that is anything over one year, the negative effects of this approach start to create an impact – potential loss of customers, loss of key staff/talent, lower employee engagement leading to lower financial performance and even more dangerous, an increase in risk.

Anyone convinced that by cutting costs you inevitably improve profitability should read Raynor and Ahmed's 2012 article[10] in Harvard Business Review. This looks at organisational performance (based on return on assets) for over 25,000 companies over 40 years to identify what the long-term high performers did. They looked at many factors and concluded that what delivered long-term top 10% performance was behaviour based on three rules:

1. Better before cheaper – in other words, compete on differentiators other than price.

2. Revenue before cost – that is, prioritise increasing revenue over reducing costs.

3. There are no other rules – so change anything you must to follow Rules 1 and 2.

Interestingly research by Ambler[11] in 2003 showed that boards spend, on average, nine times more time discussing spending and cashflow issues than where the money comes from and how it could be increased.

There is insufficient space here for deeper analysis of this revelation that key commonly held strategic assumptions could actually be wrong. But a good summary is in the article by Jules Goddard from London Business School, which won the CMI Article of the Year Award in UK in February 2014[12].

What these three rules promote is effectively Mach 1 and Mach 2 – increasing revenue and, if, along the way, people identify potential cost efficiency around them that doesn't affect 'the better before cheaper' rule, then better still. The idea of better not cheaper and total focus on differentiation by quality is also a key objective of Mach 1 and Mach 2. So it is about making the cake bigger and doing so efficiently, rather than making the portion of profit in a smaller cake bigger by reducing cost.

WHERE IS THE RISK?

Based on my experience of the way organisations work, I have long thought that the way an exclusively profit-focused organisation develops its leaders, communicates and conducts its activities, means that the key area of risk is not at senior levels but at middle and junior levels. This may seem strange as the CEO and the board are running the organisation, but they aren't the ones that make the decisions on actions that instigate problems that can turn into disasters. Middle and junior management do that. And in my view they often do so by making assumptions about, or misinterpreting, what they think senior leaders want.

Returning to the question of maximising profit – this is often perceived by middle and junior managers as the only objective from the top; the caveats to this that any sane CEO would add being 'lost in communication' – managing risk, customer service, ethics, sustainability and so on. Admittedly some senior banking leaders prior to the financial crisis did actually send that 'only profits matter' message out, but they – and we – paid the price. As a result of this ineffective communication and assumption, the middle and junior group can go on to take decisions that lead to problems that grow into disasters if not identified and prevented. Mach 2 leadership deals with this danger by making sure leaders at all levels know all the key messages and objectives from the top and all the associated caveats, so the communication and thus the risk management is effective.

Interestingly this has been confirmed by research from CEB SHL data for the Wall Street Journal (WSJ) from December 2013[13]. They examined 20,000 managers about their approach to decision-making, (understanding risk and its impacts) and communications (making sure everyone is clear on key objectives and caveats). What they found from the data in Europe, for example, was that at the most senior levels, just one in 21 leaders was perceived as presenting a risk to the organisation. The global average is one in 14. At the next level down this rose to this average of one in 14, by middle management level it was one in eight, and by junior management level, potentially even more.

Junior management levels are undoubtedly worse because of a lack of experience. But the danger is at middle management level, because they are able to make operational decisions that initiate potential disasters of many types. Moreover, they are in key position to monitor and develop junior leaders. The CEB/WSJ to some degree lays the blame for this at the door of over-promotion of technical experts. I would rather say it's a failure to make sure that any technical experts who are needed in such roles are also effective leaders. That's one of the reasons I wrote this book – to help achieve that.

We touch on this issue again as it has relevance for both individual leaders, leaders who lead other leaders and organisations who need all their leaders to be effective.

So the focus of Mach 2 is to maximise sustainable performance and profit while effectively managing risk. The performance and profits will flow naturally from Mach 2 being in place. Total focus on profit can in practice block Mach 2 from being achieved.

SO HOW CAN THIS BOOK HELP?

If further improvements are to be made to individual or organisational performance with effective risk management, what happens inside organisations has to fundamentally change. In previous years they might have been run along command and control lines, or more recently by aggressive 'macho management'. *These tactics will no longer work.*

> 'I suppose leadership at one time meant muscles; but today it means getting along with people.'
> Mahatma Gandhi (1869-1948), first president of India

Organisations must remove the traditional silo structures and be transformed into 'communities of effort and collaboration' – a phrase we will revisit again and again in this book because it is so important – that maximise effort and work together in an aligned way. They must always seek to deliver the best for the customer in an effective and efficient way that optimises organisational performance, not just do their own work.

This notion of communities of effort and collaboration points the way forward; it's about the 'we' and not the 'me' in the future, and that's the only way such slimmed-down organisations can meet the demands of employees, shareholders, customers, stakeholders, governments and society.

This approach is vital to success. Partnership working and collaboration is key. According to CEB research[8] between 2002 and 2012, the relative importance to business unit profitability of individuals collaborating across the organisation as opposed to working on their own tasks dramatically changed. The importance of individual task working fell from 78% to 51% and the importance of collaboration increased from 22% to 49%. This represents a doubling of the importance of collaboration in these slimmed-down organisations, which makes collaboration with others as important to profitability as working on your own tasks. Getting 50% of employees to contribute organisationally through collaboration could add 4% to profitability, and if all of your staff reaches that collaborative level you could add 12%.

So what do these highly collaborative people do, and how can everyone else replicate this? These high-performing collaborators add value to their organisations in a number of ways:

- 63% transfer great ideas from one part of the organisation to another
- 71% improve procedures or process based on ideas from others
- 78% transfer skills/knowledge effectively to co-workers
- 72% provide useful new ideas for products/services or improvements to process for others
- 81% improve working methods, techniques or tools for others
- The maximum rating for how any low-performance collaborators delivered in any of these areas is 22%.

Few organisations are even aware of this critical change and even fewer have done anything about it. Yet it is key to the future success of organisations and a key element of Mach 2 leadership, which will be looked at in more detail later. But there are challenges for leaders. Hay Group found that 43% of employees don't want to do anything to contribute to their organisation other than their own job[14].

LET'S BE REALISTIC!

What sort of leader do you want to be? Those at senior level in organisations often say that people should model themselves on the great leaders of history. Here is a selection of those leaders often presented as the ones developing leaders should model themselves on:

Can you name them? Answers at end of Chapter (page 28).

These leaders are considered the great leaders of history and it's true that they achieved great things and were right for their time. But they wouldn't, or indeed didn't, do well in organisational settings at junior levels – many were seen as mavericks. To get the results needed in 21st century organisations you don't have to change the face of the world and the history of humanity, you just have to get maximum effort from your people. Take lessons from what these leaders did well – their ability to inspire and innovate, their determination, courage and vision for the future, or as some might say, their propensity to break the rules. But they had faults as well, some of them quite significant. So don't simply try and copy them!

Nelson Mandela's passing in late 2013 led many to focus on his amazing world-changing ability as a statesman. However, that distracted from his real skill as a leader, which enabled the statesman to develop: the power to get the best from others. So it is not Nelson Mandela's statesmanship that has real lessons for every leader in every organisation across the globe, but his skill as an individual leader.

What he did do was to show people he cared about them no matter whether they were presidents or cleaners. He showed them that there was within them a greater self that they had not yet discovered but which they could become, and that there was value in what they did and a better way. This led people to give him their effort, loyalty, support and sometimes risk their lives. He encapsulated and demonstrated what real day-to-day leadership and humanity is about at its highest level of integrity, impact and effectiveness.

'It is better to lead from behind and to put others in front, especially when you celebrate victory when nice things occur. You take the front line when there is danger. Then people will appreciate your leadership.'
Nelson Mandela (1918–2013), first black president of South Africa, Nobel Peace Prize winner and global icon

This is the *spirit* of leadership, and not just the mechanics. The mechanics are what we learn on development programmes, in other words the processes, and this book includes much of it. But the spirit is what takes the mechanics to the highest level of true leadership. If as a leader you only ever use the mechanics of leadership you will never get the best from yourself or others. So on top of the help this book will bring, you need to think about the spirit of leadership and how you will use that to help you as well.

The spirit of leadership that Nelson Mandela used so well includes the qualities of inspiration, determination, humility, humour, forgiveness, courage, justice, integrity, charisma, clarity and simplicity, creating and inspiring vision, showing people they can be better than they are and finally bringing hope where there is little. This delivers real action that engages everyone and not just the few, and led to his power as a statesman as well as an individual leader.

YOU WON'T GET THERE OVERNIGHT!

Unlike other leadership books this one doesn't promise that you will be the CEO in a year, it won't make every reader a great leader that goes down in history, and you won't get to Mach 2 in three weeks. But if you do what the book suggests it will start your growth, maximise your chances of being the best you can be and you will start to reap the personal and professional rewards.

The principle of this book is one of 'aggregation of marginal gains', an idea that's used in areas from economics to rocket science. In simple terms, it means lots of little improvements that build up, support each other and often become greater than the sum of the parts. That's why the simple steps the book suggests can actually build into a transformative journey for you, the people you lead and your organisation.

'A journey of a thousand miles starts with a single step'

Laozi, Chinese philosopher, 4th century BCE

It may take a little time, but because it's based on very simple, practical ideas that you can implement yourself relatively quickly, it just requires a clear plan and your focus and effort on making it happen. It's good if you can also have the help of your organisation or team; it's even better if they are trying to get to Mach 2 at the same time. But even if your organisation hasn't embraced Mach 2 there is no reason why you should not. In fact if you do, it will make it easier for them to spot the great performance you deliver amongst the mediocrity around you!

Additional online resources with useful self assessments, exercises and checklists can be found on my website at www.theonlyleadershipbook.com

We all spend a large percentage of our time at work and what happens there has a massive impact on our families as well as ourselves, and on our satisfaction with life. If we are engaged, happy and achieving our potential at work, we are much more satisfied and we are also happier when with our friends and family, so they also reap the benefits. It's therefore vital to get the best out of our time at work, even if it's for our families' benefit and not our own.

IS LEADERSHIP MYSTICAL?

The ability to lead is considered vital to getting the best out of a team, an organisation or a nation, and it is seen as something that sets an individual apart from the rest. Sometimes the aura that surrounds leadership elevates it to almost a mystical quality, which leads many to believe you can only be born with it.

You will probably have heard the old myths about leadership, which may make you think that getting to Mach 2 is impossible. But these myths usually come from those who don't really understand leadership. So let's debunk some of them:

- *Leaders are born, not made*
  This is not the case. Leadership skills, like any other skills, can be developed with practice based on knowledge passed on by others.
- *Leaders must have certain, defined, qualities*
  No list of qualities has been formulated that can apply to all great leaders. The important factor is the behaviour you demonstrate, not the qualities you have.

Some behaviour may increase your chances of becoming an effective leader, as we will see later.

- *Leaders in one situation must be leaders in others*
A person becomes a leader because they are the best choice to lead the team for a specific task; they may not be the best leaders for a different task. Thus as a leader you must be aware of all the likely situations your team will potentially face and ensure you have all the skills required to make sure you are the best choice for leader in any of these.

- *Leadership can't be taught, only developed by experience*
Development of any skill is a combination of passed-on, taught knowledge and practice that builds experience. Otherwise everyone would rely on trial and error and one generation would not learn from previous ones.

- *Leadership is not a popularity contest*
No it's not, but your people must be willing to work for you and support you rather than be happy to see you sink.

In the real world, leadership skills do not automatically accrue as you become more senior, but the damage that bad leadership can cause does! Also, as you get more senior, fewer people will be prepared to risk telling you that you aren't doing a good job. So for senior leaders, getting to Mach 2 is even more vital, as is genuine self-awareness and the courage to seek honest feedback.

Despite the fact that many people say that it is complex and mystical, getting leadership right is very simple. Here is a simple example of what really matters in leadership.

Leadership in two questions

At one time in my career I served as an officer in the British Army. I had to successfully complete the assessment course at the Royal Military Academy Sandhurst. This I did and on the last night I was there I spoke to the most experienced instructor who gave me his insight into leadership. He was a sergeant major of one of the top British Army regiments with 25 years' military service. 'If you can't remember what you learnt on the course, sir' he told me, 'remember this: that whenever your soldiers look at you they will have two simple questions in their minds. You have to be able to convince them that they can answer yes to both. They will be thinking, firstly: does he know what he is doing? And secondly: do I trust him? If they can answer yes to both they will work hard for you, they will support you, and if required they will die for you.' I will never forget those words. One week later I was in front of 40 soldiers all of whom were asking themselves those two questions of me. I was able to get two yes answers.

You can't get simpler than that! And that's at the heart of what Mach 2 is about – the ability to build strong trust and get maximum effort, then know how to use that trust and effort to its full value.

IT'S ABOUT THE ORGANISATION AS WELL AS INDIVIDUAL LEADERS

Unusually for a leadership book, developing the organisation is covered as well, because while it is important for you as an individual leader to get to Mach 2, it doesn't solve the performance challenges of your organisation as a whole. As we have seen earlier, the challenges for 21st century organisations mean that there is little or no room for error, and there is no room for under-performance. Headcount and cost reductions have produced slimmed-down organisations, meaning fewer people are having to do more work, with 55% saying they have more work than they have time for. Organisations are therefore reaching the limit of their capacity to deliver their objectives. So Mach 2 is also needed for the organisation to work smarter and focus on what is key to success.

As an individual, no matter how good you are your efforts alone will not be sufficient to significantly increase the performance of your organisation and get it to be a Mach 2 organisation. This means that the organisation also has to have a plan to become Mach 2. This involves two key elements:

1. Maximising the number of Mach 2 leaders in the organisation at all levels
2. Then getting them to work well together as an integrated team through collaboration.

Too often there's an assumption that if an organisation makes all its leaders better, then by some act of fate the organisation will automatically be better. It won't. It just means that you have a lot of good individual leaders in the same place, and that doesn't make a great team. Someone has to get them to work together on a day-to-day basis just as you have to do with your people.

That's why this book also contains chapters on how organisations can get to Mach 2, which explain the foundations that need to be in place to be successful, and the steps to take to achieve that. It's about the organisation making sure that everyone is at Mach 2 and aligning their efforts onto what needs to be done to ensure success.

LEADERS AT ALL LEVELS

People often assume that unless you're a chief executive, a general or a president, you're not really a leader. This is patently untrue. If you run a team of any sort, even if you have only one other person reporting to you, if you have the ability to influence other people, you are a leader. Those who lead large groups just need more effective leadership skills. The more people you lead, the harder it is. That's primarily because you have to lead through other leaders, so it's indirect leadership. This is much more challenging than the direct leadership of the line manager.

Although surrounded by a mystique not associated with other skills, leadership is really a simple idea: it is the ability to get the best out of the people around you in any given situation. If you can do this, everyone will benefit.

Most people can give up to 30% effort if they want to. One of the keys to moving up to Mach 1 is to get this maximum 'discretionary' effort from people. The problem is that you can't tell if they are not giving it. They can still be rated as satisfactory in appraisals even if they give no discretionary effort. But if they do, their performance can rocket by up to 20%. This will deliver Mach 1, the springboard to Mach 2, which then focuses that effort onto what really makes a difference to individual, team and organisational performance.

BASIC LEADERSHIP –	MACH 1 – ENGAGING LEADERSHIP –	MACH 2 – ENTREPRENEURIAL LEADERSHIP –
Status quo 'just good enough is good enough'. Organisational performance – in the bottom 80%	Most people giving discretionary effort . Organisational performance – top 80 – 95%	Discretionary effort aligned to critical deliverables. Organisational performance – top 5%

In simple terms, basic leadership is what most organisations have, which just about keeps things running. It maintains the status quo; it stops disasters happening and keeps customers more or less content. But no one is really inspired; there is no desire or drive to be the best, just to be good enough to get by. Leaders here probably lack many of the core skills they need through no fault of their own, as they haven't been developed well. In the more challenging 21st century world this isn't a route to success. The reduced headcounts, cost pressure, demanding customers and pressure to improve performance mean that in reality this approach is a recipe for slow decline towards failure. Such failures are happening every day across the world.

So what happens in basic leadership teams and organisations?

- The customer is given pretty much what the organisational process decides they will get – more product delivery than service provision
- People are unclear on what they have to do. Time and resources may be wasted and the work may not be done properly
- The team or organisation is not motivated. People take longer than they should to do the task, or may not even complete it
- The individuals are not working as teams, and will not perform as well as a motivated team would
- Under pressure the teams and organisation will probably not do enough to get the job done and not be able to sustain workload
- More individuals, especially talented ones, will leave, as they will not wish to stay in such an environment
- Skills will not be developed and thus the organisation will be unable to deal with new situations or challenges
- There is no capability to be 'entrepreneurial'

Moving to Mach 1 is the first level to be achieved by you and the organisation. This is the foundation for the move to Mach 2. Here the leaders in the organisation are aware discretionary effort can be obtained and are starting to get it. So Mach 1 is about getting much higher effort and performance levels from everyone than in basic leadership organisations.

Mach 1 is about maximising the effort you get from everyone

- The team or organisation works as a team and not just as a group of individuals
- The team is able to understand their own objectives and how these fit in with overall team objectives
- Teams members support each other
- Everyone is prepared to put in extra effort when required
- Everyone aims for 'excellence' and not just 'doing the job'
- Everyone knows what they have to do and why
- People are developed and inspired on the job to perform even better.

Once discretionary effort is building up, Mach 2 applies it in the best way to serve your customers and make your organisation as efficient, agile and entrepreneurial as possible. Mach 2 takes all the new extra effort of Mach 1 and targets it exactly where it delivers most benefit for you, your team, the organisation and its customers. So if Mach 1 is about working harder, Mach 2 is about working smarter.

Mach 2 applies the maximum effort where it delivers the best return on investment (ROI) and customer service

- Everyone focuses relentlessly on delivering the best customer service in the most efficient and effective way
- Everyone understands the needs of the external customer
- Everyone collaborates with others to deliver what the organisation needs to achieve and not just their own work
- Individuals understand how what they do fits in with the organisation's key objectives as well as the teams and supports it
- Everyone takes personal responsibility for his or her actions.
- Risk is optimised, not minimised
- The organisation's leaders become an aligned, networked and mutually supportive team wherever they are
- Innovation, creativity and challenging the status quo are encouraged
- Every leader uses entrepreneurial leadership to underpin every action
- Support functions as well as 'front line' areas are entrepreneurial
- Leaders take proactive personal responsibility for not only delivering their objectives, but also collaborating to deliver the organisation's key objectives.

But you cannot go straight to Mach 2 from basic leadership. Mach 1 has to be in place both individually and organisationally before it is possible to achieve Mach 2. Your staff will not engage your customers unless they are engaged with you as their leader and the organisation first.

YOUR EXPERIENCE OF LEADERSHIP TELLS YOU WHAT REALLY MATTERS!

In fact you are a leadership expert as well! You have probably seen and experienced both good and bad leadership and know what effect it has had on your motivation and attitude to your boss and organisation. It's also linked to whether or not you gave any discretionary effort, and why that was the case or not. You might not have called it that at the time, but over your career there will have been times when you gave every little bit of effort you could because you wanted to get the job done to the best possible level, and your boss inspired you to do that. That was discretionary effort, and probably the reason you gave it was because your boss was someone you felt you wanted to make that extra effort for. In other words, he or she was your 'best boss'.

Those moments where you gave that extra effort were in effect you moving from basic leadership to Mach 1 and on to Mach 2. So you know what Mach 1 feels like. And what led you to do that gives you the understanding you need to start your journey to Mach 2. So take a few moments to think about that 'best boss' who you really respected, trusted and gave that extra effort for.

'It is a terrible thing to look over your shoulder when you are trying to lead – and find no one there'
Franklin Delano Roosevelt (1882–1945), US president and WWII leader

Think about what they did day-to-day that made them special; the things that this leader did that made you want to give that extra effort for them. Then write down those key actions – most people can think of half a dozen without a problem. Keep that list for later, when we look at what other people said across the world.

This list is important because it gives you a clear idea of the things you have to do to start moving to Mach 1 yourself, and then on to Mach 2. If the things this boss did motivated you, then those actions will probably be how you could motivate others as well. We will look in more detail at motivation, and the idea that what motivates you probably motivates others, and conversely what demotivates probably demotivates others. In other words, all human beings have a consistent view of what they want out of life, work and their leaders in terms of general principles.

How do I know this? Because I have asked thousands of people in organisations over the past 20 years the 'what made you give maximum effort?' question. And the list they come up with, usually containing about 20 items, is always the same in terms of general themes if not specific words. Whether the answers come from board directors of global organisations, first line managers, MBA students, cleaning staff, technical experts or charity workers, they all say they want the same things from their boss in order for them to give this extra effort. It doesn't matter where they are or where they come from, whether it's the US, Asia or Europe. It seems to be totally consistent everywhere – people are driven by common human needs.

It's these very simple things that make you give your ultimate effort at work. It's what you want from your current boss and what you measure them against all the time, even if subconsciously. It's also what your people want from you!

But as well as focusing on the task this also emphasises the importance of thinking about individuals, and indeed the team. This theme is developed later in more detail but the optimum balance of task, team and individual focus must be present to get to Mach 1 and then to progress to Mach 2.

From your organisation's perspective therefore every leader needs to be doing the same as you to get the whole organisation to Mach 2. This is why there has to be co-ordination to enable an organisation to get to Mach 2: it won't just happen on its own.

CAN YOUR ORGANISATION GET TO MACH 2?

If you are a senior leader or in HR you will be asking the obvious question about how you take a whole organisation to Mach 2. It's much easier as an individual. However, it is possible to take the whole organisation up to Mach 2. Certainly the initiative I was involved in at UBS between 2002 and 2006 showed that it is possible to get an organisation working at Mach 2 levels. This was evidenced by the various awards, including Best Company for Leaders in Europe 2005, top 10 2007, and the fact that Harvard Business School wrote a case study[15] on it, *UBS Towards the integrated firm*. Other organisations I have worked for or advised, and studies from around the world, some of which are referenced here[15], all confirm that the core elements of Mach 1 and Mach 2 can improve organisational performance.

The problem is that in most places this just isn't happening.

So this book sets out the key steps organisations as well as individuals have to take to get to Mach 2 leadership. But if you also have responsibility for others over and above your own team, for example for a department or a division within an organisation, you can also use the relevant sections to help mould your developing Mach 2 leaders into an integrated team and bring your area and organisation to the levels set out previously in this chapter. If you are in a senior leadership or HR role these sections will form the basis of a Mach 2 strategy for an organisation you can work with senior leaders to implement.

DON'T CUT CORNERS

Strangely, many people seem to think that if they were to skip to the end of a book like this and implement the last chapter it would save all the time and effort of having to do the things that came before. A clever idea, but that's like trying to build a house before you have laid the foundations – doomed to inevitable failure. Like anything else you have to make sure that the very basics are in place before adding the more complex elements. In this case the chronology is:

1. Mach 1
   1. Manage yourself – if you can't organise your own work effectively then you won't be able to organise others
   2. Manage others – you need to be able to get people to do basic tasks for you by managing them

  3. Maximise the discretionary effort the team give you by motivating and inspiring them

2. Mach 2

  1. Deliver maximum benefit by focusing that effort onto what really matters

  2. Get everyone working together as an aligned and collaborative team, including those you work with outside your team.

You can't cut out any of these stages. It's all or nothing. You may be some way down the path already, but make sure that your assessment of where you are is honest and realistic.

LEADERSHIP OR MANAGEMENT?

Some will be asking the question as to whether this book covers management as well as leadership, or if management is part of leadership, or whether there's a difference between leadership and management. Some say that leadership is part of being an effective manager, whereas others consider management part of being an effective leader. Views on this would fill the book. But I am going to concentrate on what works in the real world and not worry too much about whether it falls into the leadership box or the management box.

To help you think about the distinction, it may be a good idea to look at management as dealing with the preparation, planning and decision-making aspects of a project, and leadership as getting the people to complete the project, the inspiration, motivation, actual delivery and supervision. So you could say that management turns ideas into plans and leadership turns plans into successful action. For any job to be completed successfully, you need skills in both areas. To get to Mach 2 you need both and so both are covered when and where they need to be in this book. No matter which definition you prefer you need both management and leadership elements, but above all, whatever you call these actions, to achieve Mach 2 you have to make them work in practice!

THE NON-NEGOTIABLE PRINCIPLES

Before you, your team or your organisation start the move to Mach 2, there are some very basic principles you have to use to underpin everything you do, otherwise you simply will not get there. These basics are so simple that many people will say that they are obvious or common sense. It may be called common sense but often in organisations it isn't that common. Not adhering to these principles are some of the key reasons why people and organisations fail.

Principle – Treat others as you want to be treated. Trust, integrity, fairness, decency and honesty come first

It may seem strange but unless you are prepared to treat the people around you – and that includes those below you – with integrity and decency, you might as well throw this book in the bin now, because it's not going to work. Everyone says that they abide by this principle of treating others as they would wish to be treated, but sometimes we wander from this path and have a tendency to look after ourselves to the detriment of those around us. We can get away with that once or twice, but then those others will ask themselves why, as we seem to always be putting ourselves first, they should help us. They will then cease to work effectively with us and as a result our effectiveness is compromised. That's why working for a 'win/win' makes sense.

> 'The supreme quality for leadership is unquestionably integrity. Without it, no real success is possible, no matter whether it is on a section gang, a football field, in an army, or in an office.'
> Dwight D. Eisenhower (1890–1969), WWII leader and US president

Trust, integrity and honesty are the same: once you are seen to compromise what others see as their core values of integrity and honesty, no one will trust you again. Furthermore, these qualities are proven to encourage people to work harder for you than otherwise, by up to 27.9%[16].

This applies to organisations just as much as individuals. If your organisation does not treat people decently, lies for its own ends or fails to demonstrate integrity, then Mach 2 will never be achieved. In October 2013 the Chartered Institute of Personnel and Development (CIPD), the London-based HR professional body, conducted a survey of 3000 employees[17]. This survey found that 31% did not trust the senior management of their organisation, a figure that would doubtless impact on organisational performance. However, the findings that 92% trusted their colleagues and 80% their line manger, may help to rebalance the effect. But that then poses the bigger question: how can organisations do well if 20% of employees don't even trust their own line manager?

I have no reason to think that the UK and Europe are isolated in this respect – conversations I have had with employees across the globe confirm this reduction in trust. We will examine the organisational requirements of this basic principle in more detail later.

Principle – show humility, listen and learn

As you travel on your journey to Mach 2 the fastest way to get better is to learn from how others see you as well as what you see of yourself. It's also about listening to what others have to say and the ideas they might have – this is likely to motivate them to give you more. It's about seeking every opportunity you can to find out how you can get better. It's about accepting that people below you on the organisation's hierarchy can possess information, opinions, ideas and perspectives that are of value to you, and encouraging them to share them with you by asking them for their input, listening and showing humility.

Principle – work in partnership and collaboration for common good

It's not just about you – it's about how you can help others and how they can help you in turn. If you help other people with their challenges they will help you – and that creates an organisation that is agile and very effective when dealing with problems. In fact, as we saw earlier, it is a critical factor in success for 21st century organisations.

If everyone feels that they are working together for a common outcome this significantly increases the performance of both individuals and organisations. So you have to make an effort to help others, show your dedication to the common vision and make sure that what you do helps rather than hinders others. It's about the whole organisation being one aligned and mutually supportive team. 'We' is more important than 'me'.

Principle – beauty is in the eye of the receiver, not the giver

Just because you think your proposal, what you do, or your service to customers is excellent, it doesn't mean the person on the receiving end does. The effectiveness of what you do is not measured by what *you* think, sadly, but by those receiving it. You therefore have to make sure that no matter what you think or feel, what you supply them meets their needs as they have expressed them. This applies in particular to your customers. If you aren't sure about that, the solution is simple: ask!

Principle – keep everything simple

Recent research has shown that most organisations could perform by between 10% and 20% better if they made things simpler[18]. We have a bad habit of making things more complicated than they need to be to deliver what we want. This often comes from either trying to impress others with how clever we are, in an attempt to minimise risk, or just bureaucracy. The simple fact is that every additional unnecessary step in an action plan increases the risk of it going wrong, takes more time and reduces the chances of success. So the question you should constantly be asking is: is this as simple as we can possibly make it?

Principle – keep asking why

Why are we doing this? Why do we do it like this? Why can't we make it better? Too often we follow the normal organisational systems and procedures and do things in a certain way because they have always been done that way, and we get into individual habits of doing things in a certain way. However, in so doing, we often end up either doing the wrong thing, doing the right thing in the wrong way, or missing the point. One of the key problems is that operational teams often do things that don't support the organisation's key deliverables as much they could. Everything you do should have a clear answer to the 'why' and 'how' questions, and you should be able to fully align what you do to the overall objective of your organisation. If everyone questions everything they do in this way, then it's logical that everything done will contribute to the organisational objectives in an aligned way. As a leader it also enables you to identify things that don't so you can stop doing them.

When applying both the simplicity principle and the 'why' question in practice, I have seen too many organisations trying to implement a 'traditional' process in a situation that is not viable and that requires a totally new solution. I worked with a financial organisation that had a year-end process for setting objectives that, in the previous year, had lasted three months. Various circumstances meant they had only three weeks to do the same process that year. There were clearly steps in the process that could be removed or changed to speed it up and make it viable in terms of both the timeline and the quality of delivery. However, they insisted on trying to get the normal three-month process into three weeks – an outcome that was not as effective as it could have been, and resulted in unacceptable additional stress on everyone involved leading to mistakes and loss of some talent.

YOUR OWN EXPERIENCE HOLDS MANY ANSWERS

Earlier I asked you to list what your best boss did that made them a good boss. If you review that list you will probably find that your boss did some of the things we have just discussed. In the final analysis, the most basic principle to remember is to treat others as you would wish to be treated. If you follow this golden rule you will be using the majority of the key principles outlined above. You should think carefully about this: if you are not able to abide by the principles of leadership behaviour, then perhaps you should rethink the reasons behind your desire to be a leader.

WHY YOUR EXAMPLE IS SO IMPORTANT

These principles determine not only the way the members of your team react to you, but also the way they act as well. They will respond to your actions, and you are responsible for determining how the relationship develops – well or badly. It is important that you set a clear and positive example to your team using the principles outlined above. It sends out important messages that may influence team values.

Values and example may sound old-fashioned, but team members copy the behaviour of their leader, as it is felt that whatever the leader does must be acceptable. Much of this happens unconsciously. You need to behave in the way you want team members to behave. The old military phrase 'lead by example' is a good maxim.

Example matters – humans really don't change that much

The importance of example and its effect has been recorded throughout history. In the 16th century, Sir Francis Bacon, Lord Chancellor of England, scientist, philosopher and writer said, 'A man that gives good advice and good example builds with both hands, but a man that gives good advice but bad example builds with one and tears down with the other.'

Whether you like it or not, you will set an example to your team. The only question is whether it is a good or bad one. Don't forget, in leadership, actions speak much louder than words. But even the most senior leaders seem to forget this simple principle sometimes.

RECOGNISING WHAT YOU CAN AND CAN'T CONTROL

I have often met people frustrated and stressed by things happening around them in their organisation, as in life. As we aren't all superheroes we have to recognise that there are some things we can control and some we can't. As former US Defence Secretary Donald Rumsfeld said: 'Stuff happens.' We can all influence things and we are all concerned about things. The secret for effective leadership is to balance the two. In the simplest terms don't get too concerned about things you can't influence. There's no point – you can't do anything about them.

It's a good idea to make a list of all the things that worry you and indicate the ones you can actually influence. Concentrate on those and forget the rest. That way you'll stay sane. The ability to work with within the real world as it is, (where you can't control everything) rather than the world you'd like it to be (where you think you can) is key to effective leadership and managing change. The graphic below summarises this:

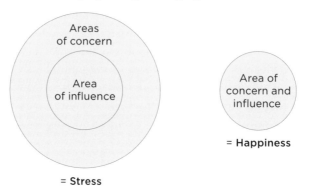

THE RESPONSIBILITY OF POWER

Finally, if you have been given the power of leadership you must also accept the responsibility that goes with it. You should always remember that you have a duty to do the best for your team, both personally and professionally, to enable them to do their best for you. 'Serve to lead', the motto of the Royal Military Academy Sandhurst where UK army officers are trained, sums it up well. To lead effectively, you must, by your actions, enable and encourage the team to do their best for you.

'Leadership is lifting a person's vision to high sights, the raising of a person's performance to a higher standard, the building of a personality beyond its normal limitations.'
Peter Drucker (1909–2005), Austrian-born American management thinker

This is confirmed by many studies, including the aforementioned October 2013 CIPD report. This summarises the views of employees as wanting 'a simple and common sense style of leadership to engender and create a climate of trust.

Employees talk about 'approachable', 'competent' and 'consistent' leaders 'who act with honesty and integrity' and 'lead by example'. This the simple and practical objective that this book will help you and your organisation achieve.

Setting your example as a leader:

• Demonstrate integrity, fairness, honesty and humility

• Listen, learn, collaborate and work in partnership for the common good

• Remember that beauty is in the eye of the receiver, not the giver

• Keep it simple

• Lead by example

• Constantly keep asking how I/we can be better and develop performance

If you keep applying these basic *non-negotiable* principles at every step, getting to Mach 1 and then to Mach 2 will be much easier. Now it's time to start that journey. Good Luck!

CHAPTER 1 KEY POINTS

- There are basic principles of leadership that respond to the basic needs of human beings and ensure success. These are common round the world but the delivery of them needs to match local cultures.

- The 21st century world has brought significant changes in the way organisations are structured, how they operate successfully and what leaders need to do. Leadership needs to be tailored to this.

- Being a leader is about what you do, not the rank or role you occupy.

- Leaders and organisations can be the best by maximising the effort of their people, then applying that effort onto what makes a real difference.

- Mach 1 and Mach 2 deliver significant operational and organisational benefits in the real world.

- To achieve this you don't have to be a leader that will change the world, just one who can get the trust and effort of your people to get to Mach 1 and Mach 2.

- You'll find a variety of supporting resources online at www.theonlyleadershipbook.com

CHAPTER 1 – KEY ACTIONS FOR YOU TO DO NOW

1. Complete your 'best boss' list of the things that your best boss did day-to-day that made you give maximum effort. Are you delivering these to your people?

2. When you have implemented Mach 2 what are the potential areas of benefit for:

   1. You?

   2. Your team?

   3. Your organisation?

3. If you review the key principles listed above how well are you doing those? Could be better, satisfactory or good?

   1. Treat others as you want to be treated – trust, integrity, fairness, decency and honesty come first

   2. Show humility, listen and learn

   3. Work in partnership and collaboration for common good

   4. Beauty is in the eye of the receiver

   5. Keep everything simple

   6. Keep asking why and could we do better?

References

1. *The Bias Blind Spot: Perceptions of bias in self versus others*, Emily Pronin, Daniel Y. Lin & Lee Ross: Personality and Social Psychology Bulletin, Vol. 28 No. 3, March 2002 (p369-381) and *Objectivity in the Eye of the Beholder: Divergent perceptions of bias in self versus others*, Emily Pronin, Thomas Gilovich & Lee Ross: Psychological Review, Vol 111(3), Jul 2004, (p781-799)

2. www.managers.org.uk/news/half-managers-misjudge-their-workplace-performance

3. *Have we earned anything about leadership development?*, R. Kramer: Conference Board Review 45, 2008 (p26-30)

4. *What we know about Leadership*, Hogan & Kaiser: Review of General Psychology, 2005 9 (p169-180)

5. *Handbook of Work Stress*, Kelloway, Sivanathan, Francis & Barling: Sage Publications, 2005, (p89-112)

6. *Innovations in Public Governance: Success stories from winners of the 2013 United Nations Public Service Awards*: United Nations Department of Economic and Social Affairs, New York, 2013

7. *Improving Public Sector Efficiency: Challenges and opportunities*, Teresa Curristine, Zsuzsanna Lonti & Isabelle Joumard: OECD Journal on Budgeting, Vol. 7 No.1

8. *Driving Breakthrough Performance in the New Work Environment*: Corporate Executive Board, 2013

9. Depressed employee engagement stunts global business performance, Hay group, July 2012

10. *Three rules for making a truly great company*, Raynor & Ahmed: Harvard Business Review, Vol. 91 (4), 2013

11. *Marketing and the Bottom Line*, Tim Ambler; Prentice Hall, Harlow, 2003

12. *The Fatal Bias: the prevailing managerial bias towards cost efficiency is seriously harmful to corporate performance*, Jules Goddard: Management Article of the Year 2013; Chartered Management Institute, February 2014

13. You'll find more information on my website: chrisroebuck.co/files/2014/02/Companies-need-to-be-more-aware-of-risk.pdf

14. *Depressed employee engagement stunts global business performance*: Hay Group, July 2012

15. *UBS: Towards the integrated firm*, Lal, Nohrai & Knoop: Harvard Business School, May 15 2006

16. *Employee engagement framework and survey*: Corporate Leadership Council 2004 (p60)

17. *Focus on trust in leaders*, CIPD Employee Outlook: CIPD London, Autumn 2013

18. *Complexity: The human paradox and how to address it*: The Simplicity Partnership, London

Answers: Alexander the Great, Gandhi, Churchill, Chairman Mao, Roosevelt, Mandela, Martin Luther King Junior, Horatio Nelson.

2

Moving to Mach 1
for individual leaders:
how to maximise efforts
from your team

2

Moving to Mach 1 for individual leaders: how to maximise efforts from your team

UNDERSTANDING PEOPLE, MANAGING YOURSELF, LEADING THE TEAM

In Chapter 1 we saw that you don't have to become one of the great leaders of history to be an effective leader in an organisation, so pretty much anyone has the potential to be effective as a leader. We also saw that leaders need to fine-tune the way they work to reflect the changes organisations have undergone in recent years.

However, you have to be at least competent and lead in the right way, which is what you will achieve if you apply the contents of this book in your workplace.

> 'Before you are a leader, success is all about growing yourself. When you become a leader, success is all about growing others.'
>
> Jack Welch (b 1935), CEO of GEC, 1981–2001

Bad leadership can be worse than you think!

Bad leaders make their own job difficult, but it's worse for those they lead: bad leadership can kill! In a 2009 survey[1] of over 3000 Swedish males, those with bosses who were poor leaders suffered 20% to 40% more heart attacks than those with good ones! And in a survey of British hospitals,[2] those with poor leadership systems had higher mortality rates than those with good ones.

In this chapter I look at how you get to Mach 1 and then get your team there, and in so doing maximise the chances of them maximising *their* effort for you. To do this you need to:

1. Understand people and why they behave as they do both in their work and in response to your actions as a leader

2. Maximise the value and quality of the work you do personally by effectively managing yourself

3. Improve your ability to collaborate with others to support the wider organisational agenda

4. Take the key elements of managing tasks you use yourself and apply them to your team to manage others effectively

There are two key parts of managing yourself and others: the principles and the toolkit. Chapter 2 concerns the principles, or the key ways of working that you need to remember to implement all the time, day by day. Chapter 3 provides the toolkit, a simple step-by-step process to getting it right every time.

Before looking at how you can improve what you do at work it's worth looking at some critical information about what makes people behave the way they do. This doesn't apply solely to other people; it also applies to you, so considering it at this point may help you understand your own behaviour better as well as that of others.

As human beings we all have certain basic patterns of behaviour that are consistent, as well as many things that are different between individuals. For example, irrespective of your job, your background, your culture or where you live, you probably want to get very much the same things from life as everyone else in general terms. This idea was developed by Abraham Maslow in his Hierarchy of Needs (1964)[3].

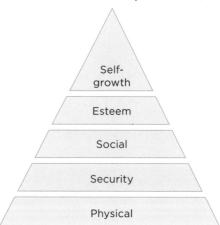

Maslow asserts that people put in effort to get what they need or want to achieve. Some of these needs are basic and some more intellectual. People tend to want the more basic first and then the more intellectual. There may be exceptions, for example the hermit who rejects contact with society in favour of solitary contemplation, but these are very few and far between. In general we all conform to the core principles. Maslow suggests that these are:

- Food and water *(physical need)*
- Safety and shelter *(security need)*
- Love, contact and group membership *(social need)*
- Achievement, status and recognition *(esteem need)*
- Personal development, growth and inner achievement *(self-growth need)*

We are prepared to put in effort to satisfy these needs and work, Maslow says, is one form of effort to achieve this. Looking at Maslow's pyramid format, it can be seen that most people move from the lower needs to the higher ones as the lower needs are satisfied.

Let's look at those needs in more detail:

PHYSICAL/SECURITY

These most basic needs have to be met first as they relate to simple survival. This is the most basic driver of the need to work – you need to get paid to survive.

SOCIAL

Human beings are essentially social animals so most of us like to be part of a group, whether that is family, friends, work colleagues, our team or the organisation or a sports club. This group membership generally makes us feel good and we like to fit in with what our group is trying to do and support it for the common good.

ESTEEM

It feels even better when other people in our group or wider society recognise us in some way for having done well. This could be by passing exams, promotion, sporting or other success; recognition by others of our good work or contribution makes us feel good – even better than just being in the group.

SELF-GROWTH

This is often seen as the highest need, and may or may not link to the esteem needs in the previous section. Self-growth happens when we achieve something that we personally wanted to do. It could be related to getting recognition from one of our 'groups', but it could also relate to something only we know we want and which does not require external recognition. An example could be learning to play a musical instrument or climbing a mountain. This has no link to work, possibly no recognition by others, but gives a great degree of personal satisfaction.

There is often an assumption that it's good if a leader's self-growth need relates to work. In some cases it is, but if they are so driven to achieve and do it in the wrong way by pushing people too hard or coercing them rather than bringing the people with them, it will have negative long-term effects, as will be explained later[4].

Once the current need has been met a new, higher need often develops, for example in social, esteem and self-growth areas. We constantly strive for more as human beings and individual leaders. To maximise that effort to everyone's benefit, our leader and organisation needs to leverage it so that it is enabling us to get what we want while doing what the organisation needs.

You should be able to better identify your own needs in each area now you are aware of Maslow's categories. Ask yourself the question: what is it that you really want out of what you do at work? You should be able to list the things you want to achieve and put them into the relevant categories of needs. Everyone else in your team and in the organisation at large, no matter who or where they are, also has needs that fit all these categories. The secret of success to both working well with others and leading them is to understand what your people's needs are.

USING PEOPLE'S NEEDS AT WORK TO MAXIMISE EFFORT

If we are seeking to meet our needs and are willing to put effort in to achieve them, inevitably some of them can be met, either directly or indirectly, while we are working. We have seen that what people – including you – want from work and from their bosses tends to be consistent the world over. So we can logically conclude that these characteristics provide the core purpose of leadership at work:

> 'We do not only go to work to earn an income, but to find meaning in our lives. What we do is as large part of what we are.'
>
> Alan James Ryan (b 1940), professor of politics, University of Oxford

1. Individuals wish to satisfy their needs and aspirations and will put effort in to achieve them

2. Organisations have to deliver objectives through the effort of their people.

Therefore leadership at its heart is about enabling individuals to meet their needs and aspirations by doing what the organisation needs to achieve its objectives. The more these two can be aligned, so that individuals can meet more of their needs by putting in more effort, the more successful the organisation will be. You know from your own experience that this is the case in the real world – you work harder when you can see that if you deliver what the organisation wants, you get what motivates you in return.

THE BEST BOSS LIST

To get an idea of what maximises your effort, here is a short task for you to do now. Think about the best boss you ever had, the boss you put in extra effort for, and write down on a piece of paper your responses to the following question:

• What did this person do each day that made them the best boss and made you want to give extra effort for them?

• When you have made the list read on, but NOT before!!!

The point of getting you to do this is to compare your list to other people's lists. I would be very surprised if what you have written is significantly different from the contents of the list shown opposite.

I have been asking this question of leaders and staff in organisations around the world for over 25 years, from first line managers to board members, from hard-nosed businesses focused on the bottom line to not-for-profits, from the US to Europe, Middle East and Asia, and across a wide variety of industries and sectors. The list they have all come up with is almost always the same; the words may be slightly different but the core drivers that make people give maximum effort are consistent. This proves conclusively that human beings want very much the same things from their boss no matter where or who they are.

Now compare your list to the 'best boss' summary list below. Are they similar – if not in the specific words then in the general principles? We'll explore the difference between (R), (B) and (T) qualities later.

1. Kept me informed about what was going on (R)
2. Set realistic but challenging targets (T)
3. Made me part of a successful organisation with good culture (B)
4. Respected me as a professional and a person (R)
5. Backed me up when required (R)
6. Developed my skills and career (B)
7. Acted with integrity (R)
8. Led by example (R)
9. Listened to what I said and my ideas (R)
10. Genuinely cared about me (R)
11. Didn't blame me for genuine mistakes (R)
12. Let me get on with things and didn't interfere – empowered me (B)
13. Was fair and treated me decently (R)
14. Inspired me with their enthusiasm (R)
15. Built trust and transparency (R)
16. Praised me and encouraged me (R)
17. Had a sense of humour and laughed with us (R)

My work in developing the above is confirmed by other studies that look at what people want at work. For example, Rob Goffee and Gareth Jones identify that it's these simple things that enable people to be most productive[5]:

- Let me be myself
- Tell me what's really going on
- Discover and magnify my strengths
- Make me proud to work here
- Make my work meaningful
- Don't hinder me with stupid rules

Comparing the two wish lists shows significant commonality of desire from people.

Unsurprisingly, the things that people *don't* want to happen are also both consistent and predictable, in fact very much the mirror image – or to reference *Star Wars*, the 'dark side' – of the things they *do* want to happen. People want to be treated with respect; therefore *not* being treated with respect has a significantly negative impact on their effort.

WHAT ABOUT THINGS YOU CAN'T CONTROL?

One issue around effectiveness at work and being effective leaders is that most people really have two brains. No, I haven't strayed into science fiction here; I'm talking about the conscious and the subconscious. More leaders need to know about the interaction between the two, and how they can affect individual and team responses, even without them realising that it's happening. Interestingly, you probably couldn't help some negative responses to bad leadership or behaviour even if you wanted to. Some are automatic and subconscious.

Neuroscience research[6] has clearly shown that there are certain subconscious 'protection' mechanisms in the human brain that initiate automatic responses if certain things happen. This is like the rush of adrenalin that automatically occurs in times of trauma. When we experience unpleasant or threatening situations our brains start to close down and go into a defensive mode. It might not be obvious but it still happens. This means that our ability to be positive and to respond with logic rather than emotion is reduced and our effort declines even if we don't want it to.

This has a much more powerful effect than we realise, and our subconscious brain is assessing everything at the same time as our conscious brain. Sometimes the subconscious responds to things we don't even know have happened. To demonstrate the power of this effect a number of experiments have been conducted, and here is one that is thought provoking.

Now you see it, now you don't – but your brain does!

Researchers[7] monitored the brain activity of volunteers while they were being shown photographs of snakes. They observed how the brain responded in each case and the patterns involved. They then replayed the experiment but shortened the time that the photographs were displayed for, until the time was so short that they no longer seemed visible to the viewer. Despite this, when the snake and other threatening images were displayed, the brain activity responded in the same way as when the photographs were visible. Thus the subconscious brain recognised and responded to this even though the conscious brain didn't even know a snake had been seen.

This research shows that the subconscious controls much more than we think.

YOU HAVE DECIDED WHAT TO DO BEFORE YOU KNOW IT!

The Max Planck Institute for Human Cognitive and Brain Sciences undertook research[8] on how people make decisions. Volunteers were asked to decide whether to use their right or left hand to perform a task, and then to do the task when they had made the decision. By monitoring brain activity, the researchers were able to predict which hand would be used by each individual up to a full seven seconds before the individual themselves moved their hand. The hand movement indicated the point at which the conscious mind had made the decision about which hand to use. Thus in reality the subconscious mind had made the decision well before the conscious mind recognised it and knew about it.

These two experiments show that there is very much more going on in the minds of the people we seek to lead than maybe even they know. What we do know, however, is that the responses to the best boss list are positive, and that even if we don't understand the subconscious mind, we understand what leaders can do to make it work positively.

But this is also why, try as you might, no one will work well with bosses that they don't believe care about them.

WHAT ARE THE IMPLICATIONS?

We will revisit both Maslow and the best boss list again as we look more deeply into how you can become a more effective leader and develop through Mach 1 and on to Mach 2 leadership.

You should now understand why you want certain things from life, work and your boss, and that actually everyone else wants pretty much the same as you do. Furthermore, if you have negative experiences, your subconscious defence mechanisms may take over automatically and reduce your performance. Being aware of these key facts will help you understand your own behaviour better, and enable you to understand better how your leadership impacts on others and drives their responses. This helps you move through Mach 1 and on to Mach 2 and become a better leader more quickly.

MANAGING YOURSELF

Before you can start to lead others, you need to be able to manage your own work first. The preparation you do prior to any task must lay a strong foundation to ensure success. The implementation must then also be effective. When you become skilled at this it will also enable you to assess how effective others are at doing their work, and you can then help them develop their skills if required.

Recurring problems in organisations are, for example, projects finishing late or not achieving the right quality or not aligning to overall organisational objectives. You need to avoid these and ensure that the benefit you deliver to your organisation is maximised. Note that this is *not* the same as just maximising the performance in your own job. To deliver your own maximum performance you must:

1. Behave in a way that makes you effective and credible as a leader
2. Focus on working in a way that maximises your effort for the organisation
3. Focus on work that aligns to the critical deliverables of the organisation
4. Plan the work so it is delivered with maximum efficiency, on time and to the optimum quality level.

Only when you are able to do these things effectively for yourself will you understand how to help your team to do them effectively as well. The next section covers the most basic elements of getting this right.

CRITICAL PRINCIPLES OF LEADER BEHAVIOUR

Self-confidence and self-awareness

The ability to understand yourself is the foundation of leadership behaviour. This means honestly recognising your own strengths and weaknesses. It thus encompasses humility, (recognising that you have weaknesses), confidence in your strengths, ability to admit your mistakes, and an understanding of how you need to improve yourself. It means that you also have to be consistent in your actions and attitudes; acting solely on your own feelings may lead you to be inconsistent or unfair. It therefore includes self-control. You don't have to be an extrovert to be self-confident, or to lead. Abraham Lincoln led the United States through some of the most turbulent times in its history, yet he was quiet and introverted. He did, however, have confidence that what he was doing would succeed, and he managed to convey this to others. You can build confidence with experience and knowledge and then basing your actions on that.

> 'A great leader's courage to fulfil his vision comes from passion, not position.'
> John Maxwell (b 1947), US author, speaker and pastor

Integrity

One of the most important things a leader has to do is to act with integrity. This implies honesty and underpins the trust between the leader and team members, allowing them to trust you. Without their trust you would be unable to lead any team. Integrity means matching your words with deeds and honesty, means being truthful and non-deceitful. Integrity sets out the rules by which you treat others and demonstrates your values. Not only that, but demonstrating honesty and integrity is also proven to improve employee performance by 27.9%[9]. Think about the bosses you have most respected over your career: did they behave with integrity? In many surveys, people say the key behaviour they look for and admire in their leaders is integrity. It also means thinking carefully about what you do to make sure you are not swayed by impulses or temptations.

> 'A true leader has the confidence to stand alone, the courage to make tough decisions, and the compassion to listen to the needs of others. He does not set out to be a leader, but becomes one by the equality of his actions and the integrity of his intent.'
> Douglas MacArthur (1880–1964), US/ Allied commander, World War II

Enthusiasm, vision and drive

Can you think of an effective leader who was not enthusiastic? Enthusiasm combined with vision creates inspiration and this provides the foundation for the team's drive and motivation. Can you imagine yourself being motivated by someone who obviously doesn't care whether a task is done or not?

> 'My own definition of leadership is this: the capacity and the will to rally men and women to a common purpose and the character which inspires confidence.'
>
> Field Marshall Viscount Montgomery (1887–1976), Allied/British commander, World War II

But it also relates to why you want to get the job done. Effective leaders are motivated by a desire to achieve, and that often goes beyond status or money. The motivation is therefore often not activated by external factors but by internal drives, as we saw with Maslow's model. It often includes the desire to make a difference or contribute to the common good. Again, think about leaders you have known as well as your own motivations. Think how quickly people who only want power or money can be identified. What is your attitude to them?

Enthusiasm and drive also embrace determination and commitment. Leaders must have the ability to take a positive approach when things go wrong, believing that problems can be overcome even if it's in the long term.

Listening

Not everyone is a good listener. One of the best ways to improve is to listen much more than you do now. Try to *listen* more than you *talk*, don't interrupt people and let them finish everything they want to say. Also, ask them why they feel as they do. This has two benefits: you are getting information you would not have got before; and you are letting them see your genuine interest. This in itself can motivate them to improve their performance, and it will also make the next principle much easier.

> 'Courage is what it takes to stand up and speak. Courage is also what it takes to sit down and listen.'
>
> Winston S. Churchill (1874-1965), British prime minister, World War II leader and statesman

Empathy

As we saw in the best boss list, and as all the evidence from real organisations confirms, effective leaders have a genuine interest in the people they lead and understand their feelings. They want their team members to develop both as employees and as people. They know how to respond to different individuals and how to get the best from each of them. Good leaders show warmth towards their team, they are approachable and go out of their way to support those they lead, whether taking time to talk to individuals when possible – 'walking the talk' – or asking if they need help.

> 'Outstanding leaders go out of their way to boost the self-esteem of their personnel. If people believe in themselves, it's amazing what they can accomplish.'
>
> Sam Walton (1918-1992), US entrepreneur and businessman; founder of Walmart

To get the team to show an interest in what you want to achieve, you have to show an interest in what they want to achieve, too. This applies to everyone, from the most experienced member to the new arrival.

Building rapport to build networks

An effective Mach 1 leader has the ability to quickly build relationships by establishing rapport, not only with the team, but with everyone he or she comes into contact with. Creating this rapport is based on the ability to show a genuine interest in other people and trying to find a common approach or mutual ground to enable something to be achieved. In many cases, leaders need to build networks in order to make things happen more easily; this is key to Mach 2 leadership and to organisational success in the 21st century. The ability to find and build on commonality is important in managing working relationships, dealing with conflict, and finding solutions to both long and short-term problems – and the foundation for collaboration.

If you do all of these things then the next stage – actually delivering what needs to be done – is likely to go much more smoothly.

MAKING SURE YOU MAXIMISE THE VALUE OF THE WORK YOU DO

No matter how powerful, a leader only has the same number of hours in a day as you. It is what you do with this limited time resource that determines what you achieve, both in your personal and your professional life. To make better use of the limited and valuable resource of time you need:

1. Appropriateness – only take on work that you know you or your team are the best people to do
2. Prioritisation – allocate work in the order of how much it adds value to what the organisation needs
3. Planning and action/implementation and risk management – ensure that work is implemented at the appropriate level to be completed to the required quality in the time you have.

APPROPRIATENESS

The work you take on must be the work that you or your team are there for and able to do. From a leader's perspective it is critical to be able to say 'no' to taking on work you don't have time to do, or which does not align to what you or your team should be doing to support the organisation's key objectives.

PRIORITISATION

Prioritise on the basis of what tasks contribute most to 'what the organisation needs to achieve and how you can make that happen'. That may not be the specific job that the organisation has asked you to do! The changes in organisations over the past few years have meant more matrixed structures and fewer people, so those who prioritise the wider organisational needs as well as their specific job requirements add significantly more value to their organisations.

In addition, if someone else can do the task, then delegate it or pass it to another team better equipped to deliver it.

Unless your team knows the overall organisational strategy and objectives, you'll need to prioritise for them so the team delivers what the organisation needs to succeed. Otherwise they may end up enthusiastically doing work that doesn't add the greatest value to the organisation.

Within prioritisation, sub-divide what is urgent or non-urgent, and important or not important. Urgent and important is priority 1; important but not urgent priority 2; urgent but not important is priority 3; and forget not urgent and not important. Reconsider prioritisations regularly. Non-urgent tasks, especially those that are important, should be specifically timetabled, as these will quickly become urgent! There is more on this in the Chapter 3 toolkit.

Prioritisation is also vital for effective collaboration – the ability to see what needs to be done to maximise value to the organisation. In fact the CEB data[10] shows that effective prioritisation of work, even if not all or part of your own job, is the factor with the highest impact for driving value to the organisation, in other words doing what makes a real difference.

PLANNING AND IMPLEMENTATION

Once you have decided what tasks you need to do, it is critical to do them effectively. Modern organisations require maximum efficiency to be able to deliver a quality output with limited resources in a reasonable time. Planning is very important. It is often said that 'failing to plan is really planning to fail'. But equally, spending all your time on planning and taking no action means nothing gets done.

It's interesting that a study of the difference between entrepreneurs and corporate executives by Saras Sarasvathy, Associate Professor at Darden School of Business at the University of Virginia[11], found that, in working on developing their organisation, entrepreneurs minimised the planning and started testing in the real world as fast as possible; whereas corporate executives liked to plan the future based on the past, assuming that reality would conform to their data.

Reality always triumphs

Even with the best planning there is nothing like a reality check. In 1996 fast food giant McDonalds launched a new deluxe burger range based on all the planning, focus group and analysis the might of the company could muster. But people didn't buy the new burgers, and the initiative lost the company over $300m. Had they done some simple testing in the real world that loss might have been avoided. There are many other examples of even the most extensive planning and development producing a failure that the most simple of pilot testing in the real world would have prevented.

The answer therefore is to plan enough to get to the point where you can real-world test, then plan for a wider roll out once you know the idea will work.

Empowering leadership
The key steps to success

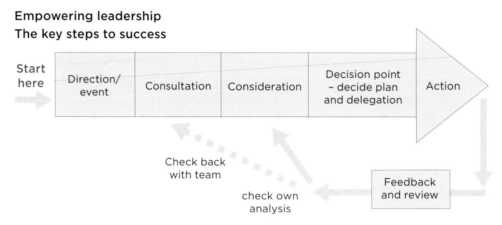

Just make sure that at each stage you're using the knowledge, skills and experience of the team to its full value, by consulting its members where appropriate. Once you've assembled all the relevant data and made a decision on the best option, you have to build an action plan you can implement with your team. The key steps are:

1. What's the problem or what's the task I have to deliver?
2. Who should I consult to get all the relevant information I need to decide?
3. Consider possible options
4. Decide on the best, make a plan for it and delegate tasks as required (including both a contingency for delays and a reserve plan 'B' if plan 'A' fails)
5. Start to take action.

No matter how inspiring a leader you are, unless you can run an effective management process that gets your own tasks planned and implemented, then you won't be able to do it for the team. So what is the process by which you get the job done in the best way in the minimum time with the resources available? These are the basic steps (more detail is given in the Chapter 3 toolkit).

INITIATION AND OBJECTIVES

Most tasks are started by either a direction from your boss or an event that needs a response. Ask yourself:

1. What do I need to achieve?
2. What are the clear and simple objectives I need to know?

If you are given a problem rather than just a simple task then more thinking is required. One of the main challenges all leaders face each day is a problem that seems to have no acceptable or easy solution. Often there is no right or wrong answer but only a 'least bad' solution. Unfortunately, this is the nature of the world and there is a limitless supply of these problems.

In many cases, we tend to jump to conclusions about how to solve problems without thinking them through logically. This often causes further problems. Our psychology gives rise to a number of reactions when we choose options based on our selective perceptions of the world around us. These are well documented in a number of studies[12] [13] and some awareness of what they are helps to warn you if they start to occur. Below are the stock responses driven by some of these biases to problems, and advice on how to create better solutions:

'We have always done it this way'

Working on the basis that what was effective in the past is perfectly logical applies if the current situation is exactly the same as the previous one. In reality that rarely happens, so reverting to past practice and failing to consider all possible options merely widens the gap between your, or the organisation's, practice and the needs of the current situation.

'We have to do something'

In some cases doing nothing is actually a better option than doing something. Always ask: 'if we did nothing what would the results be?'

'We need a quick fix'

We often seek short-term solutions and ignore long-term impact. Use the 5/5/5 assessment: if we do this what are the likely positive and negative effects in five days, five months and five years? This helps balance out any short-term thinking.

'We need one simple, clear and easy solution'

If the question is 'the building is on fire; should we leave?' then the answer is clear, but in many real organisational situations the obvious solution might not be the best answer. Double-check by asking: if we didn't have this solution, how would we solve this issue? This often reveals some other options or new perspectives.

'Maybe there is more than one way round this'

We always seem to think in single pathways, but in many cases we can do two things at once with concurrent activity and see which works out best or provides the answer first.

'What's my reserve plan if the first one goes wrong?'

In the real world you effectively need two options, the one you start with and another to change to if the first encounters problems, or at least an adaptation of the initial one. Determination to make your plan succeed is laudable; persistence with a plan that is clearly not working or fit for purpose is stupid, but historically popular.

'I will make it work!'

This relates to how we frequently over-estimate our own ability to succeed and take an overly optimistic view of the future. Yes, we are optimistic beings but within the optimism there must be some reality checks; asking the advice of your biggest critic is one way to do this!

'I don't want to know'

This is yet another tendency we have to minimise problems or to ignore information we don't want to hear because it contradicts our view or our wishes for a successful outcome. There are numerous examples from business, warfare, politics and life in general where people have not considered warnings or advice from credible sources, leading to dire consequences. For example the British explorer Captain Scott ignored advice to use dogs rather than horses or petrol-powered sledges in his race to get to the South Pole first – he and his team subsequently died on the return trip.

> **Never ignoring the warning signs**
>
> Warnings about equipment hours before the 2010 Gulf of Mexico oil disaster where 11 people were killed were ignored, and in 1984 the poor maintenance that caused the Bhopal chemical plant explosion, which killed over 4000, and injured over 500,000 people, had been predicted by earlier warning incidents.

This links back to risks posed by the decision-making of middle and junior leaders who are focused on delivering one single objective, often greater profit or less cost. They often fail to take risk management and other factors into account adequately. However, the middle and junior managers often make assumptions based on incomplete communication, so the problem is really caused by senior leaders failing to communicate all the decision-making criteria effectively. So if you are a middle or junior leader make sure you are fully aware of all the priorities for decision-making from the top and if you are a senior leader make sure those further down your organisation know these.

'One of the tests of leadership is the ability to recognise a problem before it becomes an emergency.'
Arnold H. Glasow (1901-1998), US businessman, humourist and writer

In light of the perceptions discussed above, if as a leader you approach problems in a logical way, taking a proactive and holistic view, options quickly reveal themselves and the chances of choosing the best solutions increase dramatically. All tasks you might be given need to be treated in the same way to ensure that your actions are based on reality and analysis, not guesswork or assumption. You should try to run through the process in practice, using the steps opposite for everything you do. This may seem time consuming, but with practice, and especially when dealing with smaller tasks, you will be able to apply this process in a matter of minutes. In addition, reassessing the best way to do things on a regular basis will help you to integrate change and innovation naturally into your thinking. More detail on this is in the toolkit in Chapter 3.

IMPROVE YOUR ABILITY TO COLLABORATE WITH OTHERS TO SUPPORT THE WIDER ORGANISATIONAL AGENDA

As we have seen, the financial downturn has created a tougher economic environment where organisations have been forced into a new world of work driven by cost and headcount cuts. This is characterised by fewer people doing more work per head and having to collaborate more to get things done.

This change has been significant: the importance of individual task working for adding value to the organisation has fallen from 78% to 51%, and the importance of collaboration has increased from 22% to 49%[10]. So between 2002 and 12 the importance of collaboration to profitability doubled.

There is a viewpoint that collaboration isn't always needed to maximise effectiveness – look at the world of the entrepreneur, some would say. But the world of the entrepreneur actually demonstrates the importance of collaboration, where some say new start-ups with two founders are significantly more successful than those with one[14]. Two people working to achieve excellence is often more effective than one with collaboration, providing more and better ideas.

Thus as an individual leader your ability to get to Mach 1 must start to take this into account; you can only perform well by being good at collaboration. This is focused on more in the Mach 2 leadership chapters, but there are some key factors that can help you to develop your capability in this area. Based on research findings[10], you need to:

1. Understand the organisation's wider agenda and not just what you have to do in your own job

2. Understand what the people you have to collaborate with do – not just have a good relationship with them

3. Understand the organisational context and not just the organisation's formal structures

4. Look for opportunities to change and improve things yourself and not just support change initiated by others.

This approach has additional benefits, for example understanding the wider agenda enables you to make better decisions and manage risk more effectively.

FROM BASIC LEADERSHIP TO MACH 1

The first step on the journey to success for most leaders in organisations is to move from basic leadership to Mach 1 leadership. To do this you have to take the key elements of managing tasks you use yourself and apply them to your team to manage others effectively. As explained in the introduction, this means taking your own and your team's performance from the present level to that of roughly the top 15% of performers by maximising the effort of your people. This is likely to enable you to get up to 30%

performance improvement from around 60% of your people, depending on how you are doing at present.

This is done by maximising their discretionary effort through engaging them in delivering what the organisation needs to achieve its objectives – aligning their ability to meet their needs and aspirations with the organisation's delivery of objectives. As we saw in Chapter 1, it is not possible to tell if your people are giving this extra effort from their appraisal results, as it is possible for many people to get satisfactory ratings while withholding discretionary effort.

In today's modern and more pressured organisational environment you must input sufficient positive energy through Mach 1 and Mach 2 leadership to counteract the negative forces that might cause the team to fail to deliver. We have already seen[10] that many people in the new world of work are under pressure, with 55% saying that they don't actually have enough time to do the work they are asked to do.

Within Mach 1 a series of elements builds on each other to get that extra effort and performance, and these are a prerequisite for moving to Mach 2. We have covered the self-management skills. Now we need to start to focus on managing and leading other people:

1. Core team process skills – the basic processes needed to succeed
2. Core team people skills – engaging the team for high performance – moving from basic performance to Mach 1 performance.

Again it is important to get each of these correct and implemented in the order set out above. For both individual leaders and organisations one of the key reasons things go wrong is that they try to do more advanced things before the basic foundation skills. The advanced cannot be done unless the basics are in place. Common examples include trying to develop innovation in the team when the team members don't understand how they fit into the bigger picture, or have not previously been allowed to innovate, or don't care. They can't, and won't, just switch on innovation like a light bulb.

You will recall the earlier discussion about meeting personal needs; things that made you give your boss super performance and things that stopped you performing well. We saw that these were consistent for most people. So the simple rule is that if certain actions by a boss have got you to perform at your best, then it's very likely that if you do these things it will get your people to perform at their best as well, and give you maximum effort.

This extra effort is a vital foundation on the road to achieving Mach 2 as no organisation or leader can successfully implement the components of Mach 2, for example collaboration, alignment, customer focus, innovation and creativity and entrepreneurial performance, if his or her people are not engaged in supporting the organisation with maximum effort in the first place. In simple terms, they aren't going to be interested in doing the key things needed to get to Mach 2 unless they are engaged with what the organisation is doing at Mach 1. The criticality of this cannot be underestimated.

There are two key elements that interlink and drive individual and organisational success. The first is that by engaging your team with the wider organisation their motivation will improve, and the second is that it gives them the knowledge of context, what other people do, how the organisation works, to allow them to collaborate effectively to deliver what the organisation needs. Both are critical to Mach 2 and to delivering the actions that are proven to enable an organisation to succeed in the 21st century. We will look at these in more detail when considering what the organisation has to do to succeed.

HOW AM I DOING?

Before allocating time and effort to becoming better, you need to decide what key areas you as an individual leader need to get better at. This will maximise the ROI of your time. So it's important to work through the key elements of effective leadership one by one to make sure that you have them working to a satisfactory level. Then you can quickly get to Mach 1 and on to Mach 2.

As has been said before, you don't have to be the best at everything, in fact no one can be, but you need to be good enough for the key elements of leadership to work most of the time. That means having an idea about how you are doing now and how much effort you need to put in on those specific areas to make them good enough so you can move onwards and upwards.

> 'Leadership and learning are indispensable to each other'
> John F. Kennedy (1917-1963), US president

So you need to have an assessment of how good you currently are. This can be a self-assessment but should also include some input from other people. The more input you have the more accurate the result will be, and sadly evidence suggests that our own assessments of ourselves tend to be over complimentary, so other people's views are of crucial importance! It may even be a good idea to risk asking someone you don't always get on well with; it might make them reconsider how they work with you!

The assessment is at the start of the Chapter 3 toolkit. It is designed to be quick and simple and focuses on the key areas that make the difference. It allows you to take a step back and identify those areas where you are good and those where you could improve. And everyone can improve; these questions are just as relevant for a CEO as for a first line manager. Do the assessment and then read on.

AFTER MY ASSESSMENT, WHAT NEXT?

Your score will give you a rough indication of how you are doing in the key areas of Mach 1 leadership and point to simple things you can do to get better. But it will help you significantly if you understand why doing these things will make a real difference, and the rest of this chapter will help you understand people, explain the key drivers of good day-to-day leadership and help you quickly move to Mach 1.

THE VITAL MACH 1 COMBINATION – GOOD PROCESS SKILLS UNDERPINNING GOOD ENGAGING LEADERSHIP

Ask yourself a general question: why and how does my team get the job done and not just fall apart? The answer is that you are holding it together with your leadership skills and their support. You can think of leadership as a balance. On one side is the effort that you are putting in to make the team effective (your leadership, team spirit, loyalty and collaboration) and on the other side are all those things that pull the opposite way (workload, stress, time pressure, poor interpersonal relationships).

'Example is not the main thing influencing others, it's the only thing'
Albert Schweitzer (1875-1965), French philosopher, theologian, physician and missionary

As pressure on the team builds, you have to add extra effort to keep it going by motivating and supporting them more. In all situations your team faces, you must input sufficient positive energy through your leadership to counteract the negative forces that might cause the team to fail. Your example is key to success.

CRITICAL LEADERSHIP SKILLS

So far we have looked at the need to balance positive leadership input against negative forces, the process of leadership and the key areas you have to pay attention to when leading. The question you may be asking is: what skills do I need to be able to do all this?

Over many years, writers have endeavoured to discover what it is that allows an individual to become an effective leader. Pulling together ideas from many sources, the diagram below represents probably the simplest and clearest expression of the areas involved – core process and people skills.

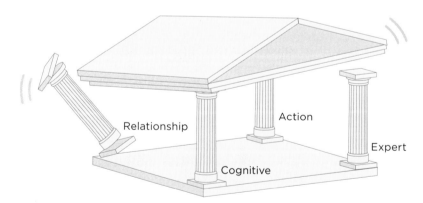

Critical skills: Cognitive, Action, Expert, Relationship

Process

Cognitive – are you able to collect and analyse information and decide on options?
Action – are you good at planning and implementation?
Expert – do you know your functional/expert role?

People

Relationships – are you good at doing the things on the best boss list? This includes collaboration – how well do you collaborate with others in your team, organisation and outside?

Just remember it as: lead with 'CARE' (as in graphic); again these fall into our categories of 'process' and 'people'.

You need to be as good as you can be in both process and people areas to become an effective Mach 1 leader. If you aren't perfect in any of these, don't worry; you can, with thought and practice, improve in any of them. Remember the two basics that will help you: an overview of the principles – the way you must try to do things every day; and the detailed steps to make sure each of the actions you undertake go well (toolkit in Chapter 3).

PROCESS SKILLS - THE BASICS

The process skills within the team are very similar to the process skills you need to manage yourself – action, expert and cognitive skills. In this case you apply them when working with others and not on only your own. But they are key to underpinning your leadership as they ensure things run smoothly and that the team has confidence in your 'hard' skills. By ensuring things run smoothly they allow you the bandwidth to apply the 'best boss' actions – people skills – for your team that will deepen the relationships with team members.

Expert skills

These are linked to 'expert power'; although not a specific way of behaving, to be a leader you need to know your job. In other words you must have the knowledge and experience to deal with situations that you are likely to face with your team. You don't need to know as much as your team does as a whole – you just need to enable them to use their knowledge and experience to the best effect. You are the architect, not the all-knowing hero. This includes understanding what is going on across your organisation and not just your own job, understanding what the teams and people around you do, and the organisational context. This is vital for you and for you to help your team understand the organisation's needs.

Cognitive skills

Leaders must have the ability to process information, to think clearly about problems, to form plans, to make decisions and to resolve other issues. They must take a logical approach to tasks, but not rule out innovation and new ideas. In this way, the best outcome can be found. You don't have to be a genius; just approach things in a structured and logical way and this skill can be developed. As we saw earlier leaders are having to process more and more information – the CEB research[10] showed that

76% of employees said that the amount of data they have to deal with went up between 2009 and 2012.

Action skills

These are the core skills around planning and delivering tasks. Effectively it is the same process as set out in the section on managing yourself but with the team involved, so there are the additional elements of getting information from the team for decision-making if required, asking for their input where you have time, then communicating with the team on the implementation plan, delegating roles and monitoring progress. The additional elements are covered in more detail in the next sections, so you will have a road map to make each task the team has to do simple and successful.

The foundation process skills of planning, communication, delegation and motivation enable your plans to be put into practice. They underpin your key leadership function of achieving your objectives through your team, so you need to be competent at these before moving on to more advanced skills, such as creating vision and values and building team spirit, which will complete your Mach 1 resources.

If you can develop these foundation skills, it not only provides you with a base for the more advanced skills of Mach 2, but also allows your team and the individuals in it to improve their performance as well by getting them to Mach 1. Because you will be communicating, delegating and motivating more effectively, they will be able to take on more work, be more motivated and more effective and focused on what really matters. This will in itself make them more receptive to you when you use your advanced skills.

PLANNING AND IMPLEMENTATION

Use the format from managing yourself, as seen before, as the core process to collect information and develop a plan.

Empowering leadership
The key steps to success

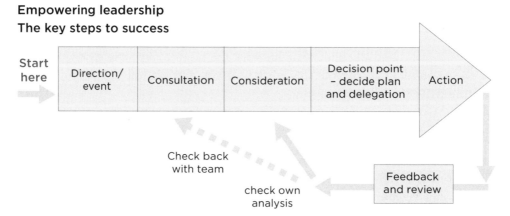

Just make sure that at each stage you are using the knowledge, skills and experience of the team to its full value by consulting its members where appropriate. Once you have assembled all the relevant data and made a decision on the best option, you have to build an action plan you can implement with your team. You have just run through the 'Direction/Event, Consultation, Consideration and Decision' process set out in the Empowering Leadership diagram (see also page 42) and are now about to 'action' your plan. So the next step is to brief the team on what needs to be done. Again more detail on exactly how to do that can be found in Chapter 3.

Now you have got the process of managing the team set up, it's about motivating your people to do it.

PEOPLE – GETTING THE RELATIONSHIP RIGHT FOR DELIVERY

When working with the team there is a new area you have to cover that you don't need when managing yourself: engaging the team to maximise effort and get to Mach 1.

This can be divided into:

1. Creating an environment for maximum performance
2. Actions for specific tasks
3. Developing even better performance in the future.

CREATING AN ENVIRONMENT FOR MAXIMUM PERFORMANCE

This is dependent on a number of factors:

1. Recognising the needs and desires of the people you are asking to deliver organisational success
2. Meeting these through core positive leadership behaviour that is commonly accepted worldwide
3. Delivering these in a way that fits with the leadership culture of the organisation or sub-section
4. Delivering these in a way that fits with the leadership culture of the country or culture you are in.

How these interact is the subject of much research and various theories, as we saw in Chapter 1. As this book aims to help you make a real difference in real organisations simply and quickly, I will summarise the voluminous debate to give a little perspective.

RECOGNISING THE NEEDS AND DESIRES OF THE PEOPLE YOU ARE ASKING TO DELIVER ORGANISATIONAL SUCCESS

No matter how good you are at the technicalities of delegation, planning, cultural awareness or other areas, unless you pay attention to what your people need – as both individuals and as a team – you are very unlikely to become an effective leader and thus able to maximise the effort of those people.

The findings from a number of sources, including Maslow, my 'best boss' list testing and other research[3], point to people across the world all seeming to want pretty much the same thing from their time at work and from their leaders.

'If your actions inspire others to dream more, learn more, do more and become more, you are a leader.'
John Quincy Adams (1767–1848), US President

The best boss list from Chapter 1 and other research confirms, in[5] the most pragmatic terms, wherever and whomever you are leading, what you need to do to engage and maximise effort from your people:

1. Kept me informed about what was going on (R)
2. Set realistic but challenging targets (T)
3. Made me part of a successful organisation with good culture (B)
4. Respected me as a professional and a person (R)
5. Backed me up when required (R)
6. Developed my skills and career (B)
7. Acted with integrity (R)
8. Led by example (R)
9. Listened to what I said and my ideas (R)
10. Genuinely cared about me (R)
11. Didn't blame me for genuine mistakes (R)
12. Let me get on with things and didn't interfere – empowered me (B)
13. Was fair and treated me decently (R)
14. Inspired me with their enthusiasm (R)
15. Built trust and transparency (R)
16. Praised me and encouraged me (R)
17. Had a sense of humour and laughed with us (R)

MEETING THESE THROUGH CORE POSITIVE LEADERSHIP BEHAVIOUR THAT IS COMMONLY ACCEPTED WORLDWIDE

Again a vast volume of research exists – Hofstede, Norhouse, GLOBE[15] – some of which is re-analysis of analysis. My objective here is to keep it as simple as possible and give you the critical information you need to be aware of to lead effectively. The GLOBE study and other research found that good leaders everywhere are generally in possession of these core attributes:

trustworthy; has foresight; just; honest; plans ahead; encouraging; positive; dynamic; confidence builder; motivational; dependable; intelligent; decisive; win/win focused; communicative; informed; team builder; excellence-focused; co-ordinator; good at administration.

Unsurprisingly, from my perspective many of these attributes underpin the delivery of the best boss list.

This is then confirmed in the global leadership behaviour identified by GLOBE[15] that again seems to be present everywhere, but note that it is not always in the same order of priority as we see in the next section. This is where cultural differences come into play. So again, from the practical perspective, these are the attributes and behaviour you need to develop to lead anywhere, but as we will see the importance of each may vary depending on the culture.

DELIVERING THESE IN A WAY THAT FITS WITH THE LEADERSHIP CULTURE OF THE ORGANISATION OR SUB-SECTION

As I have suggested and as we all know from experience organisations often have many cultural perspectives:

1. 'Main' culture driven by the business they do (transactional or relationship-based)

2. Sub-cultures driven by geography or the society in which they are based (headquarters culture) that determines the general approach and systems

3. Sub-cultures driven by what people do within the organisation, for example, sales teams do not generally think or behave in the same way as the finance department.

For example, in London Underground, station operatives, engineering staff, train drivers, and headquarters and administration staff are all aligned to different cultural groups. In the banks there are front office staff dealing with different customers; private bankers are different from traders who are different to asset managers or retail bankers. Then in the back office there are IT, HR, risk, finance, operations and facilities departments, each with its own culture. And that's just in one country. So to be effective you need to fine-tune how you deliver the core common leadership behaviour (1 and 2 above) to match the culture of the organisation or sub-section you are operating within. But that's not all.

DELIVERING THESE IN A WAY THAT FITS WITH THE LEADERSHIP CULTURE OF THE COUNTRY OR CULTURE

A global bank would have many more cultures, multiplied by, in particular, the cultures of the major business hubs it operated in, for example, London, New York, Hong Kong or Singapore. The differences in cultures may be slight but they need to be accommodated in the leadership approaches taken in those locations.

So the global leadership behaviour identified by 'best boss', GLOBE and others[15], is consistent in that it is present in effective leadership everywhere, but the importance of each attribute varies depending on 'local' conditions.

A society's cultural differences tend to revolve around the balance between the individual and the society, organisation or team. How important or how much freedom does the individual have or expect in relation to their duty or control by the organisation or society – is it *laissez-faire* like the US or more collectivist as in China? A positive leadership approach in the US might be seen as confident, forceful, clearly stating intentions, and allowing individual freedom as much as possible. In Asia the focus is on the team more than the individual and people are working hard for the team, often more than themselves.

The GLOBE study[15] grouped together a number of cultures from the leadership perspective based on similarities in cultural values and beliefs. These groupings will help you get an idea of where different cultural 'fine-tuning' may be needed.

To fully explore the differences would take a very a large book, but the purpose of this list is to make you aware that there is likely to be a difference in how you need to deliver the core common leadership behaviour if you are leading across any two of these cultures. More details are in Chapter 3 page 89, which you should refer to if you are working across cultures. This overview gives a general perspective:

1. **Anglo Saxon** – *England, Australia, South Africa (White sample), Canada, New Zealand, Ireland, United States* – competitive and result-oriented

2. **Confucian Asia** – *Taiwan, Singapore, Hong Kong, South Korea, China, Japan* – result-driven, encourage group working together over individual goals

3. **Eastern Europe** – *Hungary, Russia, Kazakhstan, Albania, Poland, Greece, Slovenia, Georgia* – forceful, supportive of co-workers, treat women with equality

4. **Germanic Europe** – *Austria, Switzerland (German-speaking part), Netherlands, Germany* – value competition & aggressiveness and are more result-oriented

5. **Latin America** – *Costa Rica, Venezuela, Ecuador, Mexico, El Salvador, Colombia, Guatemala, Bolivia, Brazil, Argentina* – loyal and devoted to their families and similar groups

6. **Latin Europe** – *Israel, Italy, Portugal, Spain, France, Switzerland (French-speaking part)* – value individual autonomy

7. **Middle East** – *Qatar, Morocco, Turkey, Egypt, Kuwait, UAE* – devoted and loyal to their own people, women afforded less status

8. **Nordic Europe** – *Finland, Sweden, Denmark* – high priority on long-term success, women treated with greater equality

9. **Southern Asia** – *India, Indonesia, Philippines, Malaysia, Thailand, Iran* – strong family & deep concern for their communities

10. **Sub-Sahara Africa** – *Namibia, Zambia, Zimbabwe, South Africa (Black sample), Nigeria* – concerned and sensitive to others, demonstrate strong family loyalty

It can get even more complex when you then start to deal with multiple leadership cultural dimensions. Imagine the cultural sensitivities needed for example, for a US-born and educated leader, operating as the head of IT for a Swiss global company for their Asian region, based in Hong Kong. This takes time and experience to develop, but it can be done. I often compare this challenge of leadership across cultures to 3D chess, where you have to do a lot of careful observation and thinking before you make a move!

But in the final analysis, and sticking to the core principle of this book by keeping things simple and practical, if you follow the 'best boss' list in a way that seems to fit in the way they like things done 'locally', then you won't go far wrong!

SO HOW CAN YOU LEARN TO MAKE THIS ALL WORK FOR YOU AS A LEADER – TO DELIVER SUCCESS?

Some people say these skills are more difficult to develop than the process areas, but there's no mystery about it. There are some simple principles and some practical steps you can take that will make you effective very quickly. They may seem daunting, but again, with thought and practice, you will be able to achieve them.

Much of this links psychology and effective leadership. These are not abstract theories; they are backed up by hard evidence that shows the type of behaviour from leaders that maximise performance and the type that degrades it. These are also supported by the real life experiences you and many others will have had yourself.

> 'It is almost true to say that leaders are 'made' rather than born. There are principles of leadership, just as there are principles of war, and these need to be studied'
>
> Field Marshall Viscount Montgomery (1887-1976), leading British/ Allied WWII commander

The best boss list is a prime example of this, so let's revisit it and dig a little deeper as it reveals some critical information you need to have to get that maximum effort. These are the actions that people say make them give maximum effort for their boss.

This time let's examine the coding: T = task-related behaviour; R = people-related behaviour that concerns the relationship between the boss and the individual; and B = both task and people-related behaviour. This coding is based on categories agreed by the 500 plus leaders and staff groups that contributed.

1. Kept me informed about what was going on (R)
2. Set realistic but challenging targets (T)
3. Made me part of a successful organisation with good culture (B)
4. Respected me as a professional and a person (R)
5. Backed me up when required (R)
6. Developed my skills and career (B)

7. Acted with integrity (R)

8. Led by example (R)

9. Listened to what I said and my ideas (R)

10. Genuinely cared about me (R)

11. Didn't blame me for genuine mistakes (R)

12. Let me get on with things and didn't interfere – empowered me (B)

13. Was fair and treated me decently (R)

14. Inspired me with their enthusiasm (R)

15. Built trust and transparency (R)

16. Praised me and encouraged me (R)

17. Had a sense of humour and laughed with us (R)

But it gets even more interesting. When you look down the best boss list and ask what is task specific (T) – part of making the task effective, and what is relationship specific (R) – keeping people motivated and maintaining a good relationship – or what are both (B), the answer is very surprising. When you ask those present to decide which behaviour falls into which category, on most occasions 70-80% are relationship; 10-15% are both; and ten or less are task specific..

Your list is likely to be the same. The lesson from this is clear: to get super performance it's not about expertise in the process – that is, the planning and decision-making; it's about making sure there is a strong and positive relationship between the leader, the team and the individual and ultimately with the organisation. And that is one of the critical success factors for Mach 1 leadership and then applying the extra effort to move on to Mach 2.

So provided that the task is well planned it will work, but if you focus on just the task you will probably only get average performance. This is the practical reality based on both your own experience and real world leaders giving their experience.

But if you focus too much on the task and getting things done without these other elements related to the relationship with people, it could actually reduce the performance of the team long term. There is a danger that too much pressure on the team from an excessive drive to deliver and achieve ends up causing short cuts, poor communications, increased risk and poor collaboration, and reduces trust and morale. Research has been done on the effects of failing to balance the desire to achieve with bringing the team with you through collaboration rather than dragging them by coercion[4]. In this study it was shown that those leaders seen as high achieving fell into two groups – those that just pushed the team hard by pace setting, which led to demotivation in the team, and those leaders who delivered results by creating a high performance environment using collaboration, vision, coaching and participation as well as pushing the pace.

This need to focus on people as well as the task is also confirmed by one of the most effective leadership models developed:

Action-Centred Leadership by John Adair[16]

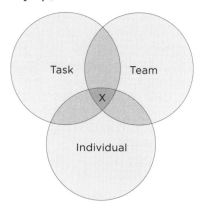

The British Army has used this very simple and memorable model very successfully for over 40 years, where it has helped turn many people into effective army officers. It centres on the simple reminder to spend time on the team and individuals as well as getting the task done. If you neglect this key message for more than a short time, your team's effort will start to reduce. If you always concentrate on the task and neglect maintaining the team and supporting individuals, the team will become unwilling or unable to do the job.

This model is an excellent foundation for all the work you do as a leader to help you get to Mach 1, in both planning, implementation and review stages of any task. Good leaders will, during the 'planning' stage, also work out how they can best balance task, team and individual needs. Say to yourself: this is the task we have to do, but while doing it, can I use it to build the team and develop individuals? Could I delegate parts of the task to provide development and challenge the team? Could I delegate it to more people to build team spirit?

So all the time keep thinking: TASK; TEAM; INDIVIDUAL.

GOOD COMMUNICATION ISN'T COMPLICATED

Too often I have heard leaders saying that it is very difficult to get critical messages down to the bottom of the organisation. In fact it is quite simple to do this without any trouble, as demonstrated by this example.

The simplicity of communication

I attended a weekly meeting with the head of a global organisation with branches round the world, and his direct reports. He said to those in the room who report to him: 'I want to make clear to everyone that the three critical things we need to get right are improving customer service, developing new business and reducing costs. I want everyone across the organisation to be aware of these. Is that clear?' All those in attendance nodded their agreement. Unusually for a leader, however, he then said: 'Oh, and by the way, as you know, I travel the world and visit your offices to see you all. When I next do this, as I walk through the office I will ask members of your staff at random how they are and what the three key things are that we need to focus on this year. I hope they will tell me what I have just told you; otherwise when I do get to your office what I say to you may not be welcome.'

An example of how being clear and simple is the most effective way to communicate a message.

Now that we know we have to spend time on the individuals and the team as well as the task, the question is: what do we do for them? Here we can revisit Maslow[3] and look for opportunities to enable them to meet their needs better, and to better deliver the needs of the organisation.

Assuming your team members have both a place to live and the ability to buy food and other basics, then the survival, safety and security needs are met. So you need to use the higher needs to increase their effort levels.

SOCIAL NEEDS

Once the survival needs are met you can focus on building team spirit through social contact. Think of examples where you have worked in a team with little team spirit, and one where there was a strong sense of this. In which did you work better? What can you do to get the team to become mutually supportive? There are many ways to achieve this, for example team meetings, team social events, or working together to discuss major activities away from the office – all building a collaborative community of effort.

PUBLIC ESTEEM

Leaders can utilise the need for public esteem at work. Most people want to achieve recognition from their peers or boss in some way, either through rewards or promotion for jobs well done, or through a boost to their confidence and self-respect. Exactly what form this takes varies with individuals and cultures: some will relish praise given in front of the whole team; others will cringe at this but be grateful for it when delivered face-to-face with you alone. Some may want visible promotion; others like to be the acknowledged team expert but don't want promotion. The public esteem motivator is probably the one that you can use most often, but you must know your team to use it effectively and fairly.

SELF-GROWTH

The self-growth need is perhaps the most difficult to quantify as it goes right to the heart of what people really want, such as personal development and the achievement of their own inner goals. This can be the most powerful motivator if you know what the individual really wants to achieve in their life. It may not all relate to work, often involving family and matters outside work, such as climbing Mount Everest or sailing the Atlantic. But helping them towards these goals through some part of their work will motivate them. The public esteem need and the self-growth need can be used again and again – once promoted, you probably want further promotion and the same applies to self-growth. Thus, by giving your team the opportunity to satisfy their own needs, you enable them to effectively motivate themselves at work.

Developing people is a key element in this as personal development often meets many self-growth needs. It can also help you get better, not just in your ability to coach, mentor or develop others, but once again it also improves effort – having an effective mentor can increase effort by 25.5%[17]. And it's not only that – having high quality direct reports can increase your own potential to go further by 22%![18]

EMOTION IS ESSENTIAL!

With all these perspectives you will by now be realising that a significant part of leadership is controlled by emotion as well as rational thought. We know from evidence[19] that an employee's decision to give high performance is 57% rational and 43% emotional. And we know that both have to be present because the rational underpins and increases the power of the emotional to get the job done. So rational gets the job done, while emotional gets things done even better. The rational acts as a multiplier to the emotional by increasing it up to 57% over and above wherever the emotional is not supported by the rational at all. If both are in place, effort is increased by 26% and intent to stay in the organisation by 36%.

Not only that, but the individual's line manager determines 80% of the emotional element. So it's the line managers and not the CEO that determine the quality of day-to-day performance in an organisation. A strong emotional link to the team can increase effort by up to 38.8%, in the organisation by 43%, in the job itself by 55.9% and to the line manager as an individual by 34%[17].

The significance of this to you and your organisation is critical. It means that it is YOU and no one else who is the main determinant of how your team performs. And you must use both rational explanation – business case, organisational strategy, potential benefits for organisation, *and* emotional explanation – inspiring vision or outcome, personal benefits, being the best. It's likely that's this part of what you do will be linked back to Maslow's[3] model and the higher needs for your team members.

EVERYONE IS DIFFERENT BUT THE SAME!

Everyone is the same in terms of their set of needs, but where the differences occur is in the specifics of what will meet those needs and drive higher performance. Different things motivate different people. This also relates to the cultural comparisons set out earlier; all the things we discuss in this section are positive for teams and individuals everywhere, but exactly how you deliver them might vary slightly depending on where you are in the world.

As a quick exercise, write down the following in the order that they motivate you to do your job: cash; holidays; responsibility; public achievement; contributing to the team and organisation; contributing to society; helping others; personal development; clear objectives; support from your boss. Other people could prioritise in a different way, not only individually but as a group or society. For example, 'contributing to society' is likely to be much more important for those in Switzerland or Singapore than in the US.

Most people think that pay comes top of the list, but research shows[20] that this is not the case. In fact the top driver of executive effort is 'connection between work and organisation strategy', with an increase in effort of 28%, whereas the highest compensation driver only delivers 7.6%. So finding out what you have to do to meet your people's needs is fundamental if you want to increase their effort. Know your team, no matter who or where they are! One of my teams in a major organisation included members from the US, the UK, Switzerland, Hong Kong, Germany, France and South Africa, with some based in London, some in Zurich and some in New York. Sometimes culturally challenging, yes, but always inspiring – and with such a range of perspectives the flow of ideas and solutions was amazing.

It can be difficult to pin down what really motivates different people. If you ask people in business, many give 'money' as their immediate response because they feel uneasy about admitting to the real factors. In the public or not-for-profit sectors, 'public service' or 'helping others' is the first response. But again that's not always the real motivator for the individual. People working in IT, for example, are often motivated by the technical challenge, irrespective of what the organisation does. So real motivations are often not as obvious as first appears, and the only way to find out what they are is to get to know your team well and, if unsure, ask them!

You should also never assume that the things that motivate you are the same as those that motivate others, but Maslow[3] can be used as a general guide. There is an easy route to getting some of the way: the qualities on the best boss list will automatically meet some of most people's needs. So that's a good start.

BUILDING RESERVES OF TRUST

By using all the ideas above to maximise the effort of others, to engage them and get them involved, you will deepen the trust that your team has in you. The importance of having the trust of your people cannot be overestimated – as was stated in Chapter 1, the two key questions in anyone's mind about a leader are whether they trust them and whether they know what they are doing.

As trust builds, it creates a 'reserve of trust', which you can call on when you need to. This is a commitment to you as the leader and will give you extra support when times are tough. If those reserves are not present, in tough times the necessary work may not be delivered. This is important, because on occasions, for example when time is short or there is high stress, you may not have time to explain why the job has to be done, and done the way you ask. Sometimes it just needs to be done, and done quickly. You may not have time to consult as outlined in the leadership process diagram on page 42, so all you can do is make a decision and tell the team what to do. But they will trust you if, in the past, you have built up a reserve of trust with them on the basis of your past explanations and consultations – we call this referent power – where a group of people will do what they're asked, based on their respect or admiration for that individual.

To build up this reserve of trust you need to give the team as many opportunities as possible to contribute and allow them to participate in decision-making processes. The trust you have shown them during these periods is returned when you have to tell them what to do summarily or ask them to put in extra effort. This is why working as a team and team meetings are as important as direct interaction with the individuals.

MISTAKES CAN HAPPEN

Sometimes, even though you are trusted, a check is required because mistakes can happen. Even with the mutual trust of Mach 1 and 2, there are times when a double check is needed, as the consequences of mistakes are too serious to allow any possibility of error.

'To make no mistakes is not within the power of man, but from their errors and mistakes the wise and good learn wisdom for the future'
Plutarch (45-120AD), Greek historian and biographer

Bang... but which way will it fall?

When I was in the UK Army Reserve and we had been asked to demolish a 40m high factory chimney in an old industrial site next to some newly built houses, we had to ensure of course that the chimney fell away from the new houses and not onto them. Thus at every stage, the calculations, drilling of the charge holes, placing of the charges and the timing of different charges all had to be checked and then checked again. Three people checked the quality of each stage independently, not just two. The moment of truth arrived on the morning of the demolition in front of a large crowd, including some anxious house owners, and the media. The button was pressed. There was a loud bang. The chimney stood stock still for about five very, very long seconds before it slowly started to fall – the right way. There are times when you cannot risk a mistake even with a team you trust.

There are many safety-critical environments where a double check is normal practice. But in reality too many organisations with safety-critical areas that require risk minimisation (for example nuclear power generation) extend the check out of the areas where it's needed into all activities, even those that pose no risk, such as HR. This is understandable, but counterproductive, and is a common problem those in such organisations should be aware of.

BUILDING AN EFFECTIVE TEAM

In many organisations, teams don't really work as teams but as collections of individuals. This is particularly true where reward is based solely on individual performance. This can reduce the potential for maximum performance from the group as a whole. In any team there are those who are experts and some who are new to the job. So, for example, if the experts in the team only do their own work and never coach the new members, it will take much longer to get the new members performing well. If coaching took place, team spirit – and thus collaboration – would be built, and we know this is critical to overall performance and getting to Mach 1.

While motivation is to some degree internal for individuals, this tends to focus on their own work, so for team spirit to flourish the catalyst needs to come from you as the leader. Some team members may naturally do this but as the leader you need to ensure everyone is involved. Building team spirit is critical to maintaining the team, and allowing it to take on challenges and still succeed, as shown in the Adair model.

Your objective should be to build an environment where the team members will mutually support each other even without your input. This ensures they are motivated even if you aren't there. The following elements make a strong team spirit easier to build:

1. Trust in you
2. Having a good team plan
3. Knowing how they are doing
4. Trust in each other
5. Celebrating mutual achievement.

TRUST IN YOU

As set out previously, we have seen that building team spirit and trust from the team is a vital part of being a good Mach 1 leader, delivered by actions, not words. This is the starting point and creates the foundation for progress. But these aren't just nice words – if the individual feels that you as his or her boss demonstrate good personal qualities of honesty, integrity and friendliness, this alone could increase potential to go further by 42.9%, ability by 36.5%, aspiration by 8% and engagement by 42%[21].

HAVING A GOOD TEAM PLAN

The value of you initiating a discussion with the team in a team meeting or at other times cannot be overestimated. This in itself builds trust for you. I have done this with many teams and it has significant impact. This helps the team to move much more quickly to Mach 1 and Mach 2.

This is because discussion can have the following benefits:

1. It gives the team an agreed common purpose above individual tasks
2. This purpose is aligned to the organisation's vision and objectives
3. It makes the individuals aware of the organisational bigger picture
4. It develops collaboration and mutual support
5. It sets the standards for behaviour within the team and the team's values.

All of the above are known to improve both individual and team performance, for example, knowing how they contribute to the bigger picture can improve an employee's performance by 33%[19]. We also know that effective collaboration accounts for 50% of what people should be doing in the new world of work[10].

COMMON PURPOSE AND VISION – LONG-TERM DIRECTION

In the rush of day-to-day activity it is easy to focus only on the short term. But having a vision gives the team a long-term aim, and this really helps with making Mach 1 work.

It will motivate and inspire the team over time, giving meaning to their day-to-day work and aligning them to the organisation's vision for Mach 2. It's a fact that if the team has a vision, and believes in it, performance will improve. The vision is based on where the team sees itself in relation to what it needs to deliver to the organisation.

> 'A rock pile ceases to be a rock pile the moment a single man contemplates it, bearing within it the image of a cathedral'
>
> Antoine de Saint Exupery (1900-1944), French writer, poet, aristocrat and pioneering aviator

The discussion of vision and common purpose starts to build understanding of the wider organisation. The evidence[19] clearly shows that enabling the team to understand the wider organisation can improve their individual job performance by over 33%. It also impacts on how well the whole organisation functions by enabling the collaboration that is now critical to success. You cannot collaborate unless you understand. The evidence already set[10] out suggests that, in the new world of work, the value to the organisation of what employees do in collaboration with others is now as important as what they do themselves on their own work.

The vision for your team should be based on where your team needs to be, or what it needs to be able to do, to help the organisation perform at its best in the future. If you have an organisational vision, use this to help build your team vision. If the organisational vision is 'We will be the leading supplier of IT services in five years', then your team vision could be, 'We will provide a top rated XXXXX team (insert what your team does, for example IT/HR/sales) within five years to support achieving the organisational vision'.

Even if there is no organisational vision, you still need to develop your team vision.

SHORT TERM – ACTIONS TO ACHIEVE VISION

The vision can then be broken down into actions that will achieve it. The next step, for example, would be to start to identify what actions need to be delivered to make the vision a reality. To help with this, use the questions in the section in Chapter 3 toolkit on page 80. It is often best to do this at a team meeting, as everyone will be more dedicated to achieving them if they have been involved in creating them. Don't forget, this is a team vision, not just your vision.

> 'Never tell people how to do things. Tell them what to do and they will surprise you with their ingenuity.'
> General George Patton (1885–1945), US/Allied Commander WWII

To achieve the vision and get to your destination, there obviously needs to be some planning and objective setting. Achieving a vision is like any journey, with a starting point and agreed stages *en route*. As well as your destination, you need to know where you are starting from and how to get there. There are some questions you might find useful in the Chapter 3 toolkit.

KNOWING HOW THEY ARE DOING

Everyone needs to know regularly how they are doing or they will never improve or peform at their best. Regular feedback is critical to achieve Mach 1. Without it you and the team are unlikely to succeed – there is significant evidence that regular constructive feedback is a driver of success[22], increasing effort by up to 25.6%.

TRUST IN EACH OTHER

If the above is the 'what' in what has to be done, this is the 'how'. Discussing and agreeing the team's common values, rather than telling them, sets a benchmark of positive behaviour the team will be more likely to observe. It also encourages trust in each other. How does it involve integrity, honesty, supporting each other, producing excellent work, dealing fairly with everyone, helping people develop, loyalty, setting an example and collaborating with others? Remember that actions speak louder than words.

The organisation will have its values; you can then work with the team to reflect those values and draw up the day-to-day behaviour that underpins those values. For example, if mutual support is our value, then the behaviour is always trying to provide help if we see a colleague in need. Again this positions the team to become an aligned, integrated and focused team at Mach 1 and ready to move to Mach 2.

Once you have had an initial team meeting to agree vision, objectives, values and behaviour, then subsequent meetings that leverage further value follow on naturally. These will help significantly in getting to Mach 1 and then moving to Mach 2, and can be both communication and brainstorming sessions on how to improve. More information and the rules for brainstorming are in Chapter 3 on page 80.

EVERY EMPLOYEE HAS IDEAS THAT ADD VALUE

In the dim and distant past of my career when I served in the military – not quite as distant as the Roman legions, but nearly! – I was once asked to develop a new method of enabling armoured vehicles to cross small streams that would allow the larger, more valuable and limited metal bridges to be used on larger rivers. This was critical to the ability of the British Army to be highly mobile in central Europe and elsewhere. We had a prototype – the pipe fascine[23] – but it needed development to be taken into full service. I took my team of soldiers out to a number of project sites for three months to test and develop it. Up to this point expert engineers and myself had undertaken the design and development. But at the project sites there were no engineers, just myself, some of my NCOs, and my soldiers. I told everyone that we needed to get the device finished and a user handbook written within the deadline, and that I wanted ideas from anyone, no matter how junior and no matter how mad.

Over a period of days, everyone took up the challenge and became more inspired, and I asked even the most junior soldier for their thoughts as we worked. One evening I caught a group of soldiers having a can of beer in their tent – not unusual – but what was unusual was that in front of them were the engineering drawings and they were sketching ideas for a release mechanism problem we were trying to solve. They were working on the project in their own free time because they felt so inspired and involved in making it work. When I asked why they were doing this, they said: 'because we want to help you get it sorted, Sir, and to be a part of something special.' So I sat down with them and opened a can of beer. The project came in under time and the British Army and others around the world have been successfully using the device ever since.

Pipe fascine

CELEBRATING MUTUAL ACHIEVEMENT AND HAVING FUN

After you have reached your objective it is very important that you take some time to celebrate the achievement and allow the team to do so as well. In such celebrations it is also possible to ask the question: 'and how could we do it even better next time?'

This also applies to individuals. If they have achieved personal goals, congratulate them and, with their permission, inform the team. This is particularly important for work-related achievements, for example, gaining qualifications or doing a good job for another team. If possible, birthdays should never be overlooked, but dealt with in a way that is appropriate for the individual concerned.

To some this may sound both simplistic and maybe even patronising. And it's hardly strategic management, but that's the reality of life and organisations: people note the small things as much as the big picture, and even simple things like birthdays count. As the statistics prove, just showing you care can improve performance of an individual by up to 23.4% – and it's on the best boss list. Your people will never care about the customers, strategy or maximising performance if you don't show you care about them.

Finally, don't forget the fun element. This is important for building enthusiasm and team spirit. Make sure you encourage a sense of humour so that you and the team can laugh at yourselves and the problems you faced once you have succeeded. You know how much humour can lift the whole mood and inject another burst of enthusiasm when things may not be going well. And that even appears on the best boss list too!

IT'S JUST AS MUCH ABOUT THE FUTURE AS THE PRESENT

In everything you do with your team the focus should be on the future as much as the past. The past is the foundation for the future, but organisations and leaders that constantly look back lock themselves into a static mindset and quickly become adrift from the world they need to operate in with all the consequences of that. Perpetually developing the capability and motivation of your people is as important as getting them to do the current task. This means you need to plan their development and make sure it happens. Some line managers see

'As we look ahead into the next century, leaders will be those who empower others.'

Bill Gates (b 1955), US entrepreneur, businessman and philanthropist, founder of Microsoft

this activity as a distraction from the real job. In fact it is central to the sustainable success of the individual, team and organisation, and that's what everyone – customers and investors included – wants.

The benefits are clear and beyond dispute. For example, a well-designed, credible development plan can improve the potential of talented staff by 37.8%, their engagement by 45.4%, their ability by 15.7% and their aspiration by 22.5%. Unachievable development plans can reduce that potential by 18.9%, and development plans that managers don't support or take seriously reduce potential by 12.5%[24].

This shows that this development doesn't just improve current performance but it also gets people more engaged and makes them want to do even better, leading to further improvements in performance in the future.

WHAT ABOUT THE DARK SIDE?

All of us, you included, have a darker side to our personality[25]. We need to keep an eye on these aspects because if we slip into them there will be a negative impact. They aren't bad enough to be seen as personality disorders but they must be avoided. Identifying and dealing with this 'dark side' has been the subject of a number of books, Hogan being a prime example but a brief overview will help you to know what to look for in yourself and others to see if it's taking over! In the simplest terms it's all about qualities and behaviour that can be positive and for which you may get promoted, but which if you exercise them too much they actually become negative. Hogan[26] identified these:

- Excitable – great empathy and deep feelings – but can take up time and be hard to please
- Sceptical – insightful and constructive criticism – but can resist compromise or trusting others
- Cautious – prudent and evaluate risk well – but can resist change and be indecisive
- Reserved – not easily distracted and can take adversity – but can be insensitive and tactless
- Leisurely – good interpersonal skills – but can be focused on own agendas
- Arrogant – energetic, fearless, successful – but can be arrogant, refuse to accept their failures
- Mischievous – charming, clever, risk takers – but can be reckless, manipulative, over confident
- Colourful – charming, dramatic, bright – but can be distracted, impulsive and unproductive
- Imaginative – visionary, insightful, creative – but can be poor communicators, self-absorbed, indifferent to consequences
- Diligent – reliable, predictable, high standards – but can be over controlling, micromanaging, fussy
- Dutiful – polite, eager to please, uncritical – but can have problems taking decisions or action.

These 'de-railers' Hogan identified have the potential to develop in anyone. It is worth taking the opportunity if you can to consider these in more detail to make yourself aware of where your risk areas might be and so avoid them. However, if you do what this book suggests and achieve Mach 2, then the chances are you will have avoided these de-railers and are maintaining the right balance in your leadership.

KEY POINTS CHAPTER 2

As an individual leader

You need to ensure that you are doing the work only you can do, that you delegate work the team can do, and say no to work that others can do better than you.

Build your skills around these areas:

- *Cognitive – dealing with information effectively*
- *Action – getting things done*
- *Relationship – building good working relationships*
- *Expert – doing your specialist work with excellence*
- Always plan your work using a structured process
- Always get and give feedback as you work through a task

With the team

- As an individual leader you control the majority of the factors that will determine how much effort your people put in at work
- Generally everyone who works for you wants the same things from you as you want from your boss to maximise your effort
- Your key role as a leader is to enable your people to meet their own needs and aspirations by delivering the organisation's objectives
- Balance TASK/TEAM/INDIVIDUAL
- Everyone and every team needs an inspiring vision to aim for

Get the team to develop vision, objectives and values with you, as a group this helps them to:

1. Trust you
2. Build a good plan
3. Trust each other and collaborate
4. Celebrate achievement.

- This will help maximise performance
- Emotion is just as important as rational analysis in maximising performance
- Watch out for possible dark side derailers

CHAPTER 2 KEY ACTIONS FOR YOU TO DO NOW

1. How well are you covering the full best boss list with your people, and if there are any shortfalls what are they?

2. When you get the team to do a task how are you doing against balancing:

    1. Tasks need – is there good planning and execution of task?

    2. Team need – are you developing the team as a mutually-supportive group?

    3. Individual needs – are you developing the motivation and capabilities of every team member?

    4. Organisational needs – are you aligning the work to the organisation's critical deliverables?

    Always make sure each of these areas is covered with every task.

3. How are you doing at building trust with your team and encouraging them to collaborate:

    1. With each other?

    2. With other teams in the organisation?

    3. With contractors, suppliers or external stakeholders?

    4. Identify three areas where collaboration needs to be improved.

References

1. *Managerial leadership and ischaemic heart disease among employees: the Swedish WOLF study*, A. Nyberg, L. Alfredsson, T. Theorell, H. Westerlund, J. Vahtera & M. Kivimäki: Occupational Environmental Medicine 66(9), September 2009 (p640)

2. *Reducing patient mortality in hospitals: The role of human resource management*, West, Guthrie, Dawson, Borrill & Carter: Journal of Organisational Behaviour 27, 2006 (p983–1002)

3. *A theory of human motivation*, A.H. Maslow: Psychological Review 50(4), 1943 (p370–96)

4. *Leadership run amok, the destructive power of potential overachievers*, Spreier, Fontaine, Malloy: Harvard Business Review June 2006 (p1-10)

5. *Creating the Best Workplace on Earth*, R. Goffee & G. Jones: Harvard Business Review, May 2013

6. *Cognitive asymmetry in employee emotional reactions to leadership behaviours*, M.T. Dasborough: Leadership Quarterly 172, 2006 (p163-178) and *SCARF: A brain-based model for collaborating with and influencing others.*, D. Rock: Neuro Leadership Journal 1, 2008 (p1-9)

7. *Pulvinar neurons reveal neurobiological evidence of past selection for rapid detection of snakes*, Quan Van Le, Lynne A. Isbell, Jumpei Matsumoto, Minh Nguyen, Etsuro Hori, Rafael S. Maior,
Carlos Tomaz, Anh Hai Tran,
Taketoshi Ono & Hisao Nishijo:
PNAS 2013 (published ahead of print October 28 2013)

8. *Unconscious determinants of free decisions in the human brain*, Chun Siong Soon, Marcel Brass, Hans-Jochen Heinze & John-Dylan Haynes: Nature Neuroscience, April 13 2008

9. *Driving Employee Performance and Retention Through Engagement*: Corporate Leadership Council, 2004

10. *Driving Breakthrough Performance in the New Work Environment*: Corporate Executive Board, 2013

11. *Effectuation: Elements of Entrepreneurial Expertise*, S. D. Sarasvathy: Edward Elgar, New Horizons in Entrepreneurship Series, 2008

12. *Judgment in Managerial Decision Making*, M. Bazerman: Wiley, 1993

13. *When to trust your gut* , Hayashi: Harvard Business Review, February 2001

14. *Is starting with a co-founder better than going solo? You Bet!*, B. Hodak: Forbes, 17 September 2013

15. *Culture, Leadership, and Organisations: The GLOBE study of 62 societies*, Robert J House et al: Sage Publications, 2004

16. *Action-Centred Leadership*, J. E. Adair: McGraw-Hill, London, 1973

17. *Driving Employee Performance and Retention Through Engagement*: Corporate Leadership Council, 2004 (p97)

18. *Realising the potential of rising talent*, Corporate Leadership Council, 2005 (p67)

19. *Employee engagement Framework and Survey*: Corporate Leadership Council, 2004

20. *Driving organisational performance through executive compensation*: Corporate Leadership Council, 2005 (p72)

21. *Realising the potential of rising talent*, Corporate Leadership Council, 2005 (p109)

22. *Driving Employee Performance and Retention Through Engagement*: Corporate Leadership Council, 2004 (p109)

23. You'll find more online at en.wikipedia.org/wiki/Fascine

24. *Realising the full potential of rising talent*: Corporate Leadership Council, 2005 Vol. 1 (p108)

25. *The dark side of charisma*, Raskin, Hogan & Fazzini: Measures of Leadership, Leadership Library of America (p343-354) and *Assessing leadership: a view of the dark side*: International Journal of Selection & Assessment No. 9, (p40-51)

26. *Hogan Development Survey Manual*, Hogan & Hogan: Hogan Assessment Systems, 2009

3

Step-by-step to Mach 1:
A toolkit for individual leaders

3

Step-by-step to Mach 1:
A toolkit for individual leaders

This chapter pulls together some of the practical tools and techniques that will help you as an individual leader get to Mach 1 and then Mach 2. But they apply just as much to your team, your department or organisation, and to those of you who are developing leaders across your organisation.

The contents of this chapter may seem too simple for some readers, but I promise you that from all my career experience I know that the majority of things that go wrong in organisations are due not to complex problems, but to the simple fact that the leaders involved lacked the most basic foundational knowledge and skills. If you try to implement the more advanced Mach 2 leadership without these in place you will fail. It's like trying to build a house without foundations: at the first problem it will fall to pieces.

SELF ASSESSMENT

This self assessment is designed to help you work out how well you are doing in the key areas of leadership.

Answer each statement with the most appropriate word for the action described that reflects what you do: *rarely, sometimes* or *most of the time.*

ALIGNING TEAM DELIVERY TO ORGANISATIONAL NEEDS

- I check if the team is really delivering what aligns to critical organisational objectives
- I make sure team members are aware of how and what they do contributes to the bigger picture
- I make sure team members are aware of the organisation's vision and strategic objectives

- I make sure we have a team vision and objectives and update as needed
- I ensure that the team vision directly aligns to the organisation's strategic objectives

MAKING SURE YOU ARE DOING HIGH VALUE WORK FIRST

- I review the work I do to ensure that I prioritise those things that align to key strategic objectives
- I make sure that I identify work that is important but not urgent and make sure it gets done before it becomes urgent
- I get the team to prioritise their work so that they concentrate on the work that adds most to the delivery of the organisation's key strategic objectives

PLANNING TASKS

- I only accept work that the team can do and which supports key organisational objectives
- I always work out how long a job will take and whether I have the resources before accepting it for my team or myself
- I always make sure I am absolutely clear on all the key information about a task before I accept it
- When the team has been given a task I make sure there is a viable plan developed to make it happen, where possible developed with the team
- I always allow a contingency element in all my planning, i.e. 30% reserve time, including a back-up plan
- I set myself and others SMART objectives: (Specific, Measurable – you know when it's done, Agreed – the person is committed to it, Realistic – it's achievable and Timed – with a deadline)
- I have both a rolling 'to do' list and diarise key deadlines and commencement dates to meet those

PROBLEM SOLVING

- When we have a problem I make sure we identify the real cause and not just the symptoms
- I ask for feedback from the team and others to identify the causes
- Where we have time we brainstorm potential solutions to develop innovative ones

EFFECTIVE DELEGATION

- I regularly check to see if any of the jobs I do could be delegated so I can concentrate on those only I can do
- I delegate work that others could do if they have the time

- I give people as much responsibility and freedom as possible when delegating
- I use delegation to develop the skills of team members by giving them new or challenging tasks
- I regularly check if I could delegate other tasks as the skill of the team develops
- I use the delegation formula to make sure I optimise my delegation
- I agree with each individual the level of supervision needed for each task, and don't just decide myself

CLEAR COMMUNICATION

When communicating tasks to the team I make sure everyone knows:

1. The background to the task and why it's being done
2. The contribution this makes to the wider organisation
3. What specifically we have to achieve and by when
4. What specific tasks need to be done and by whom and when
5. At the end of any discussion I ask if anyone has any questions.

When communicating generally, I:

1. Make sure I establish what the other person's perspectives are
2. Make sure I enable them to understand what my perspectives are
3. Try to identify a mutually-beneficial solution
4. Agree specific outcomes, actions and timelines.

We have regular team meetings, weekly or bi-weekly, that are two-way communication.

GIVING FEEDBACK ON PERFORMANCE

- Before I give feedback I ask the individual for their perspective on how they are doing
- I ask team members how they can improve their own and the team's performance
- I give feedback to individuals on how they are doing day-to-day
- I discuss performance shortfalls as opportunities to improve performance in the future
- I always end on a positive note even if I have been discussing problems
- I show the team I understand that sometimes people make genuine mistakes and treat them as a learning experience

GETTING FEEDBACK TO IMPROVE PERFORMANCE

- I ask others, including my own team, for feedback on my own performance

- I regularly ask individuals if I can help them perform better, especially by changing my delegation style
- I give everyone the opportunity to give me their ideas and genuinely listen to them
- In conversations with the team I spend as much time listening as talking
- Team members come to me with their ideas on how to improve their own or the team's performance

GETTING BETTER PERFORMANCE

- I know what motivates my individual team members
- I praise team members when they do a good job
- I set challenging but achievable targets for individuals and the team (SMART objectives)
- I show each team member that I have a genuine interest in them both personally and professionally, and that I care about them
- I talk to each team member for a few minutes every day – not just about the job, but about their wider life too
- I let the team update and contribute to the development of vision, values and plans

CHANGE

- I view change as an opportunity not a threat
- I initiate change and don't just carry out change initiated by others
- I ask the team for ideas for change
- I make sure that change has benefits for both team and individuals

DEVELOPING SELF AND THE TEAM

- I enable individuals to develop their skills through their work
- I regularly discuss how team members would like to develop further, in particular during the appraisal process, and use past performance to guide future development
- I make sure that every team member has a development plan that they have created, that I support and help them to achieve
- I match the development needs of the individuals and team to the present and future needs of the organisation
- I coach individuals to help them develop, or arrange for more experienced team members to do so
- I have my own development plan that I update regularly
- I have a mentor

CREATING VISION, ALIGNMENT AND TEAM SPIRIT

- I make sure the team knows how they contribute to the bigger picture
- I make sure the team has a detailed understanding of our end-customers' needs
- I ensure the team fully understands what the teams around us do and seek to help them
- We have a team vision and objectives that the team agreed on
- Team members take time to develop and support each other
- I get the team to have events to bring them together: briefings, social events, training sessions
- I make sure that those working remotely or sub-contractors are all fully integrated in the team

COLLABORATION AND THE FUTURE

- I make sure the team is encouraged to collaborate as well as do their own work
- I spend time building networks to establish contacts
- I always work for a win/win outcome
- I make sure that the team regularly find out more about other parts of the organisation and external best practice

LEADING WITH INTEGRITY

- I treat all team members equally, fairly and with respect
- I act with integrity
- I demonstrate a good example to the team
- I endeavour to understand the other person's viewpoint
- I never let self-interest influence my decisions
- I am happy to tell my friends I work for my organisation

HOW DID YOU DO?

When you have finished go through your answers. The more you have put 'most of the time' the better, the 'rarely' indicates an area that you probably need to do more of. So the best course of action is to start to do the 'rarely' much more and as soon as you can, and do more of the 'sometimes'. This way you will start to go in the right direction and improvements should result quite quickly.

You should also put the things you want to develop more into your development plan.

GETTING THE JOB DONE – EFFECTIVE PLANNING AND LEADERSHIP

Individual leaders have to get a number of preparatory steps right before they can get their team involved in making things happen. This first section looks at how to get these first steps right and make sure you as a leader are totally clear on what you want to achieve and plan how best to do it.

WORKING OUT WHAT YOU SHOULD BE DOING AND BUILDING A PLAN

To help you see if your team is aligned to the strategic needs of the organisation, the 'why are we here?' question is critical. Write 'Why are we here?' at the top of a piece of paper, and underneath list all the jobs and services the team provides to the organisation. This can be used in two ways. Firstly, if you look down the list and summarise in one sentence what you do, you can use this as a good basis for formulating the team's vision (long-term statement of intent) and mission (shorter-term statement of what you need to deliver).

Above all, this can then be compared to any tasks you are asked to do – just to make sure that what you allocate your time to is maximising the value to your organisation.

Empowering leadership
The key steps to success

The key stages to solving a problem or planning a task in a logical way are:

1. Identifying the real problem or requirement
2. Analysing the problem or task
3. Collecting information if required to optimise decision
4. Producing a set of options
5. Evaluating options and deciding on the best.

Running this process effectively is key. Each of these steps must be undertaken effectively to both come up with the optimum solution but also, in the process, to avoid the bias and other perception issues that creep into our decision making as leaders, as set out in Chapter 2 and well documented[1].

1. IDENTIFYING THE REAL PROBLEM OR REQUIREMENT
   (Note: only use this step if it's a problem scenario; if not go straight to step 2)

There are many complex types of analysis processes that do this, such as the McKinsey 7S[2] and using Fishbone analysis[3] (identifying issues around key categories, for example location, task, people, equipment and process.) More details on these tools can be quickly found on the internet. But for quick and simple analysis of general day-to-day problems just use the 'why' question three or four times.

For example:

'We need to improve communication in the team.' 'Why?'

'Because there have been misunderstandings.' 'Why?'

'Because my instructions have been misunderstood.' 'Why?'

'Because I failed to make my meaning fully clear.' 'Why?'

'Because my communication skills were lacking.'

Solution: improve my communication skills by a training course

At this point you should have identified the problem and this can now be turned, with analysis of that problem and planning, into an action plan.

2. ANALYSING THE PROBLEM OR TASK

You now need to examine the problem or task to see how you can go about dealing with it and to find an objective to aim for. To continue with the example problem:

Poor communication skills on my part led to me not making clear what I wanted. So my objective is to improve my communication skills.

3. COLLECTING INFORMATION

Your next stage is to make sure you have all the information you need to develop the best options to take action. You may have this information yourself or you may need to gather it from other sources. You then need to consider it, produce a number of options for action, and then decide on the best.

If it's a difficult problem you need to be sure that you get all the relevant information on the problem or task in hand within a reasonable timescale. This information can come from any source, including asking the team or others for their input. They may be aware of things that you are not, or have knowledge or experience you don't have. So if in doubt always get input from others, if time allows.

'Seek truth from facts'
Deng Xiaoping (1904–1997)
Chinese leader

79

4. PRODUCING A SET OF OPTIONS

From the information you have collected draw up at least two or three possible ways to approach the problem. Don't just go for the obvious or 'the way it always been done before' option. Just because a problem has been solved or a task done in a certain way in the past doesn't mean that this is the best way to do it this time. That might have been appropriate in the past but may not be now. In addition, having a second option can also give you a reserve plan if things go wrong.

You can develop options either by yourself or by brainstorming with the team. Brainstorming allows you to pull together all the potential ideas you have about a subject, which in turn stimulates new ideas and approaches, as well as those commonly used. All the ideas can then be assessed and the best ones used. A brainstorming session may only last 20 or 30 minutes, but it removes some of the main barriers to creative thinking. For brainstorming to be effective there are five rules you should stick to:

'The way to get good ideas is to get lots of ideas and throw the bad ones away.'
Linus Pauling (1901-1994), American chemist, Nobel Prize for Chemistry and Nobel Peace Prize winner

1. No criticism of any ideas until they are evaluated – if with the team tell them no astonished looks, giggles or hysterical laughter for others' suggestions!

2. Encourage 'freewheeling' where the group just tries to get the ideas to flow thick and fast

3. Get as many ideas as possible – it's possible to get 80 ideas in 20 minutes!

4. Write down every idea. You can either appoint someone to do this or individuals can write down their own ideas on a flip chart or board. Some groups like to write down their ideas as they go along and then put them all into a central list at the end. Use whatever works best for you!

5. If you have time, think about the ideas for a few days, then re-evaluate. Many brainstorming sessions evaluate ideas straight away, but this can mean that new or challenging ideas tend to get rejected. If everyone has a list of all the ideas for a few days, after which an evaluation session is held, the quality of evaluation is higher. Evaluate each idea, listing pros and cons, and then thin the list down to three good ones for detailed analysis.

Mind mapping

You can also do this yourself through 'mind mapping', where you put the problem in a circle in the centre of a piece of paper. Like a tree, each idea branches off into another circle connected by a line. Sub-divisions of these ideas then branch off further, and so on until you have run out of ideas.

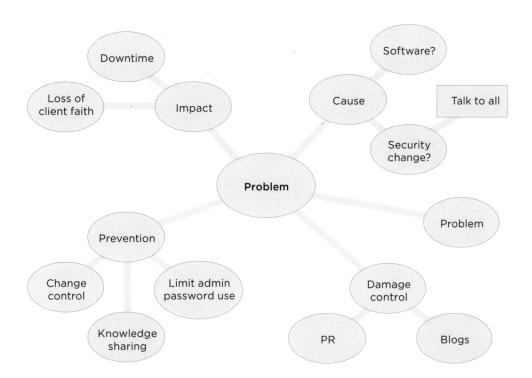

5. EVALUATING YOUR OPTIONS AND DECIDING ON THE BEST

Depending on the problem, evaluate the options to maximise benefit, whether that is to bring in the most money, to minimise costs, to minimise or maximise time, to get things in place as required. Use whichever measures you can to show the most effective option to achieve your objective. Some tools such as cost-benefit analysis can be used for complex problems, or just a simple list of 'pros' and 'cons' for each option, with some figures if possible, is enough for simple tasks. However, beware of the common mistakes we all make in decision-making, as set out on page 61 of Chapter 2.

THE PLAN

Once you have your best option for solving the problem or doing the task, you need to be clear about what needs to be done to achieve your objectives. Consider the steps or stages you have to go through, which order to do them in, and what resources are available, including a start time and a deadline. All this applies to your own tasks, as well as to teamwork.

Question	Example
What do I want to achieve?	Set up a briefing process
Why does it need to be done?	Misunderstandings have occurred costing time & money
When does it need to be done by?	The end of the month
How best can it be done?	By weekly team briefings
Where will it be done?	In the office on Friday afternoons
Who will take part?	The whole team led by me

From this example you can then go into more detail in the 'how best can it be done' section using the following guide:

- Timings: what needs to be done when, especially start and finish
- People: who needs to do what?
- Resources: financial, material
- Authority: do you need clearance or authority?

It's still true today!

There is a simple formula that may help, from the famous British poet Rudyard Kipling 1865-1936.
'I keep six honest serving-men
(They taught me all I knew);
Their names are What and Why and When
And How and Where and Who.'

IS IT WORKING? REVIEWS AND FEEDBACK

You will see that the task process diagram has 'feedback loops' that allow for reviews, both during after the task, and if you decide you can't proceed, these help you to find out what you need to proceed.

This process may at first seem impractical, but apply it to the last task you did anyway. Did you go through all the stages? Consider a task that went wrong. At which stage did the problem occur? The advice in this chapter is intended to help you make sure each stage of the process runs smoothly.

This process will obviously be the same when you plan tasks for the team, except that you have to bear in mind their skills and experience as well as your own.

CONCLUSION

All of this may seem very, very basic, if not common sense, but the main cause of people making the wrong decisions, or when things don't get done effectively in organisations, is the failure to run through the basic processes set out above.

Too many people jump to conclusions, make decisions based on untested assumptions or out-of-date information, or just take the easy way out by doing it the way it has always been done. In other cases, the project plan is not viable, the time allowed is insufficient and the result is either failure or everyone having to work very long hours when they don't need to. In 2013 an intern in the banking sector in London died after working very long hours on a project[4]. So this lack of ability to project plan effectively is an issue you need to think about.

Before you get it right for the team you have to be able to get it right for yourself!

IMPLEMENTING YOUR PLAN

Having developed a credible plan, the next stage is its implementation, which is easy if you are doing it alone, but less so when others are involved. There are particular challenges if the team is involved:

1. Delegating tasks to the right people where appropriate
2. Communicating to the team what needs to be done
3. Motivating them to do it
4. Giving them feedback as you go along and reviewing progress.

DELEGATING TASKS TO THE RIGHT PEOPLE WHERE APPROPRIATE – SHOULD I DELEGATE AND TO WHOM?

To maximise your own time and develop the skills and motivation of the team, it is very important to delegate tasks where possible and to match the level of freedom you give (the delegation level) to the situation (the individual and the task) involved. This has the following benefits:

1. It makes sure an individual or team capable of successfully completing it does the job
2. It gives the leader more time to spend on leadership functions, for example, building the team, planning development and building working relationships
3. It gives the right degree of freedom to those doing the task so that they are not over-supervised or given a task they cannot complete without support
4. It allows the individual or team to maximise their skills and knowledge development
5. It reduces sources of potential conflict within the team.

So try to delegate those tasks are often referred to as 'low leverage' tasks:

- Routine, minor and day-to-day jobs
- Jobs that other team members can do as well as you
- Jobs that team members can do better than you because of their specialist skills
- Jobs that will challenge and help develop those involved

There may be exceptions where you need to delegate some high leverage tasks, for example, to develop the skills of your deputy to cover for you if you are away or if you are leaving. But the types of high leverage tasks usually better done by yourself include:

- Jobs that require your personal attention because no one else has the authority or experience to do them
- Jobs that involve the long-term development of the team, i.e. leadership roles. These include training, planning, gaining commitment, motivating the team, setting up control and evaluation systems, setting and agreeing objectives, crafting vision and team spirit.

As a rule of thumb you should try to spend 20% of your time on low leverage tasks and 80% on high leverage ones.

WHAT SHOULD YOU DELEGATE TO OTHERS?

Delegation can save a lot of time. A very effective exercise is the 'What jobs could I delegate?' list. Write ten jobs that you do each week down the left-hand side of a page. Then draw five columns to the right of these, the first column headed 'name', the second headed 'without training', the third headed 'with training', the fourth, 'training details' and the fifth, 'time saving'. Now consider each job.

What jobs could I delegate?

Job	Name	Without training?	With training?	Details	Time Saved
1. Weekly sales figures	Paul Smith	Yes			2.5 hours
2. Liaison with minor clients	Ann Richards	No	Yes	Two weeks shadowing A Thomas	1.5 hrs
3. Sending out information to clients	Bill Dobson	No	Yes	John B to teach him	(2.5 for John B)
Total					Me 4.0 John B 2.5

Ask yourself if you can delegate each job to someone on the team, either with or without training. If you can delegate, write 'yes' in the relevant column and the name of the individual in the name column. Then assess how much time you will save each week and put this saving in the time saved column. Once you have thought about all the jobs, add up the total time you will save. In most cases leaders find that this process enables a 10% to 25% time saving each week, which can equate to an extra day to spend on high leverage work.

TO WHOM SHOULD YOU DELEGATE?

Before you delegate to anyone, you must assess existing workloads. Asking people if they have time to take on extra work is not enough; some people will take on work they cannot manage because they are worried about saying no to their boss. If it seems they may have the time, then ask them to confirm this.

Who can do it? Once you know that some of your team have time to take on the new task, you need to select the best person to do the job and delegate it to them with the appropriate degree of freedom to act on their own initiative – empowerment.

Think about how you delegate at present: would you give a task to someone with no previous experience of the job, or someone with a lot of previous experience? The answer is clear: you would choose the person with the experience. The same applies to the motivation to complete the job. Would you delegate to someone who is motivated to complete the job or someone who is not? Again, the answer is fairly obvious. You would choose the person who is committed to completing the job.

This shows the two most important criteria for effective delegation – those that you are already using – task knowledge and experience, and motivation and commitment. These factors also determine how much time you have to spend on supervision; inexperienced or unmotivated team members will need more help. The lesson for all leaders is that the more motivated and knowledgeable the team, the more you can delegate, and therefore the more time you have to concentrate on tasks only you can do. This is why you should be constantly developing their performance and motivation.

In practice, there is a formula to help you. It classifies individuals for each job by their level of knowledge, experience and motivational commitment. This helps you determine the best delegation level to allow them to successfully complete a task whilst minimising your supervision time.

Classify team members

Think about those who work for you and write down one job that could be delegated to several individuals on your team. Consider which classification each person comes under for that job. Are they a beginner, a learner, a regular or a performer? These are the classifications:

1. The beginner is new to the task but very motivated – low in knowledge and experience but high in motivation
2. The learner has some task knowledge, but is not an expert. He or she is motivated to complete the task
3. The regular has good task knowledge but medium or reduced motivation
4. The performer has full task knowledge and is fully motivated.

Also, think about one individual who does a number of different jobs. What classification does he or she come under for all the different jobs? He or she may be a performer for some tasks but a beginner in others. This emphasises the need for you to assess which category the person or team is in for each job you want to delegate. As well as helping you categorise team members into the different classifications for each job they do, it also helps you see where individuals need to develop their skills.

How much supervision should you use?

So how do you determine how much supervision each individual needs for a particular job? Or, in other words, what is the level of freedom and responsibility they can safely take on without making costly mistakes? There are four levels of supervision:

- CONTROLLER: You closely supervise the person or team, taking them through the task stage by stage, showing or telling them what to do.
- COACH: You let them complete the task using their own knowledge, but you proactively give advice and encouragement when you think it is needed.
- CONSULTANT: The consultant is like the coach, but support is reactive – you only give it if they ask for it.
- CO-ORDINATOR: The co-ordinator gives full responsibility to the team or individual, and only co-ordinates the different tasks going on within the team. A reporting system is agreed so that you are kept informed of progress and completion.

The following exercises are designed to help improve your delegation skills using the ideas introduced earlier. To help you make sure you use the right delegation level for each of your team for the job, you should complete a 'team delegation assessment'. Using the table below, write in the name of each team member together with four tasks that you regularly delegate to them. Indicate whether they have knowledge and/ or experience of the task and whether they are motivated and committed to it.

Now write the delegation level you use with them currently in the 'current style used' column; and in the 'possible future style' column put the level that the formula suggests you should use, bearing in mind the knowledge motivation assessment. Does this agree with the level you are currently using? The last column is headed 'style agreed'. This will allow you to discuss your assessment for each task with the individual and ask for their views. You can then agree a style.

		Task 1	Task 2	Task 3	Task 4
Team member's name	John Smith				
Regular tasks	Weekly sales figures				

	Task 1	Task 2	Task 3	Task 4
Knowledge/ experience?	Yes, high			
Motivation/ commitment?	Yes, high			
Current style you use?	Consultant			
Future style?	Co-ordinator			
Style agreed?	Co-ordinator			

Don't forget that where possible you should give team members a challenge, so try to be more 'hands off' than 'hands on'. Also remember that with time, people develop, so ideally you need to repeat this process for 15 to 30 minutes three times a year. Otherwise you will find that you will naturally tend to use one delegation level more often than others, which may lead to ineffective delegation. By using the formula you should get the level right, but first get the agreement of the individual concerned. Each delegation level has advantages and disadvantages that you should bear in mind. The table below gives you a summary of the benefits, risks and examples of best use for each delegation level.

Style	Benefits	Risks	Example situation
Controller	Rapid decisions if time short, clear objectives and performance requirements.	No involvement from individual/team. Takes lots of your time.	For team members with little experience, especially on critical jobs.
Coach	Builds confidence. Small risk of mistakes but encourages them to take on responsibility.	Can be time consuming and leave individual dependent on you.	When people have some experience, but still need a fair amount of support.
Consultant	Builds commitment and encourages taking on responsibility.	Decision-making process may take longer. Team can get asked too many questions.	For experienced staff, who can contribute ideas, and can work without you there.
Co-ordinator	Gives you maximum time to do other tasks. Builds team innovation and motivation.	May end up with a group of individuals not a team.	For motivated and experienced staff who can solve most problems.

Do you ask them what support they need?

While you may have assessed the level of delegation the individual or team can take on, you may not have a fully accurate picture. Ask them if they can take on the job and what level of supervision they think they need. This gives them the opportunity to take on more if they are happy to, or ask for more support if they are not. In both cases it allows you to maximise the chance of completing the task and minimise the chance of it going wrong. Simply asking them will also make them feel more motivated. Remember, you can still retain control if you feel that they are overestimating their own ability.

How does time affect delegation level?

Think of a new skill you have recently acquired. You know that by using that skill, you can go from being a beginner to being a performer on certain tasks in only a few months. The same applies to other members of your team, so you need to reconsider the delegation level you use for the jobs they do on a regular basis. In practice, if you are asking the same person to do a job they've been doing regularly and successfully for the past six months, you will be able to adopt a more hands-off approach. It is also useful to consider talking to each person about the delegation level they need for all their main jobs every six months, and agreeing it for the next six months. You should definitely try to do this at annual appraisals, at the very least.

Can people go backwards?

For individuals to go backwards they need to have a reduction in either their knowledge or experience of the task, or their motivation and commitment. In most cases, people don't forget what they have learnt, so the likelihood of a reduction in task knowledge is small. There may be occasional situations that can result in a backwards step, for example, if someone hasn't done the job for some time, or new technology or systems have been introduced. However, these reversals occur much more often as a result of a drop in motivation or commitment. This may be through boredom, problems at home, stress or other negative influences. The best response is twofold: try to find the cause of the problem and deal with it, and give extra support during this phase.

Should I encourage people to take on more freedom?

It was previously suggested that the more you delegate to your team the better it becomes, as long as team members have time to take on more tasks. It improves their skills, motivates them, gets the job done and leaves you to concentrate on the jobs that you need to do yourself. Agreeing to give more freedom to people, for example, by using the consultant level rather than a coach level, may be useful if you have an individual who you want to develop and give a challenge to. This is perfectly safe as you are still on hand if they need help. It's better to give people more challenges, otherwise they will get bored, fail to develop and assume you don't respect their abilities or talents.

Getting delegation right will help motivate individuals and match what you and they do more effectively to the task. But getting maximum effort from people is not just about process and tasks; it's also about emotion, which we will return to.

CROSS-CULTURAL LEADERSHIP

In Chapter 1 we saw that there are both similarities and differences to leadership in different cultures. It was suggested that there were common things that all leaders had to do, but that the way these might be delivered could vary from culture to culture. This was explored more in Chapter 2, which showed where the differences occurred and suggested that leaders should take time to be aware of these differences and carefully fine-tune what they do to match the different cultures.

Based on the GLOBE[5] project, these are the types of leadership behaviour again:

1. Charismatic/value-based leadership reflects the ability to inspire, to motivate, and to expect high performance from others based on strongly-held core values

2. Team-oriented leadership emphasises team building and a common purpose among team members

3. Participative leadership reflects the degree to which leaders involve others in making and implementing decisions

4. Humane-oriented leadership emphasises being supportive, considerate, compassionate and generous

5. Autonomous leadership refers to independent and individualistic leadership, which includes being autonomous and unique

6. Self-protective leadership reflects behaviour that ensures the safety and security of the leader and the group.

These are the cultural groupings:

- **Anglo Cultures** – England, Australia, South Africa (white sample), Canada, New Zealand, Ireland, United States

- **Latin Europe** – Israel, Italy, Portugal, Spain, France, Switzerland (French-speaking)

- **Nordic Europe** – Finland, Sweden, Denmark

- **Germanic Europe** – Austria, Switzerland, Netherlands, Germany

- **Eastern Europe** – Hungary, Russia, Kazakhstan, Albania, Poland, Greece, Slovenia, Georgia

- **Latin America** – Costa Rica, Venezuela, Ecuador, Mexico, El Salvador, Colombia, Guatemala, Bolivia, Brazil, Argentina

- **Sub-Sahara Africa** – Namibia, Zambia, Zimbabwe, South Africa (black sample), Nigeria

- **Arab Cultures** – Qatar, Morocco, Turkey, Egypt, Kuwait, UAE

- **Southern Asia** – India, Indonesia, Philippines, Malaysia, Thailand, Iran
- **Confucian Asia** – Taiwan, Singapore, Hong Kong, South Korea, China, Japan

Here is the prioritisation of behaviour by culture: (numbers are ranked by importance, eg 1 = 1st)

Behaviour	East Europe	Latin America	Germanic	Latin Europe	Asia Confuc	Nordic	Anglo Saxon	SubSh Africa	South Asia	Middle East
Autonomous	1	6	1	6	5	4	5	6	5	3
Self Protect	2	3	6	4	1	6	6	5	1	1
Charismatic	3	1	2	1	4	1	1	2	2	4
Team Orient	4	2	5	2	2	3	4	3	4	5
Humane-oriented	5	5	4	5	3	5	3	1	3	2
Participative	6	4	3	3	6	2	2	4	6	6

This is interesting because it confirms the overall global importance of leaders being charismatic, but there is a clear split in other areas, for example with the focus on the leader and team being a high priority in Asia, the Middle East and Africa, whereas the focus in other cultures is more on individuals.

TELLING THE TEAM WHAT NEEDS TO BE DONE

It doesn't matter if you don't accurately express yourself when you order the sandwiches for your lunch, other than that you will get a very varied diet, but if you can't get your message across when communicating with your team or major clients, then you have a serious problem. The event list (below) allows you to consider all the major communication events individually, and analyse your performance in each. It lists the main communication events that you may engage in on a regular basis and considers if you have room for improvement in these areas.

Set out the table as shown and enter each main communication activity that you engage in, together with the way you do it at present. To check you have assessed it correctly, why not ask the person you communicated with what they think? This also encourages feedback. This list will give you an idea of the communication activities you presently undertake, but also show how you could improve your effectiveness.

Event you communicate at or subject discussed	1. Weekly sales figures	2. Giving feedback to individual team members
Who is there?	The team	Individual team members
What feedback do you get?	None	Yes – sometimes I am not clear according to some

What can you do better?	I think I rush it a bit, so take it more slowly in future. Maybe look at encouraging ideas from team?	Take more time to make clear what I am talking about and what needs to be done.

It should be easy to get your message across, but unfortunately, bad communication is the cause of most problems at work. Evidence suggests[6] that when we communicate, particularly verbally, we need to repeat ourselves to ensure full understanding. Understanding the principles of communication and how to apply them in practice will allow you to make sure that you are immediately understood. The simple model below demonstrates the process and its stages. This applies both to the team and to individuals alike.

Interpersonal communication

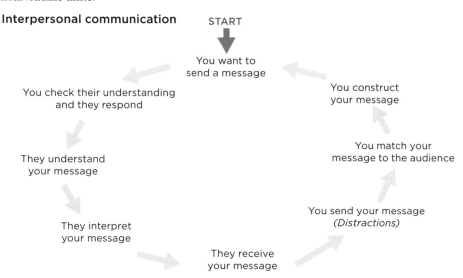

So the whole communication process is summarised by:

- You construct the message: the message you want to send is put together
- You match the message: the message is constructed to suit, or match, the other person/people
- You prepare the other person/people: you get their attention
- You send the message: you initiate the delivery
- They receive the message: do they understand it all, or only part of it? Are they listening?
- They interpret the message: do they interpret the words and phrases as you intended?
- You confirm the message has been understood: you confirm this by using feedback, via listening and asking questions.

A simple message

The message is a simple one: for effective communication, the message received must be the same as the message sent. Just think of the number of times you have heard: 'Oh, that's what you meant'; 'I thought you wanted me to...', or 'No, that's not what I said. I said ...'

Understanding the model allows you to make sure that your message gets through and helps you avoid the pitfalls. If you can do this, you won't have to worry that the people you work with misunderstand your communications. This may sound like common sense but if you look at many of the major organisational crises that have happened over the years – the Gulf of Mexico oil spill and the 2008 financial crisis are just two examples – ineffective communication of critical messages was a key part of what went wrong.

In principle, communication should happen like this, but how do you make sure your message gets across? It's simple: by planning your communications, whether they are one-to-one, meetings or team meetings. Here's a brief detail of each part of the communication process:

Constructing your message

How do you compose the message so that the other person or team will understand clearly? Even in short conversations, you need to think about this.

The first part of the process is to put together the message you want to send to achieve your objective. So the first question is: what do I want to achieve? Is it getting a specific job done, briefing a group on the plans for next year, or talking over performance problems with a team member? Apply these questions when constructing your message:

- What do I want to achieve?
- Why does it need to be done?
- When does it need to be done by?
- How is it best done?
- Where should it be done?
- Who should do it?

Matching the message

The second step in the preparation process is to fine-tune the message to match the audience. The audience could be your team, clients, or other managers, so you will need to vary your delivery to match the personalities and perspectives of different audiences. The volume or detail you include also needs to match.

Compare how you would ask an experienced colleague to do a job to how you would ask an inexperienced trainee, speaking to colleagues or top-level clients. The objective – getting the message over – is the same, but clearly you would need to include more information for the inexperienced trainee or clients whose experience or knowledge was less. Even with people of the same ability in your own team, you know that some people will listen carefully and take on board everything you say, but it's probably best to give the message twice so you are sure it's clear.

Delivering the message

Preparing the team or individual and getting your message across:

1. **Check they are ready to receive your message.** You should make sure that the time and place are appropriate for the delivery of your message. There may be other distractions that cause barriers to communication, so double check that everyone is ready to hear what you are going to say.

2. **Outline what you are going to say.** It is useful to give them a brief outline of what you intend to say in your message.

3. **Background.** Go over the background to what you want to say.

4. **Say why it is important to you, your staff and the organisation.** This is confirmation of your own assumptions and perceptions. It establishes where the message is coming from and your thoughts and attitudes towards it. This tells the receiver why you are sending the message to them and conveys your interpretation.

5. **Say why it is important and has benefit for them.** In any communication the receiver must have some motivation to take the message on board. The 'what's in it for me?' question goes back to the need for an emotional as well as rational element to leadership. You should try to do this all the time, asking yourself: what's the rational element in my message and what's the emotional? This applies even to simple tasks where gaining new experience or building networks, for example, will improve individual or team motivation to listen to the message and do the job.

Confirmation

Confirmation is your last chance to check your message has been understood. You must make sure that your message has been understood as you intended – and all of it. In the financial crisis banks will have been given the message: 'you need to make money but do so within the law and in the best interests of clients'. Some clearly only heard 'you need to make money' and interpreted that as 'you need to make money any way you can.' This checking can be done through open questioning and active listening. Asking, 'do you understand?' is not enough; the team or individual may answer 'yes' just to keep you happy. So getting the message repeated back to you is often a good safety check.

Other useful tools –

Open questioning

These are questions that do not have a 'yes' or 'no' answer. They start with 'how', 'why', 'when', 'where' and 'what'. A closed question might be: 'Do you think this plan will work?' An open version of the same question might be; 'What problems do you think might occur with this plan?' Open questions force a more detailed response and so can reveal both more information and misunderstandings effectively.

Active listening

When someone answers your question, listen to the whole of the answer: don't interrupt. If they have difficulty answering, help them with suggestions, but check the meaning with them first: 'So, what you are trying to say is...' At the end, summarise and ask them if your summary is accurate. Not listening enough is a critical failing amongst leaders, especially senior ones, their view being that they need to take action and make decisions, and listening isn't part of that. In fact it's a critical part of it, and leaders who don't listen often fail.

Showing you care

Make sure you match the time and place to the message you want to get across. Look at the time, place and conduct of how the message is communicated from the other person's perspective. Would you want to have your appraisal rushed into half the time it should have been because your boss arrived late? What message does delivering an unprepared and confused team meeting send to the team? Beauty is in the eye of the receiver, not the giver.

Summary of communication principles

You should follow the communication principles outlined above, and fine-tune them to suit your situation. Always use this basic structure to make sure your communication is effective:

1. Use clear, simple messages in a form that matches your audience
2. Make sure the environment suits the message you are trying to deliver
3. Get your audience's attention and minimise distractions
4. Deliver the message in a way that enables your audience to clearly understand it
5. Check the message has been understood by getting feedback through open questioning and active listening.

MOTIVATING YOUR PEOPLE TO DELIVER GOOD WORK

Here are a few tips to help you motivate your team:

1. Give people achievable but challenging targets that they have been involved in setting with you. (SMART objectives – Specific, Measurable, Achievable, Relevant, Timed)
2. Keep everyone informed about how they are doing on a day-to-day basis
3. Keep everyone informed about decisions or events that may affect them
4. Delegate as much as you can so that everyone has responsibility and builds expertise
5. Allow individuals as much freedom as possible within their responsibilities. Let them decide methods, speed of work, and stages within a framework where everyone knows who is responsible for defined targets, objectives or standards
6. Establish a clear relationship between effort, delivery and reward
7. Encourage the team to become involved in planning, innovating and contributing ideas to improve team performance
8. Make clear that individuals are responsible for their own task success or failure
9. Praise and recognise achievement when due.

GIVING FEEDBACK AS YOU GO ALONG

One of the main criticisms of many leaders is that they don't tell the people on their teams how they are doing often enough. Yet this is very important. Many bosses wait until the appraisal to tell people how they are progressing, but that may be months away. Giving feedback during and after every task should be part of being a leader. If the task is long, do it during the job. Your team needs your regular feedback. This is a key driver of better performance.

Giving both praise and negative feedback needs careful attention. The former we tend not to do enough (when was the last time your boss praised you?), and the latter is so often mishandled or avoided that it makes the situation worse!

PRAISE AS A MOTIVATOR

As we saw from the best boss list, praise is a good motivator and should be given when someone has made an extra effort, achieved something new or special, helped you out, or deserved it in some other way. Just because they are being paid to come to work does not mean that everything they do is 'just part of what they're paid for'. You know how satisfying it is being praised by a boss you respect. It makes all the hard work worthwhile, so try to praise your team regularly when appropriate.

Structured praise is better than unstructured. While just saying 'thank you' is a good start, you can give praise in a more structured way that further motivates the individual or team. As well as saying 'well done', try to consider the following when giving praise:

- What was good about what the team or individual did: *'You put in those extra three hours...'*
- Why it was good: *'...which enabled the job to be finished earlier than planned.'*
- The impact on the team and organisation: *'This meant that the other parts of the project could be finished early as well, which delighted the client.'*
- What it says about them: *'This showed everyone how much you have developed and how committed you are to the team. Well done.'*

Saying more than just 'well done' gives the person valuable information, reinforces the focus of the successful action and makes it more likely to be repeated. But in any event 'well done' is much better than silence!

GIVING NEGATIVE FEEDBACK

This is one of the most difficult and sensitive things you have to deal with as a team leader. If it is handled badly you can destroy the motivation and self-confidence of the person involved, have a negative impact on their performance and ruin their relationship with you.

With the stakes so high, it is important to get it right. This does not mean avoiding it altogether, which just lets the problem continue and get worse. You can't make people accountable if they don't know that they are not doing what you want. The most important feature of 'good' negative feedback is that it is designed to help the individual improve their performance in the future, not punish them for past errors.

When giving negative feedback always use 'active' listening and the other rules of communication, as above, to get your message across and make sure it has been understood. This is slightly different from getting a normal message over in that, if possible, you want the person to find their own problem and solution rather than having to tell them. The psychology behind this is that if you can identify the problem yourself you accept it more readily than if it is pointed out to you, and you also find your own solution!

This format is useful for getting your feedback across without alienating individuals by offering to solve problems for them. It also helps them to improve their skills.

1. Find a quiet location where you will not be disturbed
2. Explain the general area that you wish to talk about: *'You know that report I asked you to do last week?'*
3. Explain why the area is important: *'Well, you know that it has to go to the MD next week?'*
4. See if you can get them to identify the problem you have in mind: *'Did you have any difficulties or problems that I could help you with?'*
5. If they can't think of any, make a suggestion by pointing out the problem area: *'How about the problem analysis section?'*

6. If they confirm this, ask them how you can help, share any relevant experience you may have had, and with their agreement work out a plan to deal with the problem in the future.

7. If they still do not identify the problem, start with a positive note, then describe factually what happened, and look to the future: '*Well, although the report was generally good, you seem to have had some difficulty developing different courses of action. I had a similar problem years ago that I was able to solve; would it be of help if we discussed this?*'

NEVER delay in giving negative feedback – the problem will just get worse.

Helping individuals perform well as a team

CREATING A TEAM VISION

The team should have a team vision and it should inspire them. It should say where the team wants to be in the future. Creating this vision should be done with everyone's participation; it needs to be something that all support. You can't just impose your own ideas. Again this fits in with the key elements of the best boss list and other principles of getting to Mach 1.

However, you need to plan the process, so think about how to get them coming up with ideas on the subject. Try to bring as much inspiration to the session as you can. The first stage is to write down the question: 'Where do we, as a team, really want to be in the future?' In other words, if you could determine the future, how would you see the team in, say, two years time?

Ask the team to individually write down their own vision and then get them to split into groups to discuss their ideas. After a few minutes, get each group to produce one idea, and from this, distil a team vision that everyone can agree to. The vision should be a short statement of where the team is going.

CREATING A TEAM MISSION

The mission is different from the vision in that it asks: 'What are we here for?' 'What is our purpose?' Run through the same process as you did with the team vision. You may find that to get to the real mission you have to cut through layers of detail. To do this, when the team has come up with a mission, for example: 'To supply best practice IT support', ask them: 'Why is this important?' Ask the team to list the three most important things they have to do to enable them to achieve the mission; these indicate your key actions.

THINKING ABOUT VALUES AND CRITICAL BEHAVIOUR

To help you develop a set of clear values and behaviour for you and the team, you need to list the values that people think are important. You can do this by asking questions such as:

1. What are the core values that you bring to work?
2. What are the core values you hope your children think you have?
3. If you won £2 million on the lottery, which values would you stick to?

Some common responses are:

1. For values: honesty, integrity, respect for others, fairness, trust, openness, professionalism
2. For behaviour: professionalism, self-awareness, enthusiasm, ability to establish mutual respect, ability to establish common ground.

Again you will find that all this aligns to what was covered in chapters 1 and 2 about getting people to Mach 1 and the underpinning emotional elements of maximising performance.

GET A CONSENSUS

It may also be useful to agree what each value actually means to everyone, because they can have different meanings for different people. Ask the team to write down their own values individually and then ask them to select their top three by removing the ones they would be prepared to compromise on.

Once everyone has done this, compile a team list, indicating the most popular choices. The values can also be expressed through behaviour: acting with integrity, showing respect for others, being fair, and showing trust. In practice, it is essential for this to happen. There is little point trying to impose your values on the team. This will result in them getting a negative opinion of you, despite the fact they will almost certainly have the same core values as you anyway, so it makes sense to get the team to determine its own values.

Having established the team values you need to get the team to list the behaviour, or actions, that they need to carry out to demonstrate these values, for example value – we support our colleagues; action – if we see a colleague who needs help we will offer to help. They should be encouraged to behave according to this list, as individuals, and motivate each other to stick to it. You should also stress the importance of the team monitoring their own and other team members' adherence to the agreed values. Make sure that team activities, rewards and policies support the values. Talking about values with the team is also beneficial. It encourages an open and honest discussion, which helps improve team culture.

TEAM BRIEFINGS

Team briefings, as opposed to briefing a team, are a good means of getting two-way communication and ideas and innovation building, which positions you well for Mach 2. Team briefings are sessions, normally held weekly or fortnightly, that enable you to tell the team any news, and allow them to tell you how things are going, and about any problems they may have. They are a good time to discuss ideas and suggestions and a good source of building team spirit because the team is thinking and acting together. Even if there is no team briefing system in your organisation, it is vital that you run these briefings yourself for your team.

This simple act, if done well, will have significant benefits for both you and the team. These meetings can be used to discuss team work, praise individuals or groups, discuss departmental or organisational challenges, think about the end customers, and discuss any number of beneficial actions that help you get to both Mach 1 and Mach 2.

Planning a team briefing

You need to arrange about half an hour to an hour for the briefing. Most people find that either Friday afternoons or Monday mornings are the best times. You need to structure what you are going to say before the briefing. The best way to deal with the part of the session where you brief the team on relevant issues is by using a simple formula: progress and performance, policy and plans, people, points for action (see box). Then you hand the briefing over to them for feedback. If there are certain matters that you are expecting to come up, it may be worth preparing answers.

After this you can introduce information about the wider organisation, the future or things the team would benefit from knowing: remember that an individual or team being told how they contribute to the bigger picture can increase performance by +28%. If there are questions you can't answer, then undertake to find out and let everyone know at the next meeting.

Your notes should be written down under these headings:

1. Progress and performance – tell the team how things are going

2. Policy and plans – why things are being done in a certain way and what is planned for the future

3. People – changes in responsibilities and roles, not only in the team but anywhere it may affect them and the jobs they do

4. Points for action – what needs to be done by the team in the future, setting specific objectives if required?

5. The bigger picture – what's going on with other departments, the wider organisation, customers, competitors and the market?

Fill in the information the team needs to be told under each heading. The general rule is that you should give out the information unless there is a very good reason for not doing so. Giving out information builds trust in you and enables your team to do the job because they know what's going on.

RUNNING OTHER MEETINGS

It's a fact that many team leaders spend a lot of their time in meetings of one sort or another. In many cases you will not be running the meeting, but when you are, it is very important that you get the maximum benefit from it; if you don't, you've wasted your time. Try to keep meetings to under an hour – otherwise people tend to get bored!

There are seven important pointers to making your meetings effective:

- PURPOSE: why are we meeting?
- PLANNING: plan and prepare what you want to happen in the meeting
- AGENDA: put the agenda out well before the meeting and make it flexible to change if required
- PEOPLE: don't just invite everyone automatically if they don't need to be there. There is no point wasting other people's time.
- TIME: make sure you stick to start and finish times. Starting late with eight people waiting ten minutes will cost your organisation a lot of time and money.
- VENUE: often forgotten, but it has a significant effect on how the meeting goes. Consider whether there is enough seating, whether the room is too hot or too cold, whether the table is the right shape to encourage participation, whether the AV systems work if required and if refreshments might be needed.
- MINUTES: make sure that a secretary is appointed to take notes; you cannot chair effectively and take notes at the same time.

Key action points for running meetings:

- Stick to start and finish times
- Make clear what the purpose of the meeting is
- Stick to the agenda, but be prepared to update if new circumstances have arisen.
- For each issue, deal with facts, discuss interpretations, and draw conclusions
- Be neutral and deal with conflict
- Ensure everyone one has their say; bring out the quiet people
- Listen to everyone
- Build a consensus during the meeting to gain support for proposals – get people to verbally confirm their commitment to action – silence does not demonstrate commitment
- Provide an end-of-meeting summary
- Detail responsibilities for action; make sure everyone knows what they have to do.

Decide on what is critical to success

In 2000 I worked with the executive committee of London Underground, where the team was engaged in the part privatisation of the 50-year-old institution that moves 3.5m Londoners to work every day. The sheer volume of decisions, both operational and change driven, coming to the committee was overloading the system, with meetings scheduled for two hours often taking four or five. An agenda sent out a week before a meeting was studiously followed, and anything else that arose was included in 'any other business'. This, filled by decisions needed on things that had arisen after the agenda had gone out, took longer than the rest of the meeting.

Working with the MD, I changed the meeting format to facilitate it and focus on what really mattered. The new approach would consider all the items that needed to be decided, both on agenda and those arisen since. They were divided into a number of categories:

1. Those that should never have got to this group and should have been decided lower in the organisation, which was a common problem. These were sent back down for action.

2. Those that had to be decided in that meeting to deliver the actions needed before the next meeting.

3. Those that could be delayed until the next meeting.

This then cut the number of decisions needed dramatically and meant the meetings could be strictly limited to two hours. Each item that had to be discussed at that particular meeting had a set time limit, which we stuck to. I facilitated the meetings to make sure that the agenda was kept focused and on track, that everyone contributed and that all potential issues were uncovered. Furthermore, for each group action, every member of the committee had to verbally confirm their commitment to deliver, with no nods or silence accepted. Not one meeting went over time, and staff at the levels below started to take responsibility and more decisions were effectively made than ever before: simple, yet effective.

Developing the performance of yourself and others

UNDERSTANDING HOW YOU LEARN

'The growth and development of people is the highest calling of leadership.'

Harvey S. Firestone (1868-1938), founder of Firestone Tyre Company, USA

Throughout life, we learn by a combination of passed-on knowledge and experience. Even animals can do this. We are shown how to do something; we practise it and are then able to do it. If there is no one to show us, we will try different ways until we get it right, trial and error, but the process is really the same no matter what is being learned: experience–learning–review–next step. This process is summarised by the diagram on the next page:

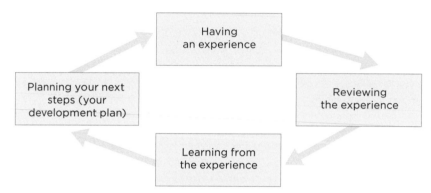

This is the process you need to use regularly to constantly improve your skills: use your new skills (experience); see how it goes (review); learning lessons; planning how to do it better next time. This is not just a one-off; you should do this after any major task and review all your skills every six months or annually. The self-assessment you completed earlier will have helped you find out some information about your abilities, but before embarking on your development plan you may need more help. But you may be missing some key information, and most people do not realise that this is often the case.

The 'Johari Window[7]' (below) helps you to collect and understand all the information you need to improve. It contains four areas of information about yourself, and you should think about each of these and how you could use them to help improve your performance.

	Information known to self	Information not known to self
Information known to others	PUBLIC KNOWLEDGE	OWN BLIND SPOT
Information not known to others	SECRET KNOWLEDGE	TO BE DISCOVERED

INFORMATION KNOWN TO YOURSELF AND OTHERS – PUBLIC KNOWLEDGE

This is public knowledge about you, for example how good you are at the technical aspects of your job. You know you can do it and you have shown your team you can. This is the easiest information to get.

INFORMATION NOT KNOWN TO OTHERS – SECRET KNOWLEDGE

These are the things that you know about yourself but which others don't know: your fears, weaknesses, feelings, and ideas for the future, job preferences, who you trust. Much of this information relates to the critical leader behaviours, much of it is emotional as well as rational. This 'hidden' area of your character has a major effect on the way you act at work and must be considered to ensure that positive behaviour and attitudes and are strengthened and the negative ones avoided. This area of information may reveal problems or concerns that you have before they become obvious to others – this gives you the ability to address them before other people notice them!

INFORMATION KNOWN ONLY TO OTHERS – BLIND SPOT

We all have blind spots – doing things that we are unaware of but that others notice. Have you ever watched yourself on video? Did you see yourself do something that you didn't know you did, but when you asked others, they said you always did it? This shows the importance of getting feedback. Or you may be doing things that, unknown to you, are in some way restricting team or individual performance. A classic example is failing to delegate to people who could easily handle a task because you didn't ask if they could do it.

Here you can, if you wish, take a first step on your development road by asking key members of your team, whose judgement you particularly value, for their views. The question to ask is simple: 'Is there anything that I could do to help the team be more effective?' If you have the courage to ask this then you will be respected. If you have never done this you might worry about possible replies. Don't worry, as you will be given information that is of value, that is, information you need to know but at present don't. In many cases, the information gained this way has been of great help to team leaders and has enabled them to perform better than before. Furthermore, those you have asked will trust you more as you asked for their insights.

INFORMATION NOT KNOWN

This is the information about you that no one knows yet. If you think back over your life you will have discovered at various times that you are either good or bad at doing certain tasks. As we get older, more and more of these reveal themselves, but some do not because, although the signs are there, we never take time to look for them. For example, you may feel intimidated by certain people. As a result, you probably avoid them. And giving presentations or public speaking is another favourite fear. You may not like being in front doing the talking, but you probably never bothered to find the 'unknown' reason why. Once you analyse these areas you discover the real feelings you have and the real problems. Once you recognise the problems, you can tackle them.

Having got as much information as possible on how you are doing – from your own perspectives and other people's views, you need to think about how best to improve. How can you deal with any weakness and build on your strengths? To do this, you need an objective, based on the intention, for example: 'to make sure I brief the team on the task effectively'. Then think about how this can be achieved, and using the formula in this book, write out briefing notes for yourself with headings such as '*before the next team briefing – update myself on organisation's strategy*', – together with a deadline by which you have to do this, eg *by March 13th*. You may also benefit from support from your manager or from people in other parts of the organisation. If they can help then you should include this in your plan.

No one is perfect so expect to find weaknesses as well as strengths – that's why teams need a variety of people in them. But you need to ensure that your weaknesses are managed in a way so that they don't create any risk for yourself, the team or organisation.

PERSONAL DEVELOPMENT PLAN

'There is no one who cannot vastly improve their powers of leadership by a little thought and practice'
Field Marshall Viscount Slim (1891-1970), British commander, WWII; Governor General of Australia

This all needs to be consolidated into your overall development plan. This is an action plan to deal with each skill you need to improve. Too many development plans are vague and do not include the key steps for success. So they fail.

For each skill you see as a development priority 1, download a development plan from www.theonlyleadershipbook.com, and write in the name of the skill at the top. Then write down:

- The exact skill that you need to improve. This may be: need to take more care in delegating to more experienced staff/tend to use the wrong style/too controlling.
- The steps you need to take to improve this in the 'actions by you' section. This may include actions such as: fully assessing an appropriate delegation style before giving out jobs, attending a course, completing a team skills summary to see who can do what, holding meetings with team members to discuss their views on taking on more responsibilities or seeking a mentor. Each action you undertake should fit in with a specific area that needs improving. It may not just relate to time at work – you could benefit by reading a book on an appropriate area in your spare time as well.
- Whether your boss or organisation could help you to improve in this area. This could involve discussing with your boss how they may have dealt in the past with problems similar to the ones that you now face.
- 'To be completed/achieved by' date. You must set yourself a deadline by which to complete your actions, and stick to it. If you don't, there is always something that needs doing instead and you will suddenly find that it is two years down the road, you've done nothing and as a result someone else has been selected for that promotion you wanted.

Development needs

Development needs should include technical training, management competencies and any skills you may need to develop for the future.

Development priorities (in order of priority if possible)

For each development priority, actions by:

• You

• Your boss

• Organisational support you need

• To be completed/achieved by

FURTHER DEVELOPMENT IDEAS

As well as the obvious operational development priorities for doing your job, there are more development opportunities to help you get to Mach 1 and Mach 2. These ideas should focus on building your ability to collaborate and help the organisation deliver its wider objectives. Broaden your knowledge of your organisation, so that you understand how it works as a whole. This is a preparation for Mach 2. The ability to take a corporate overview rather than a narrow functional view distinguishes the potential strategic leader from the rest.

Do I need a mentor?

Finding a mentor is one of the most effective forms of development you can undertake. A more experienced person, who is not on your direct reporting line, can provide general advice and perspectives on improving skills and resolving problems, particularly those relating to relationships at work. As we saw earlier, better understanding of the relationships you have with others at work is key to effective leadership. It's also good for you to be a mentor to a less experienced person. You will learn just as much from being a mentor as being mentored! Having helped set up many mentoring programmes in a wide variety of organisations from investment banks to orchestra and theatre leaders, I assure you mentoring is highly effective. In a survey 80% of FTSE chief executives in the UK said that having a mentor at the right time was key to their success in getting to be the CEO[8]. There is evidence it may also increase your potential to go further by 22%[9].

DEVELOPING BETTER TEAM PERFORMANCE – COACHING

Most learning takes place through experience, as we know. The speed with which team members learn can, however, be greatly increased if the leader or a more experienced person guides the process, rather than leaving it to trial and error – coaching. Training – generally knowledge or skills and development conducted off the job – is effective, but not as effective as coaching on the job.

Coaching on the job is the best way to improve performance, motivation and skills, not only for the individual, but also for the team as a whole. It allows the individual to take on more responsibility, builds their confidence and sometimes enables them to achieve things they never thought possible. It may also increase loyalty and reduce staff turnover. It is key that while learning, the individual is still delivering what needs to be delivered, which isn't the case if they go on a course.

Coaching is a key leadership skill. Unfortunately, when coaching is suggested, many leaders say they have no time to do it – they have too much to do already – and that's a fatal mistake. Coaching your people on the job is one of the best routes to help you get to Mach 1 level because it accomplishes so many of the areas critical to Mach 1 success.

When do you coach?

If you think of the many ways in which either you or your staff needs to develop skills to enable the job, or new jobs, to be done, then the need for coaching can come up at almost any time. The team or individual's opinion of you as a leader will be shaped by how you respond to this development need.

How do you coach?

You can't just tell people they're going to be coached. You need to ensure that they agree to the proposed development and are thus committed to making it work. You need to use some of the key skills introduced earlier in the book: asking questions, making suggestions, giving feedback and actively listening. Be careful how you make suggestions. It is much better if people can find their own solutions rather than use yours. Don't make suggestions until the individual you are coaching has run out of ideas first.

Make sure that you won't be disturbed and that you are relaxed and supportive at all times during the session. You should spend about 80% of the time listening and only 20% talking! Prepare notes before the session under each heading below:

- *Agree the topic for coaching*
  This may happen naturally or you may need to discuss the areas in which the individual has the greatest need for coaching. Both appraisals, development programmes and changes in skills requirements for the team often reveal coaching needs.

- *Identify goals*
  As with all goals, these should be SMART.
  Beware of over-generalised goals, for example: *to be better at using the word processing package on the computer.* This is too vague. It should be: *to be able to produce 75% of documents successfully by myself using the word processing package by the end of the month.* Beware of imposing your own goals for team members on them. Try and let them find their own if possible. Then they have an emotional commitment to them.

- *Promote discovery*
  This comes in three stages:

  1. Active listening

  2. Drawing out consequences from their suggestions: help them to think through their ideas

  3. Sharing experience: show them that you are human and have had problems like theirs. Share solutions. The objective is to help them discover the best way to approach the task on their own, with the minimum input from you.

You should still provide a framework that includes details of:

- Resources available – personnel, finance and time
- Processes and systems that have been used in the past
- Previous problems

This will allow the person you are coaching to think of a set of possible options.

- *Set parameters*
Now they have a set of options, you need to agree objectives, with guidelines for what needs to be reported back to you.

- *Authorise and empower*
The individual will now have a set of tasks to perform. In some areas of coaching, for example, where the individual has to work outside the immediate team, he or she will need the backing of your authority, as well as the co-operation of others outside the team. So you must give him or her clearance to do these things, and notify those involved.

- *Recap*
To make sure you both remember what has been agreed, ask him or her to recap, particularly the action points. Remember that these are objectives and thus need SMART goals (Specific, Measurable, Agreed, Realistic, Timed).

Steps	Questions
Agree the topic	What is the topic you would like to discuss?
Identify the goals	What would a solution to this problem be? What would you like to gain from this session? Why do you think that would be beneficial for you? How long do you think it will take for us to do this?
Promote discovery	What is the present situation? (Where are we now?) What has been achieved already? What has happened as a result of that? What evidence is there of any problems? Has anyone had this or seen the evidence? Where is the problem? Who else is involved or responsible? How do they view the situation?
Promote discovery	What options have you thought of? (What are the options?) What would you do? What would be the first step? How have others tackled this task in the past? What other ideas or opinions do you or others have? What are the costs, risks or chances of success of the options? Without asking for a decision, which option do you think seems most viable?

Steps	Questions
Recap	What are the next steps? When will you start the process? What problems or issues can you foresee? What support will you need from others? Who can help you?
Giving feedback/ideas	I have some/ideas/suggestions/feedback. Would you like to hear them? How do you feel we are progressing towards our goals? Is there anything else that you would like to do or think we should cover? Do you feel we are going in the right direction?

You can use this framework to help you think about how you might act not only as a coach for your team but also as a mentor to others outside your team. The skills you need are identical.

WHAT NEXT? TEAM SWOT ANALYSIS

Having assessed how good you are as an individual at meeting the needs of the organisation, you should also feed this into an analysis of where the team is now and what it may generally need to do in the future. One way to do this is to do a SWOT analysis – or strengths, weaknesses, opportunities and threats. At the top of a piece of paper write the key objectives of your team and underneath write the four headings. Under each, list the factors within the team that are strengths and those that are weaknesses. Under opportunities and threats write down the factors, both internal and external, that may affect the ability of the team to do the job.

From this SWOT analysis you can now determine the general skills or knowledge shortages in your team. You need to identify how you are going to address them. Discuss how you will address the results of your analysis with the team. Preparing your own notes beforehand will help you in this.

MATCHING SKILLS TO TASKS

To go from the general concepts of the SWOT to the more specific needs of team skills, you need to compile a list of all the team skills needed to function effectively. The easiest way to do this is to go back to the list of tasks the team does for the organisation (see page 78) and work out what skills are required to do each of those jobs. It is important that you do this because although all the people in your team may be well qualified in the areas they deal with, there may be another area the team is working in where no one has the relevant skills, or only one. The solution here is to either recruit a new person to cover this area (which can be expensive) or to provide further training for some of the existing team.

Some important questions you should ask:

1. What skills does the team need? Link this to the specific tasks the team has to do

2. What skills does the team have? Break this down into individual skills

3. Do the skills we have match the skills we need in the team both for now and the future? Identify any shortfalls.

TEAM DEVELOPMENT PLAN

So you should now have a list of skills shortfalls in the team. Go back to the personal development plan and use it as a basis for a team development plan. For each team skill requiring development, write out a form detailing your plan to address the shortfall. In this way you should be able to build up the skills within your team to make sure that you are able to fully meet clients' or bosses' demands.

Additional day-to-day tips

WORKING WITH YOUR BOSS

At this point don't forget your own boss needs managing. Your relationship with him or her is critical. You need to 'lead upwards' with your boss. All those things that your team might do that worry or annoy you will also, if you do them, annoy or worry your boss, such as giving bad news at the last minute. If your boss has more experience than you, you might also think about being coached by him or her, though this may take some encouragement. You can set an example upwards by using the critical leader behaviour in your dealings with him or her. Key rules for keeping your boss happy: high quality work on time, every time, no surprises and help them help you.

IDEAS FROM EXPERIENCED LEADERS

Here are some very simple day-to-day tips passed on from successful leaders:

1. To-do list – list the tasks you have to do each day. If you don't get them done, carry them over to the next day. You can also prioritise, so do the important ones first, and change the prioritisation as the deadline nears.

2. Avoid procrastination: set a specific date to start a task and get on with it! You can put time in your diary to do specific tasks as well as appointments, for example: two hours to finish project, one hour for telephone calls, and one hour for planning next week.

3. Always set yourself and the team SMART goals – specific, measurable, agreed, realistic, timed.

4. Tackle large tasks in small stages and reward yourself, or the team, for completing each.

5. Paperwork and email take up a significant amount of leaders' time: deal with it, delegate it, file it or bin it, but don't leave it sitting on your desk or inbox.

6. Always delegate as much as you can, bearing in mind the skills and experience of your team and the time they have to take on extra work.

7. Always work out exactly how long a task will take before telling someone how long it will take – never guess – you will always be over optimistic and then have problems meeting the deadline. So if you have to guess, think of your time to deliver then add 30%. Better to say longer and deliver early than underestimate and fall short.

CHAPTER 3 KEY POINTS

- Planning your tasks well sets you up for success – always include your 30% safety buffer
- Delegate work that others can do for you if they have time
- Delegate tasks to those who have the skills, knowledge and motivation to do them and use the formula to determine how much freedom you give them
- Communication is key – be clear, simple and understandable, and check the message has been understood as you intended
- Use all the techniques you can to motivate people to give greater effort
- Every team and every individual should have a vision, just the same as every organisation
- Use regular team meetings to pass on information and wider knowledge, and get feedback and ideas together with building team spirit and collaboration
- Constantly develop your own skills and knowledge and that of others, especially your team
- Everyone must have a development plan – and you should support the plans of those in your team
- The best development is often coaching on the job by you or by other experienced team members
- Be a mentor; get a mentor
- People you have helped to develop will be inspired by you and will willingly give you their maximum effort

CHAPTER 3 KEY ACTIONS FOR YOU TO DO NOW

Identify three areas from Chapter 3 where you could use the tools to improve your own or your team's performance. Put together a SMART action plan to make it happen.

References

1. *Judgment in Managerial Decision Making*, M. Bazerman: Wiley, 1993 and *When to trust your gut*, Hayashi: Harvard Business Review, February 2001

2. *Structure is not Organisation* Peters & Waterman: Business Horizons, Vol 23; Issue 3, June 1980 (p14 -26)

*3. *Guide to Quality Control*, Kaoru Ishikawa: JUSE, Tokyo, 1956 and *Guide to Quality Control* Kaoru Ishikawa: Asian Productivity Organisation, 1976

4. You can see more in this TV interview I did on the subject: wp.me/P1ONcQ-PX

5. *Culture, Leadership, and Organisations: The GLOBE study of 62 societies*, Robert J House et al: Sage Publications, 2004

6. *The effects of repetition and levels of processing on learning and attitudes*, Alan G. Sawyer in *NA - Advances in Consumer Research*, Volume 9; eds. Andrew Mitchell & Ann Abor: MI: Association for Consumer Research, 1982 (p 439-443)

7. *The Johari window, a graphic model of interpersonal awareness*, J. Luft & H. Ingham in *Proceedings of the western training laboratory in group development*: UCLA, Los Angeles, 1955

8. *Tomorrow's Organisation: New Mindsets, New Skills*, Rajan & Chapple: Centre for Research in Employment and Technology in Europe, 2001

9. *Realising the full potential of rising talent*, Corporate Leadership Council, 2005

4

Moving to Mach 1 for
teams and organisations:
how to maximise the effort
from all your people

4

Moving to Mach 1 for teams and organisations: how to maximise the effort from all your people

The basic principle of Mach 1 for the individual leader is being able to maximise performance by enabling his or her staff to achieve what they want by delivering what the organisation needs.

In chapters 2 and 3 we looked at how individual leaders could move from basic leadership to Mach 1 by maximising the effort of their people and potentially improving their performance by up to 30%. We also reflected on the changes the 2008 financial crisis brought about. We are in a new world of work where fewer people must deliver that performance in more matrixed and dispersed organisations.

In this chapter we will discover how it's possible to help our people deal with this more challenging world and encourage them to give that maximum effort. Once a few key leaders have reached Mach 1, we will see how it can permeate through the organisation in a consistent and quality-assured way to support the organisation's objectives.

It's important to understand that the Mach 1 approach applies to the individual as much as to the organisation, that is: *you*. If you are in a role such as a departmental or divisional head and you have other leaders working for you, you need to make sure that they are getting the best from *their* people and delivering what you need to achieve *your* objectives just as much as you do for the wider organisation.

All this is summarised in the simple concept underpinning Mach 1: that people need to have both the skills and the willingness to deliver the best for the organisation, and the organisation has to facilitate that. The way this is delivered and the support provided by the organisation is particularly crucial in the new world of work.

In Chapter 1 we saw that[1], between 2009 and 2012, 88% of employees had experienced an increase in workload, 56% had increased hours of work, and 78% had experienced an increase in the team workload. 55% of employees said they did not have sufficient time to complete the work they were expected to do.

Not only are we seeing people reach their limits in terms of the amount of work they can do, we also saw that the importance of individual task work has declined as the need for collaboration with others increased. Between 2002 and 2012, the balance changed from 78% individual against 22% collaborative, to 51% individual against 49% collaborative. So the environment needed to drive organisational success has significantly changed.

Thus part of getting to Mach 1 is dealing with this challenge by helping employees to do their own work more efficiently and effectively, to help them collaborate with others, and to do both in a way that focuses on organisational priorities. But despite what many senior leaders think, many employees have no idea of what the organisation's strategy is, so they obviously can't support it effectively[2].

Chapter 2 suggested ways a team leader could get significant improvements in effort from individuals. These were simple day-to-day actions such as[3]:

1. Explaining to an individual or team how what they do fits into the bigger picture (+30.3%)

2. Making sure that they give fair and accurate day-to-day feedback on performance (+39%)

3. Making sure that every team member has a plan to develop them and their performance that the line manager helps them implement (+38%)

4. Showing they respect their people as people can increase performance by +26.1%!

In addition we also know that emotion is key, and that an employee's decision to give high performance is 57% rational and 43% emotional. Furthermore, 80% of the emotional element is under the control of the individual's line manager. Giving a rational business case to do something is sufficient to get base level performance, but providing an emotional driver will get the best from people. But it's also about building loyalty. A line manager operating at Mach 1 level can reduce the risk of you losing your best people to competitors by up to 87%!

In the new, more collaborative world of work, it is vital that CEOs and the top team create a good culture through their behaviour, and through this drive Mach 1 and then Mach 2. CEOs and senior managers can influence[4] how much discretionary effort their staff make if they show that they:

• are open to new ideas (+22.9%)

• care deeply about employees (+20.7%)

• make employee development a priority (+19.7%)

• are strong in leading and managing people (+15.6%)

- are strong in strategy selection and implementation (+15.6%).

It is even more powerful if the organisation can create a strong emotional link with the employee – it can increase their effort by up to 43.2% – loyalty at work, in simple terms. So this isn't just about being nice to your staff, it's about delivering the best performance possible[5].

Mach 1 delivers better outcomes for the public sector

The benefits of Mach 1 don't only apply to commercial organisations; they can accrue just as much in the public sector as well, for example in the government-funded UK National Health Service (NHS), which employs over 1.4m people across more than 400 organisations. In 2011 the King's Fund, the leading UK organisation on expertise in healthcare, asked me to write a report[6] on how better leadership could improve the service delivery of the NHS, and which would provide the UK government with potential solutions to the challenge of having to cut funding to the NHS while demand was rising. In this report I said that engaging staff effectively was key to getting better patient care at lower cost, effectively Mach 1.

Further research in 2012 by Mike West[7] confirmed this, showing that there was a direct link between the quality of delivery of service to patients, financial performance and even reductions in infection rates. This is also reflected by other studies from around the world[8]. Thus, in the simplest terms, getting to Mach 2 not only improves service quality and finances, but can also save lives in some environments.

To get such benefits the organisation has to enable people to: (The bold text sets out what the individual has to do and the italics what the organisation has to do to facilitate this.)

Want to do the job well – *rational and emotional case for action* – they must also:

Be able to do the job well and get even better – have *core capability through training and development*

Know what they have to do and why – *clear communication of strategic and operational objectives to prioritise effectively*

Be given the resources to be able to do it – *effective resource management focused on outputs not process*

Be given support to do it in the new world of work – *helping people understand the need for collaboration as well as individual work and developing performance management systems that can measure how people are doing.*

If your organisation can facilitate this simple set of requirements, it should result in optimum performance, which in turn will mean beating the competition in the commercial world or delivering better service in the public sector. But for this to happen, these things have to be done by every leader at all levels in your organisation, and not just those at the top. So it is vital to have a plan for facilitating and co-ordinating it top to bottom and across the organisation. If there isn't one, you will have Mach 1 leaders and teams randomly distributed. That's better than nothing but it's not enough to get the whole organisation to Mach 1 and reaping the benefits.

It's noteworthy that it's often the tasks that fall into the category of 'important but not urgent' (see page 41) that are the very things needed to make an effective transition to Mach 1 and on to Mach 2. As we saw in Chapter 2, these are the tasks that can easily be put off, but which have a significant long-term impact if not addressed, or just make life more difficult than it should be. These could be, for example: developing the skills of the team and individuals; motivating them to perform better; identifying future customer needs; and building networks across the organisation.

The ability of an organisation to get its leaders to be able to identify those 'important but not urgent' tasks increases its chances of getting to Mach 1 and 2. Many of the key success factors for this journey fall into this category – no wonder so few organisations get to Mach 1, let alone Mach 2. In practice, this means that the culture of an organisation must often be realigned, with senior leaders prioritising those longer-term objectives that will help them get to Mach 1 and on to Mach 2 higher than currently.

As the ancient Chinese philosopher Lao Tze recognised, involvement is central to success. Lao Tze lived over 2,500 years ago, but his insights still apply today: how people respond to leaders hasn't changed over all this time, and it's not likely to. Yes, they may want leadership delivered in a different way, for example by more electronic channels, but what people want remains remarkably constant, as set out in the best boss list. No matter what level your people are at in the organisation, how old they are, what business they are in or where they are located geographically, every leader needs to be involved in helping get their organisation to Mach 1.

'Tell me and I forget, show me and I remember, involve me and I understand'
Lao Tze (604BCE–531BCE), Chinese philosopher and poet

To revisit the figures we saw earlier, we know that up to 60% of people in most organisations, if they were benefitting from Mach 1 leadership, might give up to 30% more effort. Therefore, by implication, roughly 60% of leaders aren't at Mach 1 and aren't getting maximum effort from their people. Few will even be aware that they could be leading more effectively; few will have the skills to do so and some may not have the desire or understand why they should do so. Yes, some might stumble on the answer to this challenge by chance, but it's unlikely to be more than 10% of leaders who do this.

Another problem is that when people try to measure this additional effort by engagement surveys, if it is present at all it is assumed that it is there all the time – in one survey 35% of employees were said to be rated as actively engaged to give full effort. But that's not the reality of the real world. As we all know personally, motivation and commitment can change both day-to-day and month-to-month. In the same survey 59% of employees said they were engaged only once a week, 23% even less frequently – not enough to deliver their best performance – and only 18% said they were giving full effort every day. Hence the 20% figure I use in the book, as this is the group that may be giving full effort everyday – the real objective – not the 35% or more often quoted.

Part time effort isn't good enough. So be wary of survey figures on engagement that may hide the 'part-time' givers of effort[9].

Yet with such massive potential improvements, it is sheer madness for an organisation *not* to take systematic steps to encourage better performance from all its leaders and thus all its staff. Furthermore, as noted previously, the significant changes in how slimmed-down organisations work mean that these performance improvements delivered by Mach 1 and 2 must be implemented even more.

WHAT BENEFITS CAN THIS PRODUCE FOR THE ORGANISATION?

The potential benefits for the organisation systematically trying to maximise the performance of its people by developing Mach 1 leaders can be both direct and indirect. An example of direct benefits would be staff working harder. Indirect benefits include the view taken by the market, investors or other external stakeholders of the organisation's ability to deliver its objectives, its sustainability, its brand, its reputation as an employer, and the general perspective of the organisation in society or the local community. Let's have a look at some of these, starting with the highest-level financial benefits and working down to operational performance.

Benefits in share price

In the simplest terms, the market and individuals assess the share price in relation to the perceived current value of the organisation and its potential future value. This assessment is based on physical tangible assets, for example stock, money in the bank, property and so on; and intangible assets, such as the quality of its brand, its current and future leadership, the goodwill of its customers and so on. Over the past 30 years analysts have been taking more and more notice of this 'intangible' element, as it is a predictor of future performance. There have been several research studies[10] on this but it is clear that the importance of intangible assets has increased so much that for some they are now more important than tangible ones.

Why is this important? Because the quality of the organisation's current leadership is bound up with these intangible elements. Current leaders determine the organisation's potential future performance because they develop and implement strategy, motivate the staff (or fail to), develop future leaders (or fail to) and represent the organisation in the market.

Furthermore, the organisation's ability to develop a system to support all this by leaders' activity is also critical. If the organisation is seen to be able to move to Mach 1 and on to Mach 2, it can have a positive impact on the share price.

The above may seem a little daunting for those not from a financial background, but essentially what it's saying is that your ability to 'deliver the goods' in the future is seen as more and more important than what you have done in the past.

Those who deal in investments sometimes recommend that their clients buy, sell or continue to hold shares in specific organisations. Changes in these recommendations indicate the confidence of the professional investors in that organisation and its future, and why. The quote below[11], about the global financial services firm UBS, shows how much the development of leaders and the identification of future leaders matters to the shares of an organisation:

Empowered people deliver success

'The integration of the Wealth Management units in one Business Group is the conclusion of the UBS one brand, one platform, one bank strategy. The synergies are obvious, and significant: increasingly sophisticated clients need increasingly similar specialist services around the globe. This is not only a cost issue; it is a quality of service issue... The fact that all management changes are done with successors from within UBS highlights the broad talent pool, carefully thought through processes, and motivating empowerment within UBS; for us UBS talent management and successful career planning are key aspects of our BUY recommendation.'

Sol Oppenheim, July 2005

The reason I include this quote is that it refers back to what we said at the outset of the book about the challenges facing organisations in serving clients who are increasingly sophisticated and demanding, and in some cases globally distributed. It also specifically mentions the value of 'motivating empowerment', which is a direct result of a large percentage of the organisation's leaders reaching Mach 1 leadership.

Furthermore, the mention of the organisation's talent and career planning system being a KEY part of the buy recommendation is extremely rare. But it shows unequivocally that if the organisation has the right system to get the best out of people both now and in the future, it will have a direct and positive effect on the market value of its shares.

It's reasonable to ask the question whether this effect was a direct result of the company's focus on Mach 1 and Mach 2 and what effect it had on profitability. Well, the headline[12] figures for UBS during this period (2002-2004) include:

Operating profit	+235%
Basic earnings per share	+266%
Return on equity	+286%
Market capitalisation	+130%
Headcount (total employees)	−3%
Distribution per share (pay out to shareholders)	+50%

Other example chang es:

* Increase in brand value +51% 2004 – 2007[13]

* Increase in Human Capital ROI (profit + wages costs/wage costs) 2002 – start of 2007 +24%[14]

* Rising from 7th to 4th place in global investment banking fees from 2002 to 2003, an increase of 33%[15]

- Top Global Private Bank 2003 – 2007[16]
- Euromoney Awards for Excellence 2003 – World's Best Bank[17]
  Best Company for Leaders Europe 2005 and in the top ten in 2007[18]

These are just a selection; the bank also achieved improved rankings and many first places in specific areas of financial activity over the years 2002 to 2006.

What UBS achieved is now a Harvard Business School case study[12]: *UBS: Towards the Integrated Firm.*

Although a very small number of individuals in UBS and its competitor banks subsequently made mistakes that led to the wider financial crisis, the success and size of the performance improvements achieved by the vast majority of staff being empowered and inspired at UBS is clear.

Another aspect of the benefits that Mach 1 and Mach 2 bring is the impact on customer service and thus your brand. Staff who are maximising their effort for the organisation will also be maximising the quality of what they deliver to customers, and this will reflect not only in customer satisfaction but also feed through as above, to the finances and brand value.

With engaged staff you don't even need a system

I did some work with a colleague from Cass Business School on branding and customer service at the iconic British car manufacturer Aston Martin, famous for making the cars used by James Bond in the many Bond films. They were about to introduce a new and more technologically based customer relationship management (CRM) system to try to improve service globally. I had spoken to some Aston Martin clients and their verbal feedback indicated that most of them seemed to feel that the customer service was world class. I met Markus Kramer, the marketing director, to discuss this. This is how the conversation went:

CR: So Markus, before we discuss your new CRM system, tell me about your current one.
MK: We don't have one
CT: Sorry... you don't have one?
MK: No
CR: So are you telling me that the impression that you are delivering world class customer service round the world is not down to a system at all, but to the individual actions of thousands of your staff, and your dealers, who are so determined to give maximum effort for both Aston Martin and their customers, that they make people think you have a world class customer service system?
MK: Yes...

In the broader sense, research on organisations across the globe confirms that there will be more general benefits if the development of people's performance is co-ordinated through good leadership. It shows that organisations that maximise the effort from their people are:

1. 71% more likely to outperform their peers in sector[19]

2. Able to produce earnings per share 2.6 times higher than those with low engagement[20]

3. Potentially able to increase revenue by up to 43%[21]

4. Able to improve operating income by 19.2% compared to a decline of 32.7% in those with low engagement due to poor leadership over a 12 month period[22]

5. Could halve days lost through sickness[23]

6. Could have ROE and profit up to 7% higher than competitors who do not[20]

7. Can outperform their peers in Total Shareholder Return by over 10% in a three-year period, thus also increasing their market capitalisation by this amount purely through developing good leaders. (Those who are bad at this are likely to lose 6% over the same period.)

8. Even in tough times organisations get better performance – posting shareholders' returns 22% higher than average[24]. Those where employees did not maximise effort were 28% lower than average.

So there is clear evidence that having Mach 1 leaders across your organisation makes you more money![24] As one finance director of a major organisation said to me, '*Why wasn't I told about this? We should have been doing this for years, it's a total financial no brainer!*'

As yet, the 'risk of underperformance' is never thought of as a risk, but it should be. If you are not getting the maximum performance from your staff, that is a potential risk to your organisation's success, profitability or however else you want to measure it. Not only that, but employees who are giving more effort are more likely to spot things going wrong and either do something about it or tell someone, and this means that operational and reputational risk is managed better day to day.

So risk management becomes more effective, applicable to legal, regulatory and operational risks. Furthermore, it can also mitigate reputational risk, which rules and regulations can't, as many things you don't want your people to do aren't actually illegal. They can be very embarrassing and damaging to the brand, however, if they get into the media.

So no matter which way you look at it, whether from the strategic or operational, customer service or risk perspective, the indisputable fact is that organisations which develop good leaders who engage their people and maximise effort through Mach 1 are more likely to be top performers than those that don't.

CO-ORDINATION IS VITAL

Having everyone individually maximising their own and their team's performance is very positive, but the organisation needs to co-ordinate and align that performance via every leader onto organisational priorities. This means focusing on a myriad of things from strategic alignment and customer service to risk management, cost efficiency, appraisal and skills development, recruitment, health and safety.

It's unlikely that individual leaders, especially at operational level, will have sufficient awareness to identify all these key areas of focus on their own. Consistency of approach has to be present to make the process efficient, effective and to manage risk. Only the organisation can co-ordinate this.

This also relates to the increasingly important collaboration agenda. This will be focused on in detail in chapters 5 and 6, where we look at how it relates to Mach 2, but it is worth mentioning here because it is crucial to help employees maximise their effort (Mach 1) as well as focus that maximum effort on what needs to be done for the organisation (Mach 2).

The importance of what employees do is increasingly through their collaboration with others – both in their team and outside – as much as doing their own individual work. The facilitation of collaboration and the emphasising of its importance in all communications is a central element for the organisation in getting to Mach 1. This is driven and embedded by the simple mantra: *do what the organisation needs most first.* This is in contrast to the traditional message: *just do your job.* They aren't always the same thing, and recognition of that difference is an important first step to getting your people on the road to Mach 1 and then Mach 2.

Research shows[25] that currently only 55% of employees take this mantra on board; the remainder focus on their own job requirements. It's unlikely that these are totally aligned to organisational priorities; therefore nearly half the workforce is missing the key organisational objectives.

In Chapter 2, individual leaders developing Mach 1 performance for themselves and their team were advised to use John Adair's[26] very simple and practical 'Action Centred Leadership' to balance the TASK, TEAM and INDIVIDUAL to achieve maximum performance. Too much focus on the TASK to the neglect of the TEAM and INDIVIDUALS was likely to mean performance would never reach Mach 1 levels. As we saw in Chapter 2, allowing or encouraging leaders to just focus on getting the job done without bringing the team with them through vision, inspiration and collaboration in the end is counterproductive. Yes, initially the job gets done, but the demotivating climate created by focusing on just task (achievement) without the people element (affiliation) causes lower quality work, short cuts, increased risk, potential talent loss and other problems[27]. The organisation must ensure that leaders at all levels understand that achievement of objectives must go hand in hand with the development of the team and individuals. Either get them to develop the right approach to deliver achievement or help them to find an achievement or self-growth target outside of work.

So the organisation is critical here, as all of this has to be delivered by individual leaders – but within the context of what the organisation needs, so from that perspective the model can be adapted to look like this:

The importance of leadership balance

As we said, good leadership has to occur at all levels and not just at the top. Also, as we saw in the previous chapter, the line manager is responsible for most employees' decisions about whether to give their best or not. The line manager plays a key role in helping employees align effort to organisational priorities and foster collaboration. So even if all the senior leaders in your organisation are excellent, but your boss is a poor leader, your performance is likely to be poor. Thus all leaders in the organisation, and not just those at the top, have to maximise performance to get to Mach 1, and in so doing balance task, team and individual, and all the other elements we looked at in the previous chapter.

SO HOW CAN THIS BE ACHIEVED FROM THE ORGANISATION'S VIEWPOINT?

Not all leaders are good at getting the best from their people. However, some are. Let's quantify the size of the task by looking at the rough distribution of the ability of leaders to get maximum effort. Generally it is thought[27] that maybe 10% of leaders are excellent and are getting this already; perhaps another 10% are getting some effort; probably 60% to 70% are not getting very much; and 10% are so bad at it that they demotivate their team and reduce the effort of those joining it.

'No institution can possibly survive if it needs geniuses or supermen to manage it. It must be organized in such a way as to be able to get along under a leadership composed of average human beings.'

Peter Drucker, (1909-2005), Austrian-born American management thinker

If we could get the 10% of leaders who are getting some effort from their staff, and the 60% to 70% who are getting a little to improve, the return of the resources would be significantly increased. In simple terms, if we could get the 60% to 70% to be good at getting effort from their people, that would mean that 60% to 70% of people would deliver up to a 30% improvement. This transition is summarised in more detail opposite:

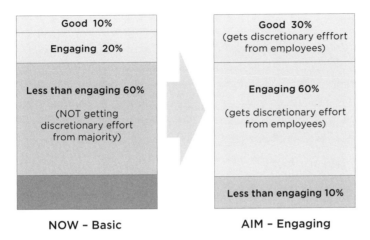

NOW – Basic   AIM – Engaging

Note: % of total leaders at each ability level

So we need to concentrate on the majority of line managers who, as yet, aren't getting the best effort, in order to get a very large improvement. This can be done quite simply, but the organisation needs to plan and implement a system that enables this transformation to happen. Despite its simplicity, few organisations have achieved this, in particular those at middle and lower levels. When I am asked how I think organisations are doing on this 'system building', I segment them into a number of categories that I think reflect the reality of what's going on inside day-to-day, which is not necessarily what the HR director might like to say. The segments are as follows:

Which is your organisation?

It's worth having a look at each of these to help you identify where your organisation is, or where the different parts of it may be. The percentage represents my estimation of the approximate number of organisations in each category.

NOT CONCERNED

These organisations aren't worried about the performance of their people. They work on the basis that they will automatically maximise their profitability as long as they minimise their employee costs. This in reality is counterproductive to profitability. They are characterised by low wages, poor employment conditions, command and control-style management and poor retention. In the end they will always fail to compete against organisations with staff engaged through Mach 1 and Mach 2 leadership.

JUST STARTING THE JOURNEY

These organisations have started to focus on people as a valuable resource, normally prompted by a problem or realising they are behind other organisations. The initiatives introduced tend to be restricted to either senior levels or others perceived as being valuable to the organisation, and are often driven by the need to develop talent for future leadership roles or the loss of talent to competitors. There is often no planned system, but rather a number of unconnected activities driven by the operational demands of different parts of the organisation.

FINDING THEIR FEET

Here the development of people and their performance is starting to become systematised, that is, there are links and information transfer between initiatives that increase the value of the output more than the individual components. For example, day-to-day feedback is fed into development planning and coaching. Here the jigsaw we will see later is slowly being assembled.

STRATEGIC VENEER

By this time in an organisation's development, it will probably have a development team of some type, which will be doing a good job. However, in-depth analysis often shows that the majority of resources are focused on either high potentials or senior leaders, and so the majority of employees do not get the full support they need to maximise their performance and get to Mach 1. Furthermore, there are often gaps in the system that no one has noticed, in particular where there is a complex organisational structure and/or a geographical spread. In these cases if you look at strategic level, all the key components seem to be in place, but in reality a significant number of employees lower down are not getting what they need.

WORLD CLASS – MACH 1 ACHIEVED

Here the system has been co-ordinated and aligned. It is led by example from the CEO and other senior leaders, and the development of employees' performance maximisation is seen as a key part of delivering the organisation's strategy and objectives. It is not seen as an HR initiative. The system is integrated with one activity feeding into and supporting another, so that a delivery chain is in place that consistently and over time develops employees' capability and desire to give the organisation their best. This includes integration of critical messages and support to employees from senior leaders, their own line managers, key influencers and HR. Implementation is done in an aligned way so the employee is given both the capability and motivation to maximise their effort for the organisation at the same time.

From the categories above you will be able to assess which most closely matches your organisation, and also the difference between where you are and the world-class group. This suggests in the simplest terms what steps you need to take to improve how your organisation adds value though leadership and moves up the iceberg model to the integrated system.

And that's the challenge from the organisational perspective: to put in place both a system and culture that will achieve that transition to maximise employee effort. As we said earlier it's about enabling each leader in the organisation to be Mach 1: able to do what is set out in Chapter 2 and Chapter 3 as quickly, simply and effectively as possible (assuming they are able and willing to do it).

So first let's look at what the organisation has to do to build the system to enable this. At the start of the chapter we said that what was needed was people who:

- **Want to do the job well** – *rational and emotional case for action from their boss being at* Mach 1
- **Are able to do the job well and get even better** – *core capability through training and development*
- **Know what they have to do and why** – *clear communication of strategic and operational objectives*
- **Have been given the resources to be able to do it** – *effective resource management focused on outputs, not process*
- **Have been given support to do it in the new way to meet the needs of the changed world** – *helping people understand the need for collaboration as well as individual work and developing performance management systems that can measure how people are doing.*

So the strategic system has to achieve several critical objectives, and it's worth asking yourself if your organisation's systems do this. (The action and the system components are in italics)

- Want to do the job well – *being inspired by their boss so making sure all leaders are at* Mach 1 *level.*
- Are able to do the job well and get even better:
  - Measuring how people are performing – *day-to-day feedback and performance management*

- Knowing what skills people need – *job criteria/requirements, especially for key roles*
- Identifying how people could perform better – *identification of development needs*
- Enabling them to get better – *development activity*
- Enabling them to progress as they get better – *pipeline of performance and potential linked to succession plans.*

What the organisational system must do at all levels

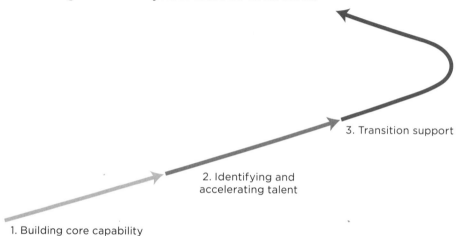

3. Transition support

2. Identifying and accelerating talent

1. Building core capability

So what that means is that at each level the system needs to:

1. Make sure everyone can do the job and wants to do it
2. Spot those who can perform even better and help them to do so
3. Move them to the right place when appropriate to maximise benefit to the organisation and support them in the transition to this new role.

The organisation has to have a system to do this as well, not only to maximise the current performance of everyone, but also to make sure everyone has their ability and potential maximised to get better and go further. But this graphic only shows what is happening at one level in the organisation. The organisation has to build a system where this happens at every level from top to bottom. So at each of these levels, specific actions must occur to make sure that capability is built to maximise performance, talent is identified and accelerated and then transitioned successfully, as we will see later, in a whole system model. You don't have to be the CEO or in HR for this to have value for you. If you have leaders reporting to you, then you also need to ensure that those leaders are having their core capability built, you are identifying and accelerating talent and supporting them through transitions to greater responsibility. This will allow them to help their people maximise their effort and get their teams to Mach 1 for you.

HOW DO WE MAKE THIS HAPPEN?

As we said above the system for the organisation has to make sure certain things happen and for this to work, 'critical' components have to be in place:

1. *Measuring how people are performing*: Performance Management:
   1. Feedback on performance both day-to-day and annually
   2. Assessment of potential for additional responsibility
2. *Knowing what skills people need* – role/job requirements/criteria, especially for critical or key roles
3. *Identifying how people could perform better* – development needs
4. *Enabling them to get better* – development plans and development activity
5. *Enabling people to progress as they get better* – creation of a pipeline of performance and potential up the organisation including succession plans
6. *Making sure people know what to do* – clear communication of both operational and strategic objectives
7. *Making sure people want to do it* – clear personal and organisational case for action to motivate individuals.

This has to be provided in a way that delivers consistency, quality, transparency, fairness and clarity across the whole organisation and integrates all of the above so it is not just a set of unlinked activities. You can view the above factors as the 'critical' components, but they are not the only components required. They form the basis of what needs to happen, but there are many other components around the 'critical' ones that have to be effective in order to facilitate, integrate and align with them to maximise benefit.

Know what they have to do, why and how – clear communication of both operational and strategic objectives

This is key to everything: delivery of short-term objectives; alignment; wider organisational objectives, and the management of both cost and risk. People at all levels must be clear on what you want them to do, the WHAT and the WHY that needs to be done, and the framework of acceptable behaviour within which that needs to happen, and the HOW. The latter ensures that a 'means justifies the end' mentality doesn't prevail, for example, 'as long as we make money that's all that matters', which would compromise effective risk management or the organisation's values. This was the attitude of some in the financial services sector that led to the 2008 crisis.

In relation to WHAT, this is best done by communication from both line manager and other sources, for example, senior leaders, organisational communications, internet sources and other organisational systems – and alignment of these messages is critical, or confusion will be created as we will see later.

The line manager is the key part of this jigsaw, given their role in day-to-day supervision and ensuring the team delivers what the organisation needs. Line managers can get much of this information themselves, but the benefits are significantly greater if the organisation provides it in a consistent way to them all together. This means everyone receives, and then passes on, the same messages about what needs to be done. Not only does this ensure that tasks get done more effectively, but also, because everyone has consistent information, it provides the foundation for collaboration.

While the WHAT is seen by many as essential, the WHY is often neglected, that is, the organisational or business case for this action, in other words, the bigger picture and the personal benefit for those involved. Including this information has the potential to increase employee effort by up to 32.8%[28], so if people are being gathered to be told the WHAT, then with such potential benefits, not including the WHY seems to me madness. The WHY will include information on the organisation's vision, strategy, what is happening in the market and anything else that helps employees understand the context.

It is also important to include the HOW; not exactly what steps have to be taken, but more a framework around the organisation's values that sets standards of behaviour for the delivery of the WHAT. The communication must be absolutely clear about this element, that is, the values within which the delivery must be made. Too many organisational disasters have occurred because communication from the top did not set out the values clearly, or they were 'lost' as the message cascaded; so the message was assumed by those at lower levels to be that profit was the priority and that what was meant by those at the top was that it was to 'make profit at all costs'. The people lower down in the organisation then interpret this to mean that, for example, the following are acceptable: reductions in maintenance to save money; cost cutting in construction to save money; or excessive risk taking to make money – all to make more profit – with inevitable and obvious consequences.

At some point something will go wrong, and this communication problem was one of the key drivers of significant corporate disasters over the past 15 years.

As mentioned in Chapter 1, my view, supported by CEB/WSJ research[29] from December 2013, is that the critical area of this type of risk for most organisations is often in middle management and not the top. It is here that the operational decisions that initiate potential disasters are made. This is confirmed by the CEB/WSJ data, which shows increasing levels of risk being shown by leaders as you move down the organisation.

Thus, for future risk management, leaders must take the utmost care to ensure that the objective and its values framework are communicated clearly. It is not only the outcome that is key, but also the values within which that is delivered, for example, 'we want to make money but in a way that adds value to our customers as well, that preserves the values of the organisation and that puts no one at personal risk.'

The delivery of this core, and indeed critical, information is relatively simple. The line managers are the most important source of this information but the organisation needs to proactively provide them with the information and tools to deliver this message. The simplest way to do this is to put in place a team briefing system. This is a two-way communication which facilitates the constant cascade of critical information, tailored to the relevant delivery point within a timed period, and with the ability for questions or feedback to return upwards to the level required for effective response.

This system is made up of regular team meeting discussions at each level run by line managers, and deals with operational issues but in addition allows the insertion of strategic and common information that the organisation needs to be distributed to everyone in a consistent way. Thus the key elements of the WHY and the HOW are given to all employees with the associated operational and strategic benefits.

The implementation of such a system should be normal practice for any organisation, but this is not the case, despite its benefits, simplicity and ease of implementation.

Team Talk gets things done

I have implemented a number of team briefing systems over time, the most notable being 'Team Talk' in 2000 for the London Underground. During a period of break up and privatisation of 75% of what was previously a publicly-owned organisation with 17,000 staff, it was critical that consistent, accurate and timed communication cascaded from the executive board to all employees, as well as providing a vehicle for teams to discuss their operational challenges.

Working full time with the board, I was able to put the system in place within three months. The communication 'cycles' started with the managing director speaking to the top 400 managers every three months, and presenting his key messages. Those attending were given copies of his slides, and also blank slides with clear instructions that they could not change the strategic messages on the first slide, but could tailor subsequent slides to identify actions their teams needed to deliver to support the strategic objectives. They then had to deliver these to those others reporting to them within three working days, thus ensuring that the messages reached the bottom of the organisation within a month. A feedback system then allowed the transmission of questions and other feedback that would be responded to within ten working days.

Ten years after the system was launched, I met the new HR director at London Underground, who informed me that it was still working effectively in virtually unaltered form.

In addition to this, other channels also need to be used to cascade these critical messages, whether these are town hall meetings led by senior leaders, intranet communications, or any other channel that effectively gets to the employees that need to hear them.

Confirming these simple key messages will ensure that practical actions which benefit everyone will always be embedded and spread across the whole organisation, and become day-to-day ways of working. That is what is required for Mach 1 and Mach 2 to work.

Be given the resources to be able to do it – focus on output not process

Organisational resources are too often focused on running the process from which it is assumed the required result will be delivered. Even worse, if the outcome is a failure, as long as the process was delivered correctly, then the view is taken that everything that could have been done was done. This is a particular problem with public sector organisations, where the measurement of outcome has not been an historic focus. Even where outcomes are measured, it is often via a target of some type that reflects only a small element of the outcome and therefore doesn't give the bigger picture. So this gives an inaccurate measure of the outcome. For example, a patient's discharge from hospital is not necessarily an indicator of the desired outcome of the delivery of good patient care, but has often been used as a target to show this.

Thus, the challenge for the organisation is to ensure that measures reflect outcomes, and that resources are focused on delivering those outcomes, and not just on the processes or targets, neither of which always accurately reflect the outcome desired.

Be given support to do it in the new way to meet the needs of the changed world

As we have seen, the world of work has changed and leaders need to be helped to understand what these changes are and how to respond to them effectively. Leaders and employees have to be more holistic when looking at what they have to do. It is no longer enough to focus solely on your own job. Understanding and collaboration with others in the team, the wider organisation and even outside is now critical to success. And to deliver this, people need to be aware of what the organisation is trying to achieve, its critical objectives, what other people do, and how they can work together to make all of this happen.

The organisation therefore has to make sure that the critical knowledge of the wider picture required by leaders and employees is easily available, that the organisation facilitates and encourages people to build relationships with those they need to collaborate with, and to understand better what they do. This is effectively moving towards the idea of communities of effort and collaboration set out in Chapter 1 as the destination for Mach 2.

So for organisations, the Mach 1 key deliverables are:

1. Maximising the effort given by employees
2. Ensuring everyone is aware of the organisation's vision, values and critical deliverables.
3. Building greater awareness of the need to collaborate with others
4. Facilitating the spread of knowledge and building of relationships to achieve this
5. Creating a system where all the components align to this end.

This then gives the organisation the foundation required to move to Mach 2, where all the effort is focused on delivering what the organisation needs for success.

CREATING A SYSTEM TO DELIVER MACH 1 AND THE FOUNDATION FOR MACH 2

There are many components needed to create a system that will ensure all of the things set out above will happen, and to allow the organisation to get to Mach 1 and then to Mach 2. We can build up the organisational jigsaw to achieve this, but many organisations fail to progress because key components are either missing or not up to the required quality standards.

Critical components

Role criteria/succession planning	
Development needs	Performance measurement
Development activity	Succession and performance pipeline
Business/personal case for action	
Effective communication	

Let us have a look at each of these critical components in more detail and then look at the others that might be needed around them to maximise the chances of success. I don't intend to go into detail on the core process or structure of these components, as there are many other books that do so. Suffice it to say that all of these critical components need to be in place, they need to be of high quality and they need to be used effectively by all involved. They also need to align to the organisation's strategy and longer-term vision and integrate with each other to deliver a consistent message to all employees about what the organisation needs to be done.

They must not be a half-completed 'tick box' exercise that people either ignore or try to avoid; all of them must be seen as key elements in delivering success. I will cover the key points about each of these that my experience tells me need to be acted on to maximise the chances of the organisation reaching Mach 1 and then Mach 2.

Knowing what skills people need – role/job requirements

Every job in the organisation, especially those that are key to the organisation's success, needs to have a list of the skills, knowledge and behaviour it requires. Furthermore, this needs to cover the actions that a Mach 1 leader needs to do as set out in Chapter 2 and Chapter 3. This includes making clear that collaboration is required, and that the prioritisation must focus on what the organisation needs to be done, not just what the individual's job says they should do. Including just the technical or functional requirements and not the leadership ones is a key reason organisations are technically excellent but never reach high levels of performance. This list then means those being considered for the role can be assessed for suitability effectively.

However, this listing should be as simple and practical as possible and focus on outputs or other visible measurable behaviour. In too many cases the role criteria that some large organisations develop are over complex, long-winded and difficult for even the post holder to properly understand. The critical point here is that if the job/role requirements are expressed in such a complex way that no one other than the HR function really understands them, then the chances of anyone actually delivering them is not great.

So, as with all elements of the system, less can often be more. You also need to be sure that what is being measured, be that appraisal, departmental performance data or a management report to the board, is what contributes directly to organisational success.

Measuring how people are performing – Performance Management

There are many books that cover the key elements of the setting up and operation of performance management systems in detail. Performance management is often assumed to centre on the annual appraisal process in an organisation, but making such an assumption is where the ability to get an organisation to Mach 1 starts to break down.

In fact, what appears in the annual appraisal should only be the summary of all of the day-to-day feedback that an individual is given over the year. Effective day-to-day feedback is critical to getting to Mach 1[30]. However, in too many organisations the end of year appraisal effectively replaces much of this and often presents individuals with surprising feedback that is not clearly linked to actions they can recall.

The critical point to note is that, unless the team leader gives regular feedback to members of their teams on a day-to-day basis, the annual appraisal will have little relevance. Furthermore, annual appraisal plays a small role in getting individuals to deliver maximum effort, compared to the good day-to-day feedback that can improve performance by up to 39.1%[31]. So all leaders must be capable of giving constructive feedback day-to-day to get maximum effort. See page 62 for explanation of how this can be done.

Too often the annual appraisal is used as a purely backward-looking 'calling to account' for past actions. It is much more effective when used in a forward-looking way. Moreover, there is no reason why giving appraisal feedback should only happen annually – often that's much too long between discussions for people to remember or to connect the feedback to real events and learn from it. So organisations should try to get mini-appraisals done quarterly rather than just the big annual one. Furthermore, where possible the appraisal should include the views of individuals other than the team leader to get a more accurate result; '360° appraisal' and other variations can help in this.

Identifying how people could perform better – development needs identification

The annual appraisal process can be used as a means to identify opportunities to maximise individual performance. This should rate current performance and identify where and how it could be improved. These areas for improvement should be agreed with the individual and taken onto the next step: the development plan.

This use of the performance management process to constantly seek to develop the performance and capability of employees is the hallmark of inspirational leaders and organisations. Organisations that fail to look to the future in this area and focus on the past create a backward-looking culture where getting better in terms of change, performance, customer service and so on, is more difficult than in forward-focused organisations.

'Performing better' means minimising poor behaviour as well as strengthening good. You will recall in Chapter 2 we saw that 'derailers' existed – characteristics and actions that if done in moderation were positive, but if done to an extreme were negative. Thus in helping people perform better this is also critical for the organisation to do, especially for senior leaders who might have slipped into bad habits, in other words derailed, or about to do so. So development needs identification but also has to keep an eye out for any emergence of the dark side, and even before then help developing leaders, and indeed even all employees, recognise where these might be for them[32].

Enabling them to get better – development plans and development activity

Once you have identified what people need to do to get better, the next challenge is implementing the actions. Again there are many books on this subject, but there are some key points that are often neglected when implementing development activity, which reduces the organisation's ability to get to Mach 1. Developing people is vital for success – it significantly increases their effort and performance – an effective mentor can increase effort by 25.5%, and an effective achievable development plan by 25.4%.

1. The most effective development is often on the job with the line manager and team colleagues, as this delivers it alongside the organisation's objectives, so this should be the prime means of development.

2. Off-the-job development should only be used where it cannot be delivered on the job.

3. The development activities should, in addition to developing the individual, specifically aim to deliver a measurable benefit to the organisation within a maximum of six months.

4. Development activity should therefore be aligned to the organisation's needs as well as the individual's.

5. The successful delivery of the individual's development should, where possible, be part of their team leaders' objectives.

The benefits, as set out in Chapter 2, are significant: the line manager can increase an employee's effort by 25.5%[33] if a development plan for that employee is challenging and implemented. But this is not the end of the potential benefits. A well-designed, credible development plan can improve the development of potential talent by 37.8%; engagement by 45.4%; ability by 15.7%; and aspiration by 22.5%[34]. Unachievable development plans can reduce potential by 18.9% and development plans that managers don't support or take seriously can reduce potential by 12.5%.

Enabling staff to progress when appropriate – creation of a pipeline of performance and potential up the organisation with succession plans

As people develop, there may come a time when they are performing sufficiently well to move up the organisation. This should be assessed against a) performance in the past and b) potential in the future. The performance in the past will be indicated by the annual appraisal, and potential in the future can be indicated by the demonstration of certain behaviour, including:

1. Engaging others – getting things done through other people and being able to establish rapport and effective working relationships quickly.

2. Learning agility – learning from experience to improve your own performance and that of others. Proactively seeking feedback and helping others develop as well.

3. Managing change – being effective in fast-moving situations and considering the needs and implications of the future as well as the present.

4. Strategic understanding – understanding, leveraging and improving the whole organisation and not just your own role responsibilities

5. Resilience – being able to deal with the pressures of challenging environments and maintaining positive behaviour with others in such situations and helping them to do the same.

Potential is potential

No matter what your organisation or where, the criteria for successful leaders are the same. These criteria were originally developed with colleagues at UBS in 2003. They were used, with proven effectiveness, to consistently identify high potential leaders across the world. But what also became clear was that these criteria did not only relate to the financial industry or commercial organisations. They were transferred successfully without any significant changes to part of the UK National Health Service (400 organisations and 1.4m staff) where, in 2009, they were used to identify those with potential from 20 organisations employing over 140,000 people.

They were subsequently taken up by further NHS organisations in 2010, so that they are now used in some way by over 120 NHS organisations. They have also been successfully taken up by other organisations in other sectors. This demonstrates that Mach 1 and Mach 2 leadership is what is required for success in any organisation no matter what the sector, industry or location. Furthermore, good practice from one sector can be effectively transferred to another.

PULLING IT TOGETHER INTO A PRACTICAL APPROACH

All of the above then needs to be pulled together into a simple, practical system that works, and which everyone in the organisation can understand and is happy to use. Below is an example of a top-to-bottom system that does this. There is a model that some in HR use called the 'talent pipeline'. I have adapted this, as organisations need not only talented people who can be promoted, but they also need everyone else to give maximum effort. Both have to be combined in a seamless system. After all, the 'everyone else' is the reservoir from which 'talent' comes, so developing future talent in this reservoir is key to Mach 1 and 2.

Performance and talent pipeline

	Core development for all, inc HP&P	Development for Talent	Transition/selection and support
Senior leaders	• Board Development • External mentors • Effective CE Programme	• Top level programme	
			• Selection interview board + p/p review • Support: 100 days programme
Department heads	• Effective Director Programme	• Aspiring CE Programme • Internal mentor	
			• Selection Assessment/interview + p/p review. Support: 100 days programme
Middle managers	• Effective Asst Director	• Aspiring MD Programme • Internal mentor	
			• Selection 2 stage interview + p/p review
First line managers	• Effective Manager	• Accelerated Asst Director Programme	
			• Selection interview +p/p review
Load Self	• Effective working and partnership	• Accelerated Management Programme	
			• Interview and/or graduate programme

It can be seen here that core capability is developed for everyone at each level; the system looks for those with potential to progress and has the processes to make this happen, and where appropriate they are supported during this transition to ensure success. This latter point is key. Even if people are accurately identified for promotion in terms of performance, this means about 50% fail at the next level. Of this group 28% fail for personal reasons, for example changes in family circumstances, 51% because their commitment or ability has been incorrectly assessed, but more importantly 21% fail because the organisation has not given appropriate support[35].

Making sure people know what to do – clear communication of both operational and strategic objectives

'Where there is no vision, the people perish.'
Proverbs 29:18

This falls into the high level principles and then the communication specifics: both need to be in place, both need to be clear and both need to align to the organisation's strategy and objectives. So at the highest level, what should be happening to move to Mach 1 is that all leaders must ensure that:

1. They are Mach 1-inspiring leaders themselves
2. They set direction and example to their teams and others in the organisation – personal high performance and collaboration with others
3. All the leaders in the areas below them are developed to Mach 1
4. Everyone in their area knows the organisation's strategy, objectives and values and how they fit in with it
5. A good system to support and enable Mach 1 exists in their area as set out in this chapter

And all employees must take responsibility for their own performance and development with the support of the organisation.

At operational level, this must be linked to the specific actions that the individual, team or department needs to deliver. But the higher-level principles are key to ensuring that people develop organisational awareness as well as delivering their objectives, which will help with collaboration and the move to Mach 2.

Making sure people want to do it – clear personal and organisational case for action to motivate individuals.

This should answer the 'what's in it for me?' question, which is part of the emotional element of the decision to give high performance. You remember that this was said to be 57% rational and 43% emotional in Chapter 2. This question has to be answered from the perspective of every individual, because the organisational benefit is unlikely to motivate people to maximise their performance. Remember the principle introduced earlier that 'beauty is in the eye of the receiver, not the giver', meaning that the person receiving determines the value of what they are being asked to do, not the person telling them.

If you think back to Chapter 1 and the discussion about why people do things and Maslow's hierarchy[36], the 'what's in it for me' will be probably related to the types of 'needs' identified. It's the job of team leaders to have some idea of the 'needs' of their people, based on their experience of working with those individuals and one-to-one discussions.

However, all too often the 'what's in it for me?' question is never properly answered by leaders for their people, whether it's when the CEO addresses the employees, or even when team leaders ask for more effort or a change in the way the team works.

But one thing is clear: if a team leader does get to Mach 1, his or her people will put in significant effort even if this question hasn't been answered. This is because they have been inspired and respect their leader. If the leader isn't delivering Mach 1 leadership, then they aren't going to be anywhere as keen.

BUILDING THE ORGANISATIONAL JIGSAW

As well as the critical components that have to be in place to get to Mach 1, other components will need to be present to ensure that the critical components can deliver the maximum benefit required. Too many people assume that as long as the critical components as set out in the system jigsaw below are present, then Mach 1 can be achieved. This graphic shows how the additional components in the organisational jigsaw must be aligned to support, or at least not hinder, the critical components. If they send contradictory messages to the critical components, the chances of success will be significantly reduced.

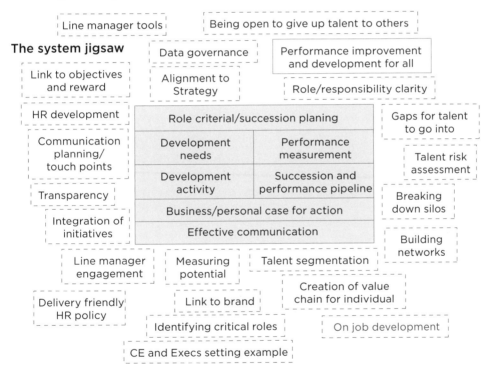

As you can see, there are many other 'facilitating' components of an effective system that enable the critical components to work more effectively. Hopefully as a reader you are beginning to see, and your own experience confirms it, that organisations, despite the nice organisational charts we produce, aren't divided into boxes. They have to be a dynamic community underpinned by a system of interaction that aligns everyone and integrates all the components to achieve Mach 1 – an *aligned community of effort and*

collaboration. So in the graphic all of the facilitating components play a role in making sure that the critical components can work effectively.

This can be achieved by simply having a checklist of the facilitating components and asking a) is this present, and b) is this supporting our critical components and aligned to the organisation's objectives and strategy?

This is effectively about sending a message – even though a process cannot talk, it can say a lot to those who observe it in relation to:

1. What is this saying the organisation wants me to do and how?

2. How important or not is this compared to other priorities?

3. Does this align with other things I am being told or asked to do? If not which do I do?

4. What's in it for me?

So with alignment in place, consistent messages are sent out, but without it, confusion will occur and this will divert effort onto the wrong things. To make this work there often needs to be a change in mindset among leaders at all levels in the organisation. It's one thing having both critical and facilitating components in place; it's quite another for leaders to use them effectively. That depends on them thinking in the right way about the organisation.

Too often the use of organisational charts makes us think that an organisation is a collection of discrete boxes that don't interact, and where information and action moves vertically not horizontally. This subconsciously starts building barriers in people's minds that create silos, which we then have to spend so much time trying to break down to get our organisations to work well.

This is the way most leaders think about how their organisation is structured and what it delivers:

Traditional leader's view

As this indicates, people, leaders included, often think of the organisation as a set of boxes that are responsible for different functions, and also that there is some HR activity based around leadership that somehow does, or does not, seem relevant to what they have to do to deliver their objectives. This disconnect between the ideas of leadership and day-to-day activity is key to why leaders: a) don't always see leadership development as relevant; b) don't have the skills to deliver it; and c) neither they, nor their organisation, ever get to Mach 1.

To change this perspective the organisation has to think, not of discrete functional boxes, but as an ***aligned*** *community of effort and collaboration*, focused on the customer with leadership as a key element of the delivery of everything that everyone does.

New aligned delivery chain view

Here the perspective is different; no matter what part of the organisation you are in, you are clear that everything you do must be underpinned and driven by Mach 1 leadership, otherwise it will never be the best, and only the best is good enough. As from the Aston Martin example – and supported by many other examples – this delivers the best customer service and the associated benefits be they financial, brand, reputation, networking or other. When leaders at all levels start thinking of the organisation as 'one' organisation all going in the same direction and all at Mach 1, often the results achieved are MORE than expected.

The same process can be used to review or challenge existing legacy systems or approaches. Breaking down the 'boxes' and looking at redesigning both the process and the way people think can have significant benefits. And this applies not just in the commercial world.

Rethinking the system improves patient service

Like many healthcare systems the NHS in the UK is under severe pressure from funding restrictions and ever increasing demand. In 2011 University College London Hospitals (UCLH) launched the productive outpatients programme in an effort to 'do more with less and do it better'. This was a structured approach to engaging, training and empowering frontline staff to redesign and improve outpatient services. The results were very significant. In many clinics waiting times were halved, unnecessary meetings removed and duplicated data entry was removed, allowing the time to be used for patients and resulting in nearly 600 additional hours per year for patient care from just two clinics. This innovative programme has been so successful that other hospitals across the UK and abroad now send their people to learn how success was achieved through engaging employees at UCLH.

Building a sustainable system

The objective in improving the performance of the organisation is to create a momentum, so that as more and more people become engaged, the effects become greater and greater. In reality, it is likely that only about a third of any group of key stakeholders that you encourage to adopt a new way of working – which Mach 1 and 2 effectively are – will initially put in effort to do so. But this is not a serious issue. It is highly unlikely that everyone will willingly take action to implement it at first. In some respects, in this kind of initiative, if everyone is happy to adopt it from the start there might be a question as to whether the change is challenging enough.

There is likely to be a third who are neutral and will wait and see, and another third who probably don't like what is proposed or don't think it is relevant to them. The diagram on the opposite page shows that even with a small group of initial adopters, sufficient momentum will build up to spread and embed the change, and the system should become self sustaining. This will then move those in the other groups to become adopters, either by the evidence of success or through peer pressure.

As each group of leaders develop other leaders for the future, and those recently developed go on to do the same, this will naturally spread and embed Mach 1 around the organisation. But again the graphic confirms the need for both an organisational system that supports the adoption of Mach 1, and the actions of individual leaders to make it happen.

'I start with the premise that the function of leadership is to produce more leaders, not more followers.'
Ralph Nader (b. 1934), US political activist

Interestingly, this cycle also introduces further benefits to the organisation. If leaders do what Mach 1 requires, not only is there an increase in the individual's effort by up to 30%[37], but this also creates an environment that actually increases an individual's potential to go further in the organisation. This then develops even more high quality people to feed into your performance and potential pipeline. But there are even greater benefits because if the line manager develops his people into those with potential to go further this can, in return, help them to increase their own potential by 22% and intent

to stay by 30%. Thus continuous development of performance brings significant benefits to individuals, team and organisation[38].

Working across cultures

There are challenges where leaders work across cultures, and this includes employees, but also suppliers, customers, potential customers, and indeed anyone the organisation needs to help it be effective. In some cultures, the US for example, consensus is not generally considered important in decision-making at the most basic level of meetings. But in Switzerland or Germany it is. However, making an effective decision is required in both.

As was covered in Chapter 2 and Chapter 3, various studies, including the GLOBE[39] study and Hofstede[40], show that there is core common leadership behaviour that all leaders need to deliver in any culture, for example, some of the things set out in the best boss list, but that these might not be prioritised in the same order in different cultures. In other words, they all have to be present, but the degree of focus on each may vary.

The cultural groups and their different priorities are given on page 54. Thus there are two organisational imperatives in this area:

1. Ensuring all leaders are up to Mach 1 in their own cultural environment – this will ensure they maximise the performance of their own people and encourage behaviour in them that will facilitate more effective learning when in contact with other cultures, for example, proactively listening and seeking to understand the bigger picture and context.

2. Helping those in areas of multiple cultures understand the need to use core Mach 1 behaviour in a way that meets the needs of the local culture and what the

different priorities are. For example, many cultures value the ability to inspire as the most important leadership skill, whereas Arab, Asian and Confucian cultures value leaders who protect themselves and the group most. As second priorities, Nordic and Anglo Saxon cultures value participative leaders – that is, those who get individuals involved in decision-making – whereas Latin and Confucian cultures value leaders who build the team. Thus, while the core skills all leaders need to use are the same, the one to focus on as the key skill varies depending where you are in the world.

It is only if the organisation has a system for ensuring that those in cross-cultural roles are given the support they need by way of the above, that effective cross-cultural working and collaboration will occur with the significant benefits this brings, for example, better innovation and creativity, more effective and efficient customer service, or the creation of a 'global yet local' presence. Understanding the cultural contexts around the decisions those destined to be future strategic leaders will make is central to their development.

What about new arrivals?

We have so far considered how to get more effort and thus performance from those already in the organisation. But most organisations may have a departure rate (staff turnover) of employees of at least 10% per year, if not significantly more. So if everyone else is performing well, how do you get those arriving up to speed as quickly as possible? Every day they are not is effectively a cost in lost performance.

The answer is to give them the Mach 1 components as quickly as possible, with their line manager taking the lead and additional support coming from HR and senior leaders. This can have a significant impact on their performance. If the following is included in the 'onboarding' process – what new employees are given when they arrive – the following potential increases in effort could be obtained[19]:

- Clearly explaining the importance of the job +23.4%
- Teaching about the organisational vision and strategy +21.9%
- Teaching about the group or division +21.5%
- Clearly explaining performance objectives +20.9%
- Clearly explaining job responsibilities +20.3%
- Introducing the new employees to each other +19.2%

The Mach 1 approach ensures that even those who are new to the organisation can, if given the right support, deliver benefit quickly.

The importance of senior leaders

While I have emphasised the importance of the line manager as the key factor in getting employees to Mach 1, the CEO and senior leaders also play an important role. This is not by directly interacting with employees day-to-day, but in building the organisational system and making sure it functions in a way that maximises the leverage of what line mangers do and helps them do it well. CEOs and the top team can have an impact, and demonstrating 'good' behaviour is vital if the right culture is to be created to drive Mach 1 and then Mach 2.

Below are the potential increases[41] in discretionary employee effort delivered by each of the factors and aspects of behaviour influencers if the CEO and senior management show they are:

- open to new ideas +22.9%
- care deeply about employees +20.7%
- make employee development a priority +19.7%
- are strong in leading and managing people +15.6%
- are strong in strategy selection and implementation +15.6%

Interestingly, developing employees' potential by way of senior leaders' commitment to development has an even higher impact, at 29%. So the visible actions of this group, for example to become visible mentors, have significant impact[42].

None of these things cost money and can be initiated very quickly if the desire is present. They simply emphasise the reality that achieving the transition to Mach 1 is simple, practical and speedy. But not only are these benefits possible, if the CEO and senior leaders set the example and make sure that this is cascaded down to create the right culture, it will support those line managers trying to get to Mach 1 and then Mach 2 with their people.

Once this becomes prevalent, then the organisational culture will become closer to Mach 1, with the following elements[43] in place delivering yet more benefit as indicated by the +% increase in employee effort:

- effective communication +29.2%
- a reputation for organisational integrity +27.6%
- a culture of innovation +26%
- a culture of flexibility +24.7%
- customer focus +23.3%
- future orientation +23.1%
- internal equity and recognition +21.5%
- overall company success +21.5%
- a culture of risk-taking and lack of a blame culture +20.6%
- community involvement +18.6%

Having Mach 1 and then Mach 2 leaders at the top of the organisation therefore has a multiplying effect on those lower down also trying to be Mach 1 and Mach 2. The senior leaders create the environment where it can grow, spread and embed faster. Without the organisational co-ordination of Mach 1 and then Mach 2 this cannot happen across the organisation. Any islands of excellence that do exist will get lost in a sea of mediocrity.

SUMMARY

There is an irrefutable case for the organisation planning and taking action to try to get all its leaders to Mach 1 and align their actions to the organisation's objectives. Senior leaders setting example and building the system, line managers at all levels delivering and inspiring their people, will achieve objectives, make money, improve customer service, manage risk and build for the future. The system does not need to be complicated; it just requires the following abilities from individuals and thus the associated elements from the organisation to make it work:

- **Wanting to do the job well** – *rational and emotional case for action,* inspiration and support *from their boss. So ensuring all leaders are at* Mach 1.

- **Being able to do the job well to get even better** – *core capability through training and development*

- **Know what they have to do and why** – *clear communication of strategic and operational objectives*

- **Be given the resources to be able to do it** – *effective resource management focused on outputs not process*

- **Be given support to do it in the new way** – *helping people understand the need for collaboration as well as individual work and developing performance management systems that can measure how people are doing.*

This has to be made possible across the organisation with a simple and effective system that has the sole aim of taking all leaders to Mach 1. This in turn will enable people to maximise their performance, which then maximises that of the organisation to take it to Mach 1. Once this is achieved, the organisation should be getting maximum effort from its people, and the journey to Mach 2 can start, where that effort is focused on what really matters to transform the organisation to reach its full potential.

CHAPTER 4 KEY POINTS

- To maximise organisational performance all leaders at all levels must be at Mach 1. People must:
  1. want to do the job, be able to do the job and know exactly what they need to do it and why – and also know that the key focus is on delivering not only their job but also what the organisation needs in the holistic sense
  2. be given the resources to do it
  3. be enabled to understand the new world of work and the best way to work effectively in it.
- If the organisation can get to Mach 1 there will be significant financial benefits.
- To get all leaders to Mach 1 the organisation must have a strategy to make that happen in a co-ordinated way. It will also need systems to monitor how the strategy is going and measure performance, assess skills and knowledge needs and help people get better, for example through performance assessment, succession plans, development activity and plans, performance and potential pipeline.
- Everything else the organisation needs to align to the objective of getting to Mach 1 and inspiring people to want to get there. Leaders must think 'leadership and working together' underpins everything; not the 'my job' silo mentality, but the *aligned community of effort and collaboration*. The objective of Mach 1 is sustainable and ever-increasing performance, not delivery of a short-term project.

CHAPTER 4 - KEY ACTIONS FOR YOU TO DO NOW

1. Make sure your senior leaders are aware of the business and personal benefits of achieving Mach 1 and have a plan to make it happen

2. Does your organisation take a consistent and systematised approach to developing Mach 1? Are any key components missing? Where could it improve?

3. Does your organisation take steps to proactively develop leaders' ability to take a holistic view of the whole organisation and its needs, and to collaborate to achieve them? Where could it improve?

References

1. *Driving Breakthrough Performance in the New Work Environment*: Corporate Executive Board, 2013

2. *An Accenture point of view on employee engagement*: Accenture (produced for MacLleod Report) 2008

3. *Driving Employee Performance and Retention Through Engagement*: Corporate Leadership Council, 2004

4. *Driving Employee Performance and Retention through Engagement*: Corporate Leadership Council, 2004 (p67)

5. *Driving Employee Performance and Retention through Engagement*: Corporate Leadership Council, 2004 (p37)

6. *Developing effective leadership in the NHS to maximise the quality of patient care*, Chris Roebuck: The King's Fund, London, 18 May 2011

7. *Employee engagement and NHS performance*, West & Dawson: The King's Fund, London, 2012

8. *Leadership: improving the quality of patient care*, Angie Clegg: Nursing Standard 14(30), 2000 (p43-45) and *Improving the quality of healthcare in the United Kingdom and United States: A framework for change*, Ferlie & Shortell: Millbank Quarterly Vol 79, No 2, 2001

9. *Working Life: employee attitudes and engagement*, Truss, Soane, Edwards, Wisdom, Croll & Burnett: CIPD, London 2006

10. *Intangibles: Management, Measurement, and Reporting*, Baruch Lev: Brookings Institution Press, 2001 and *New Metrics of Corporate Performance: Profit per employee*, Bryan: McKinsey Quarterly No.1, 2007

11. Sol Oppenheim, July 2005

12. *UBS: Towards the Integrated Firm*, Lal, Nohrai & Knoop: Harvard Business School, May 15 2006

13. Interbrand Top 100 brand rankings

14. UBS Corporate Social Responsibility Report 2007

15. Bloomberg 1/3/2004 reference Freeman & Co, New York data

16. Euromoney

17. Euromoney Investment Dealers' Digest 2003 – Bank of the Year (IDD)

18. Hewitt

19. *Driving performance and retention through employee engagement*, Corporate Leadership Council, 2004

20. *Engagement predicts earnings per share*, Gallup 2006

21. *Engage employees and boost performance*: Hay Group, 2001

22. *The ISR Employment Engagement Report*: Towers Perrin-ISR, 2006

23. *Annual Absence and Labour Turnover Survey*: CBI-AXA, 2007

24. *Q12 Meta Analysis – The relationship between engagement at work and organisational outcomes*, Harter, James, Killham & Agrawal: Gallup, 2012

25. *Driving Breakthrough Performance in the New Work Environment*: Corporate Executive Board, 2013

26. *Action-Centred Leadership*, J. E. Adair: McGraw-Hill, London, 1973

27. *Leadership run amok, the destructive power of potential overachievers*, Spreier, Fontaine & Malloy: Harvard Business Review June 2006 (p1-10)

28. *Driving employee performance and retention through engagement*, Corporate Executive Board, 2004 (p93)

29. You'll find more information on my website: chrisroebuck.co/files/2014/02/Companies-need-to-be-more-aware-of-risk.pdf

30. *Work Survey Report, Continuous Engagement: Key to unlocking the value of your people in tough times*: Watson Wyatt, 2008-9

31. *Managing for high performance and retention*: Corporate Executive Board, 2005

32. *Assessing leadership: a view of the dark side*, Hogan & Hogan: International Journal of Selection and Assessment 9, 2001 (p40-51) and *Hogan Development Survey Manual* (2nd Edition), Hogan Assessment Systems, 2009

33. *Driving employee performance and retention through engagement*: Corporate Leadership Council, 2004 (p97)

34. *Realising the full potential of rising talent*: Corporate Leadership Council, 2006 (p109)

35. *Realising the full potential of rising talent*: Corporate Leadership Council Vol.2, 2005 (p9)

36. *A theory of human motivation*, A. H. Maslow: Psychological Review 50(4), 1943, (p370–96)

37. *Engage for Success: Enhancing performance through employee engagement*, MacLeod & Clarke: Department of Innovation and Skills, London, July 2009

38. *Realising the full potential of rising talent*: Corporate Leadership Council (p67)

39. *Culture, Leadership, and Organisations: The GLOBE study of 62 societies*, Robert J House et al: Sage Publications, 2004

40. *Cultures and Organisations: Software of the Mind*, Hofstede & Geert: Administrative Science Quarterly (Johnson Graduate School of Management, Cornell University) 38 (1), March 1993 (p132–134) JSTOR 2393257 and *The GLOBE debate: Back to relevance*, Hofstede & Geert: Journal of International Business Studies (Sage Publications) 41 (8), 2010 (p1339–46) SSRN 1697436

41. *Realising the full potential of rising talent*: Corporate Leadership Council, 2005 (p77)

42. *Realising the full potential of rising talent*: Corporate Leadership Council Vol 2, 2005 (p64)

43. *Driving employee performance and retention through engagement*: Corporate Executive Board, 2004 (p103)

5

Moving to Mach 2
for individual leaders:
how to focus team effort
onto what really matters
and delivers success

5

Moving to Mach 2
for individual leaders:
how to focus team effort
onto what really matters
and delivers success

By now, if you have done all the things suggested to get yourself performing better as a leader to get to Mach 1 (chapters 2 and 3), and getting your team to do the same (Chapter 3), then your people should be increasing effort day by day, potentially by up to 30%[1]. But this will only happen if you've given them the tools to give you maximum effort and motivated them to deliver it.

Now you need to go up a gear from Mach 1 to Mach 2. This extra step, often never taken by leaders or organisations, is critical. The fact that your people are giving maximum effort for you does not mean that this maximises the benefit of that effort for the organisation. You will recall that right at the beginning of the book I said that leadership was about enabling individuals to meet their needs and aspirations by doing what the organisation needs to achieve. It is possible for people to work at their best, but be doing either the wrong work, or the right work in the wrong way.

'The first responsibility of a leader is to define reality. The last is to say thank you. In between, the leader is a servant.'

Max De Pree (b.1924), US businessman, CEO and writer

This is also what has now become more vital in the new world of work. The slimmed down, more matrixed and more pressured organisation of the 21st century need people to focus on doing what the organisation has to deliver overall, and not just their own specific work. It demands much more collaboration – collaboration has more than doubled since 2002[2] in its importance to profitability, up from 22% to 49%. Compared to the current 20% of employees norm, if you get 50% of employees to be able to deliver overall organisational contribution through collaboration this could add +4% to profitability, and getting 100% could add +12%. Thus this is an imperative for you as an individual leader.

So the objective of moving from Mach 1 to Mach 2 is to ensure that all the extra effort that you are delivering yourself, or getting from your team, is being applied to those things that are most critical for the success of organisation. The first step is to maximise *your* value to the organisation. When this is done, you can apply the same principles to your people.

GET TO MACH 2 AND MAXIMISE YOUR VALUE TO THE ORGANISATION

Mach 2 is not just about delivering your job objectives but doing other things as well to make the whole organisation perform better, collaboration being the most important. Most individual leaders find their ability to get to Mach 2 restricted, because they assume that they just have to do their own job well in the functional or technical sense, and nothing more. Mach 2 is much more than that, and most organisations look for much more than that from their future senior leaders. So it's in your interest to do it.

If you look at the 2012 CEB research[2], the key elements that maximise your ability to contribute to the organisation are:

1. Prioritisation – the ability to prioritise what you do based on its benefit to the organisation and not just the requirements of your role

2. Collaboration – the ability to not only know others in teams you have to work with, but also to know what they do

3. Organisational awareness – being aware of the context of what is happening in the organisation and not just the formal structures.

4. Proactive change – the ability to identify change opportunities and implement them, and not just support change initiated by others.

It is interesting that the ability to do these things is not greatly influenced by age, gender, education (degree level or not), or whether those involved are working remotely or are in the office. Thus everyone can be helped to do these things. We have seen[2] that the need for collaboration versus focus on one's own work to maximise profitability has doubled between 2002 and 2012 from 22% to 49%. However, do not infer that this means you need to double the time spent working with others. In fact, the CEB data[2] shows that there is only a three-hour time difference per week spent working with others, between those who are highly effective collaborators and those who are not. That confirms it is just as much about WHAT you do as with WHOM you do it. This returns us to the Mach 2 core principle – WHAT you do must focus on what is critical to the organisation's success. This is what you need to deliver as an individual leader.

For those in support functions such as HR, IT, finance, risk, and marketing, Mach 2 is also key in ensuring that what you do is aligned to what the external customer needs from the organisation. All too often, while those interacting with customers understand them and what needs to be done to deliver the best service for them, those more remote from them, such as support functions and their senior leaders, tend not to think much about the customer when doing their jobs.

This makes life difficult for those delivering customer service, as it creates a gulf between their attempts to serve customers and thus the organisation's needs, and others who just want to make the organisational process work efficiently. As meeting customers' needs is the desired end result, those in support services should be even more keen to take up the challenge of Mach 2 than those who are customer facing.

There are two key elements in the Mach 2 hierarchy that you need to be good at:

1. Mach 2 knowledge – widen and deepen your knowledge so that you understand what you and your people should be focusing on so it better aligns with what your organisation needs

2. Mach 2 skills – additional skills that allow the knowledge to be used in a more targeted way to maximise the benefit you and your team deliver. This allows you to add benefit to the wider organisation as well as your own team.

First let's look at the Mach 2 skills/knowledge:

And for entrepreneurial support functions!

These are the key areas you need to focus on:

Excellent functional knowledge

Being good at your functional role is the basic foundation for delivering what the organisation needs. But there are other things you have to do to get to Mach 2. This is where the value of Mach 2 has such an impact on the support functions, which tend to take a narrower technical or professional view of what they need to do to support the organisation. But these principles apply to all leaders. These are:

Core organisational knowledge

You also have to have a basic understanding of how all organisations work and how to make them work better. So you need to know about the basics of finance, project management and the principles of business. This helps you understand how any organisational 'machine' works and helps you to integrate what you do with principles of good organisational operation. So do those in HR understand the basics of finance? Do those in finance understand the basics of HR or marketing? And does everyone understand the basics of project management? These are things that all organisations do to make them successful, and are therefore the basic building blocks of organisational knowledge.

Operational understanding

You have to fully understand what goes on around you day-to-day at your level of the organisation. Do you really understand what the parts of the organisation around you do, and what their objectives and challenges are? If you do, this helps you to a) understand how you could help them better, b) understand how they could help you better and c) how the organisational 'machine' integrates or not, as the case may be!

This is central to building the collaboration that is now so important at operational level for good working partnerships. Your organisational understanding needs to be based on the reality of what happens day-to-day, and not official organisational silos that will often obstruct effective delivery of success. This is the all-important 'context' that both you and your team need to know.

Strategic understanding

You have to understand what the organisation is trying to achieve at strategic level: what are the key objectives, the vision, and its values? You need to know what these are so that you can make sure that what you and your team do is aligned to them as closely as possible. This is of the utmost importance. It allows you to see where the balance lies between your own work and the work you do with others, and which the organisation needs most. That way you ensure that all the effort you and the team put in delivers maximum benefit to your organisation. This is perhaps the most important of the additional things you need to know.

Market and environmental knowledge

Further information that you need to be aware of includes the market and environmental knowledge about how your organisation relates to the world around it – its market and other environments. This is not just about the environment in the 'green' sense, but all the external factors that might impact upon the organisation: political, regulatory, technological, social, economic, cultural and so on. For example, the education system of the country you are based in may have an impact on the supply of people with a certain skill set you need for the organisation. This helps you understand the external factors that affect your organisation and where its future opportunities or challenges may come from.

Mach 2 skills and knowledge

Finally, at the top of the pyramid is the key Mach 2 behaviour that takes all the knowledge and understanding below it and applies it day-to-day by focusing it on what the organisation really needs. This behaviour is made up of actions that a) focus on maximising the value of what the team does and b) help the overall organisational system work better. Again prioritisation and collaboration are key here. We know that this approach works, and works well, as it was implemented at UBS between 2002 and 2006[3], where it delivered significantly better performance than other sector comparators.

KEY MACH 2 SKILLS

For you and then the team:

Entrepreneurial leadership

Using the skills of the entrepreneur to focus on critical organisational success factors and reinvigorate what you do.

For the organisation:

Role model for collaboration and values

The role model for partnership is a key element in collaboration. By demonstrating your ability to collaborate and work in partnership, you show that it is not only possible but also beneficial, and in doing so encourage the team to do the same. A leader that encourages respect from others, and shows that integrity, respect, decency, trust and humility are core to being an effective leader, is leading by example and putting their values and ethics into practice.

Collaboration is global

Leaders and organisations need to think globally. Even if you aren't global, someone somewhere is wrestling with the same challenges you have! Strategic relationships and innovative collaboration can help here. For example, the UK India Education and Research Initiative (See ukieri.org) fosters educational links. Its three main objectives are higher education and research, schools, and professional and technical skills. Achievements include 103 new research collaborations, 380 schools linked between the two countries, 88 travel grants, 67 research awards, six major research awards, and numerous doctoral and post-doctoral fellowships.

Also, multi-national business is creating innovation hubs in the developing world, with companies such as Microsoft, Intel, Nokia and Accenture[4] establishing research and development centres in China and India. These companies are tapping into a vast new pool of skills and resources, and developing 'global leaders' to use Mach 1 and Mach 2 in a multi-cultural environment.

Being a leadership ambassador

A leader who acts as a champion for the organisation, its brand and its strategy both inside and outside. Spreading the word so that as many people as possible inside and out know what the organisation stands for and is trying to achieve and how, and encouraging them to become engaged as employees, customers or brand supporters. Again spreading understanding that enables prioritisation and collaboration.

Driving alignment and integration

A leader who looks for opportunities to better align activity to organisational objectives, and to seek opportunities to integrate and drive effectiveness and efficiency where possible. In other words, making the organisation simpler, slicker, and more focused on what really matters. This is a key part of strategic leadership where your role is in transforming not just your team, but also the whole organisation.

Let's look at each in more detail:

ENTREPRENEURIAL LEADERSHIP

This is the application of the behaviour of the entrepreneur to the larger organisation. Why is this important? Knowing how the organisation works and its environment is only useful if that knowledge is applied day-to-day to make the right decisions and improve performance. But how to do this is the subject of much debate and disagreement. However, there is a lesson for the larger organisation from the entrepreneur, both in terms of what individual leaders can do better and what the organisation can do as a whole. Here we will concentrate on what you as an individual leader can learn.

Entrepreneurs have to get things right or they don't survive in the market. They don't have the financial resources of larger organisations to help them weather problems or to recover from errors. They have to make sure they really focus on what is important, and get it right. There are no second chances. So what are these things?

1. Total focus on delivering to the customer
2. Optimising risk, not minimising it
3. Constantly being creative and innovative to get better
4. Taking personal responsibility for organisational as well as personal results
5. Understanding the wider picture
6. Keeping things simple
7. Inspiring people around you with a clear vision to collaborate.

The entrepreneur recognises that the customer needs to get what they want in a way that drives organisational success. They understand that you have to take risks to succeed, that you have to always strive to be better and beat the competition, and that you have to take responsibility for results. All of this is underpinned by prioritising success and the collaboration needed to deliver it.

Speaking to leaders of organisations across the world has taught me that the understanding of what 'entrepreneurs' do varies hugely, depending on where you are. Some people really understand what being entrepreneurial is about on a day-to-day basis, whereas some have real difficulty. The biggest difference seems to be between long-established and large corporate-based economies, where few people have experienced any form or entrepreneurial environment, as opposed to those in developing economies where the significant presence of SMEs, in particular family businesses, means that more people have been in an entrepreneurial environment at some point. In Asia, many within the corporate world are also involved in running a family business, in contrast to Europe and the US. For example, when speaking to the top leaders of two major Chinese government corporations, I asked who in the room had personal experience of the entrepreneurial world through a family business of some type. Over 80% of the audience put their hands up.

That said, in the vast majority of economies, even in Europe and the US, SMEs employ more people than large global corporations. That is why I find it strange that so many major organisations have lost much of their entrepreneurial spirit.

As organisations grow larger, the 'bureaucracy' also builds up, so compliance with the systems becomes more important and being entrepreneurial gets less important. Furthermore, as these systems get more complicated they actually obstruct the organisation's ability to deliver its own objectives. This can mean losing between 10% and 20% of performance[5] – so can present a big challenge.

If you are in a large organisation then it's likely your organisation has lost some of this entrepreneurial behaviour and you, by virtue of the way your corporate career may have developed, may never have been told that these were vital for success. Conversely, those who have run their own business successfully will know exactly what these approaches are and why they are so key to success for any organisation.

If the large organisation can get back to using the entrepreneurial behaviour and skills that its original founders used to create such a success story, it will be re-energised and significantly improve performance. But that's for the next chapter; for you as an individual leader it's enough to know that the application of entrepreneurial leadership will enable you to focus on exactly what the organisation needs to maximise its performance. If you get that right, your appraisal results and profile will be much better, you will become more effective and confident and your chances of either a pay rise or promotion will increase. You will also be happier at work and those benefits will extend into your personal life, so you will see all-round improvements.

So how do the key elements of entrepreneurial leadership for the individual leader translate into day-to-day activity?

- *Total focus on delivering what the customer wants*

  Irrespective of where you are in the organisation, even if you are not in day-to-day contact with the end customer, you need to think clearly and understand what they expect the organisation to deliver. Only that way can you make sure that what you and your team do helps to make that possible.

- *How does this add value to the service we give to the customer?*

This should be the question you ask before undertaking any action. There should be a clearly visible path from that action to customer benefit – if you can't be clear on what it is, maybe the proposed action is not really going to benefit the customer at all. If there are other people in the organisation between you and the final customer, then you also need to make sure they are getting value from what you do. Remember that 'beauty is in the eye of the receiver, not the giver'! In other words, that it's their view of the value of what you provide that matters and not yours.

- *Optimising risk, not minimising it*

As organisations get larger there is an increasing desire to make sure that mistakes don't happen – ever! Although this may seem a good objective, it has to be accepted that statistically mistakes will happen. But the impact can be minimised, not incidentally by control systems – these only catch mistakes before they become disasters – but by good leaders and engaged staff who care about the organisation and know what needs to be done.

Moreover, it has to be accepted that to enable change, to meet customer need, to improve, and to be an effective organisation, risks must be taken. If you minimise risk to the point where no one is taking any at all, or by making it too difficult to do anything, then the organisation will grind to a halt, or at the least its ability to respond to customers, markets or other external changes will be severely restricted. This will eventually cause it to fail. As a leader therefore, you need to take calculated risks and allow your team to do the same – the sayings 'nothing ventured, nothing gained', or 'who dares wins' are as true in organisations as much as in life.

- *Constantly being creative and innovative to get better*

The reality is that nothing stands still; there is constant change around us, be that developments in science, technology, economies, organisations, customer needs or social attitudes. Some people may not always be comfortable with constant change, but it is a strong driver within the human mind to seek to better oneself and to try to do the same for society as a whole where possible. Given that the world is constantly changing around us, it is essential that an organisation changes at least enough to keep up, whether that's with competitors, the environment or technology. As an individual leader you have to do the same. What was good enough in the past – 'the way we have always done things round here' – could well be not the best way to do things now. So challenge legacy systems, processes and attitudes.

How can you tell what needs changing? This is a frequent question and the answer is simple. Ignore how you currently deliver your product or service. Then simply ask, given the current and anticipated environment – whether that be the technology, customer needs, market or situation, costs and other circumstances: what is the best way to deliver your service or product? If what you think is the best solution for doing that now is not what you are currently doing, then you need to change it.

This simple process requires just one sheet of paper and 15 to 30 minutes of thought – not huge amounts of investment. There are significant potential benefits to doing this, and from the many leaders I have done this with around the world, I can assure you that it works. It is often a revelation to them just how far away they have grown over a few years from the optimum way of delivering objectives without realising it.

Change is an opportunity, not a threat. It allows you to be creative and innovative in response. But here again some themes we have seen before hold the secret to successfully dealing with change. There will be more details in Chapter 6 on getting the organisation to Mach 2, but the key points apply just as much to individual leaders. If you want your people to think about and then do things differently, remember that the decision by employees to change will be driven by a mix of rational and emotional elements, most of which you control.

Getting them to change successfully brings back some of the other success factors we have seen before – a clear vision/destination, a reason to do it, a simple plan, clear communication. It also includes making sure that people have time to do their day-to-day job as well as delivering the changes needed. This is linked to entrepreneurial leadership in that change entails innovation and creativity, and optimising risk. Change has inherent risks, but success brings benefits to all.

So it's interesting that if you implement the ideas set out in this chapter and in Chapter 2, you will be doing the very thing that will make change work for you, and not against you all the time. You won't have to think of 'managing change' as something different; it will be part of what you do day-to-day. This also relates to the critical capabilities needed to deal with the new world of work.

- *Taking personal responsibility for organisational as well as personal results*

  The attitude that 'I am only doing a job and have no responsibility outside my own objectives' is one that inevitably causes inefficiency, poor communication and poor alignment in any organisation. It also tends to reduce the performance of the individual leader; if they are doing 'only' their own job they are clearly not engaged with the organisation's overall agenda. As we have seen earlier, this attitude is just not viable any longer in the new world of work. We have to focus on what drives wider organisational success and that is individual working *and* collaboration with others, and the collaborative element is now as important as the individual in terms of impact on profitability.

So to get your performance and that of your team to the highest level you have to be committed to the wider organisation's agenda – its vision, values, strategy, critical objectives – just as much as your own personal objectives. Entrepreneurs inherently do this in their own organisation, as they have the final responsibility for overall success or failure. But to get larger organisations to perform well the same applies, and responsibility rests with leaders at all levels not just at the top. Senior leaders can provide the tools and information but it is you that has to deliver. The team is unlikely to commit to the organisation's agenda if they perceive that you don't. We return yet again to the idea of leading by example – or rather the team following your example whatever that may be.

◆ *Keeping things simple*

Sadly we manage to make things more complicated than they need to be in organisations: people wanting to impress others with their technical expertise; the desire to minimise risk; the development of legacy system on top of legacy system; everyone wanting a say in decisions, but not wanting the responsibility – these are just a few of the many reasons why.

As has been said, we know that the effect of this is to reduce organisational performance by 10% to 20%[5]. As an individual leader you may not able to remove all of this from the organisation, but you can minimise it within your team and point out where it exists elsewhere. At its most basic level every additional step in any process increases the time it takes and increases the risk of something going wrong in delivering the outcome. Some steps will be necessary to optimise risk management, but any more than the minimum will reduce efficiency and responsiveness.

So it's about you as leader within the team, making sure that everything is kept as simple as possible to achieve the outcome needed. This applies to approval processes, meetings, project planning, delegating and virtually everything you do. The key question is: 'If we didn't take this step, would it seriously impact on our ability to deliver or make the risk too high?' If the answer is no, then don't do it!

> 'Great leaders are almost always great simplifiers, who can cut through argument, debate, and doubt to offer a solution everybody can understand.'
>
> General Colin Powell (b1937), US/Allied military leader

This simplification is NOT about you editing or restricting the flow of information to your people. That is counter-productive, as they need a variety of inputs from wider sources to help them maximise organisational benefit. From who we will see later.

- *Inspiring people around you with a clear vision*

  People need a direction, otherwise it's like driving round and round in circles with no destination – frustrating and confusing. People like a vision or some form of end destination – for themselves, for their team and for the organisation. It gives meaning to why they do things, which engages them with the agenda. We also know[6] that if individuals are clear about the organisation's vision, and how they fit into, their performance is up to 32.8% higher than where they are not. They also need step-by-step targets to help them visualise the journey to that destination, and see that it's possible to achieve it.

  But it's not just about stating the organisation's strategy, business case or vision. Resonance is key – this means that what you say resonates both rationally and emotionally with your people. You will recall in Chapter 2 we saw that people's decision to give high performance is 57% rational but 43% emotional as well[6]. So you have to find something that locks into that latter 43%, some form of inspiration that makes them want to achieve the outcome the organisation needs. Where possible this should inspire both the team as a whole and the staff as individuals.

  You probably have a vision of where you see yourself in the future, but you also need to help the team understand what the vision is for the organisation and how they fit into that. This can be done by way of a team vision or operational targets that align to the organisational one, and showing how that all adds both professional and personal benefit to them will inspire them. It's quite simple to develop this in a team meeting and looking at how the team can help deliver what the organisation needs, as we shall see later.

HOW DO I SUPPORT THE ORGANISATION BETTER?

The entrepreneurial leadership area of your activity is mostly specific to you as leader and the team, but you will see that it also links into the wider agenda of the organisation. As we have seen, the increase in the importance of collaboration and alignment to overall organisational objectives is critical.

But even if all the leaders in the organisation were entrepreneurial and maximised employee effort to the benefit of the organisation, these benefits would not be as great as their potential. To get to this level of performance the organisation must enable all of this maximised effort to be focused on what matters to achieve the benefits set out earlier in this and other chapters. The system to co-ordinate this must be effective enough to leverage what you are doing with your team and what all the other leaders are doing as well in an aligned way.

Entrepreneurial leadership on its own is great for an entrepreneur who employs five people, but for a large organisation there has to be a system to co-ordinate and align all that entrepreneurial activity. This is dealt with in more detail from the organisation's perspective in the next chapter, but as an individual leader, knowing what the organisation will be seeking to achieve gives you a head start – the prioritisation and collaboration themes – but this must co-ordinate with what others are doing or the collaboration won't be effective. Behaviour for an individual entrepreneurial leader that helps the organisation focus and align the efforts of all leaders in a co-ordinated way includes:

Role model for collaboration and values

From your perspective this has two simple and practical key elements: first demonstrating that you seek to work proactively in collaboration and partnership with other leaders, teams or parts of the organisation to achieve what the organisation wants, and where the common good, that is, organisational success, outweighs personal interest. Second, that feeds into the values, where you show that at all times you act with decency and integrity in your dealings with others, in other words treating others as you would expect to be treated yourself.

This behaviour is important, as it is likely to a) be copied by your team and b) in time, adopted as a set of standards for the team to adhere to. So to reiterate what was said earlier in the book: you have to act as a leader who works by a set of values, and those values have to reflect those that most reasonable people would hold, in particular your team, and which are probably the same as your personal values you apply with your friends and family. These hopefully also reflect the overall organisational values. If they are different then, to be blunt, there is a problem – you cannot leave your personal values at home when you go to work.

This collaboration and value system are critical as a mindset. It's not enough that they are 'nice to have', they are a 'must have', as it has significant impact on every area of your work: efficiency and speed of decision making; improving individual and team performance; motivating your people; and dealing with customers or suppliers.

This then poses the interesting question about whom you should collaborate with. It is interesting that the added value collaboration brings spreads much wider than most leaders predict. This is the impact[7] that different groups have on the organisational contribution:

- Immediate team colleagues up to +34%
- Line Manager up to +29%
- Co-workers in business unit +17%
- Co-workers outside own business unit +5%
- External (vendors, partners, professional associations, alumni) +24%

The line manager and team figures are less surprising, but the value of an external perspective at +24% shows the results collaboration can bring. This is important because so many organisations now have a significant number of suppliers for what previously would have been internally-delivered services. However, despite its importance, only 17% of employees[7] say they work effectively with individuals outside the organisation.

This creates another opportunity for individual line managers to develop this capability and by doing so help their teams meet the needs of the new world of work. Being able to collaborate where required delivers organisational success.

Being a leadership ambassador

As a leader of a team you have more than just a leadership responsibility for your team. Others in the organisation see you as a leader as well, and – whether or not you think you do – you represent the organisation. People will watch what you say and do and draw conclusions accordingly. As you get more senior and more visible, this 'strategic leadership' role becomes more important. You are seen as an ambassador for the organisation both inside and out.

This is not a role you are given; this is a role you have whether you want it or not, and the more senior you are the more conscious of it you have to be. Even if you are a first line manager, your views on the organisation's culture, strategy, vision, values and objectives will be critical to your team's belief in those things. At board level this is even more significant. And your attitude to your organisation outside of work, and among your friends, will affect its brand. You have a role as an ambassador to proactively spread the word both inside and outside about what you and the organisation is trying to achieve and why.

If you can also encourage your team to do the same, the concept of every employee enthusiastically championing the organisation is a very powerful tool that can add significant benefit to its potential brand and performance. But this will only happen when employees are truly engaged by their line manager, you, and the organisation.

Can this have such an effect? Certainly, in many organisations I worked with, the idea of every employee boosting your brand even if not selling services was an objective, but one rarely even half achieved. It was a key part of the UBS transformation introduced earlier and where more detail is provided in Chapter 7.

Driving integration and alignment

As we have seen, the 21st century has placed significant pressure on organisations to become much more efficient and effective. Integration and overall alignment should be pursued where possible, as this will maximise the effectiveness of the team and indeed the whole organisation. The goal is:

1. alignment of activity and effort onto what really matters by everyone, leading to its wider co-ordinated application, that is, having the same priorities across the organisation

2. integration of what are currently disconnected activities, communications or organisational structures, to ensure more effective delivery of the organisation's desired outcome. This refers back to the 'simplicity' principle, where you seek to reduce complexity wherever possible.

Again, as an individual leader you can look for opportunities to do this within your team, and ask them to do the same. If you see opportunities to integrate and align between your team and other parts of the organisation in its systems or processes, you should identify them so that action can be taken to collaborate.

So while the wider success of the organisation in these areas will rely on how successful it is in encouraging all leaders to focus on them, you can, as an individual leader, use them effectively within your team and elsewhere. Even if the organisation is not being effective in doing this itself, it will demonstrate that you have some of the key predictors of a leader who could go further in the organisation. More detail on what these are, which will allow you to develop them, were in Chapter 4.

MAKING IT HAPPEN DAY-TO-DAY

The Mach 2 pyramid (see page 155) comprises three imperatives that worked well in many types of organisations. Other leaders in the wide range of organisations I have worked with across the world have also taken them up successfully. These can be simply developed both by yourself and by your team with your help where applicable.

The three Mach 2 imperatives are:

Understand and leverage the whole organisation

If you understand all about your organisation at operational, strategic and market/ environment level, you can better leverage it for the benefit of yourself, your team and your customers. You can also see where you can help others leverage your capability for their benefit elsewhere in the organisation. This will naturally help you break down silos and work in collaboration. To leverage the whole organisation, the next step has to be to break down those silos and ignore barriers of any type that restrict your ability to deliver the best outcome. Then work in collaboration with those people in the other parts of your organisation to create an aligned system that now focuses more effectively on what needs to be delivered.

Deliver world-class service to the customer

This is the critical driver for all of the areas included in Mach 2, if not the reason for developing Mach 2 itself. No matter what level you are at in the organisation, you must understand what the end customer wants and the way they think, and then align your activities to support the organisation in this, even if you aren't delivering directly to the customer.

One of the reasons that organisations never reach their full potential, from my observations, is that probably less than 20% of staff really interact with, understand, or put significant effort into giving the customer what they want. If more than 80% are working away without fully understanding the customer, it is very difficult for the remaining 20% to deliver world-class service. If the 80% understood the customer and what needed to happen day-to-day, then the 20% would have much more effective support. The organisation would focus its resources better on the customer, which would improve service, make more money and improve the brand.

Be a world-class leader

We know from earlier chapters that Mach 1 takes you to the point where your people are maximising their effort for you. By following the advice in this chapter, and aligning that Mach 1 effort on to maximising organisational benefit as well as delivering team objectives, they will get to Mach 2 performance.

> 'A great person attracts great people and knows how to hold them together.'
> Johann Wolfgang von Goethe (1749–1832), German philosopher and writer

Your first challenge is to get yourself to Mach 2. Continue with the actions that got you and the team to Mach 1, and then add the Mach 2 actions, firstly to your own work, then to the team's.

If you can achieve this you could well be in the top 5% of leaders in terms of effectiveness. It will certainly enhance your career prospects. That's one reason why this book doesn't need a chapter on career development – you will make it happen via Mach 2.

By assessing how one or other of these three Mach 2 imperatives supports every action you or the team takes, then you will, step by step, get used to thinking in the Mach 2 way and it will become a natural way of working for you and the team.

Benchmark yourself and your organisation and seek out the best

Too often leaders assume that, provided they consider themselves at least as good as their peers, all is well. You should always seek to be the best, and better than your peers. But even that's not good enough as your peers may not be anywhere near the best there is. Seek out the best even if it's from other sectors, industries or countries.

I have judged many awards for excellence in leadership, HR, customer service and management writing over the years, from different sectors and countries. I am constantly astonished at the amazing and innovative success stories being created by leaders across the globe. These could have value and inspiration for you. They are easy to find: a simple Internet search of awards for excellence in different areas from innovation to leadership reveals a myriad of success stories you can learn from. Whether you look for awards from professional bodies, consultancies, the UN or governments, in just a few minutes you can find inspirational ideas: using IT to enable better community healthcare in China; helping female offenders avoid reoffending in northern Canada; identifying and helping children with special needs in Thailand; developing driverless cars in Europe; or a Greek hospital winning a European Employer of the Year Award[8]. The private Hygeia hospital in Athens, against the backdrop of the greatest economic crisis in Greece since the Second World War, successfully protected salaries, safeguarded employee benefits, increased staff numbers by 14.2%, boosted revenues by 14% and delivered a 30% increase in patient satisfaction. All of these award winners, even if from different sectors than your own, may hold lessons for you and your organisation.

What about my career?

You obviously aren't going to be doing this for the benefit of your team and the organisation without getting anything out of it for yourself. But this is where it gets interesting. If we examine the things that organisations look for in people with potential to go further, they are often all the things I have suggested are key to implementing Mach 1 and Mach 2 leadership. So not only will achieving Mach 1 and aiming for Mach 2 get things done and make your life easier, it should also directly help you to advance your career.

At UBS we developed a quick and accurate test, based on simple criteria, to identify those in the organisation who were likely to have the potential to go much further than their current roles, particularly those at middle and junior management. This was found to be both accurate and very effective. Furthermore, it has transferred successfully to other organisations, including not-for-profits. Page 136 in Chapter 4 sets out the criteria organisations need to use to make such a selection. If you look at these it a) confirms that some of these criteria directly link to or align with the Mach 2 actions and b) provides you with some idea of the key areas you need to develop to go further in your organisation.

HELPING MY TEAM TO GET TO MACH 2

By focusing on all the areas covered in this chapter you should get Mach 2 as an individual leader. But there is one more step that you can take which will make your professional life more rewarding and add even more value to the organisation: to get your team to Mach 2. They can then fully support you in what you are doing to make the organisation perform more effectively and succeed, as well as focus on this independently as individuals.

Moving from Mach 1 to Mach 2 is relatively easy if Mach 1 has been achieved. People are already engaged with you and the organisation and will want to improve their performance still further. Therefore moving to Mach 2 is to some degree an 'open door'. All you have to do is help them think more holistically about the organisation and how to deliver what it needs for success, that is, prioritisation and collaboration.

Taking them to Mach 2 also gives them an opportunity to show that, as individuals, they have the potential to develop and go further just as it has for you. It makes their working life more interesting and more likely to reinforce your ability as a leader to get more effort from them. Go back to the John Adair[9] leadership model on page 57 where we said it was critical to balance TASK, TEAM and INDIVIDUAL. This was confirmed in Chapter 1 as linked to getting maximum performance.

Once you are confident that you are achieving this, then it's about making sure everything the team does, all that extra effort from Mach 1, is focused on maximising organisational benefit. You have a key role in helping your team understand and deliver this by becoming effective collaborators and prioritisers. They can do some themselves but your help can boost the chances of success. Maximum impact on organisational contribution happens where line managers help employees:

1. Prioritise what contributes to organisational success
2. Deliver this as effectively as possible through collaboration.

Help employees prioritise what contributes to organisational success

In general, about half of employees prioritise on the basis of the needs of their individual work and ignore organisational priorities. You as their line manager have to change this by making them aware of the organisation's priorities and helping them balance individual work and collaboration better to meet those organisational priorities.

CEB global data[10] shows that 80% of employees, whether high or low individual task performers, have low collaboration levels.

High individual task performance	40%	17%
Low individual task performance	40%	3%
	Low collaboration	High collaboration

To make your team effective in the new world of work, the main challenge for you as a line manager is to get those *40 + 40 = 80%* low collaborators to become high collaborators.

Help them deliver this as effectively as possible through collaboration

Once you have made them aware of the priorities and identified what they need to do, the key is doing it as effectively as possible. This is about helping employees to use the organisational environment better, not by filtering and simplifying information, but by helping people 'navigate' the system more effectively. This revolves around (figures are impact on organisational contribution[10])

Facilitating relationships:

1. Connecting employees to co-workers +8%
2. Helping employees manage stakeholders +6%

Providing context and advice:

1. Explaining why organisational decisions are made +7%
2. Explaining how organisational decisions affect me +7%
3. Helping me understand my role +6%

If, however, you are the only source of information and you filter that information, this can actually reduce the ability of your people to contribute to the wider organisation's objectives by 4%. This is because employees need multiple sources of information to help them create accurate context, and not filtered perspectives based on just your view. This facilitates the development of connections and collaboration, from which point you will start to move the team to Mach 2.

How to build team awareness and start the transformation

You need to make all the team aware of what Mach 2 is, what you are trying to achieve by using it, and how they can become Mach 2. The best way to achieve this is to have team meetings with the focus on becoming Mach 2, where you engage the team with the idea and produce a plan to make this happen. This is a very simple and logical approach where you can get the ball rolling in a couple of hours, then follow up with regular reviews. Below is a suggested structure:

Mach 2 team event

• Practical two hour team event you can run to start things moving.

• What is Mach 2 Leadership and why we need to be entrepreneurial? – You

• What is the business and personal case? – You

• How do the team think they are doing at present? – Them

• How could they be better in the key areas? – Them

• What specific things could they do as a team and as individuals? – You and them

  • Remember the idea that Mach 1 and 2 underpins all actions

  • Can you review and improve legacy systems and process?

• Get them to agree an action plan that is the team's plan, not just yours

---

It is important to get team members to come up with their own ideas about how they could be more entrepreneurial and get to Mach 2. Once you have introduced the idea, they need to drive the discussion with you present simply to facilitate. By the end you should have an action plan for the team and the individuals within it. You can then discuss this with those individuals and integrate it with areas such as their objectives and development plans. You need to make Mach 2 a day-to-day reality for the team. As such it needs to be discussed in relation to team activities and the imperatives that will drive it forward: prioritisation for organisational success; collaboration; customer focus; understanding the whole organisation and so on.

You might think that it is only you who can add value to the organisation, but the whole team can play a role in this by demonstrating Mach 2 behaviour and championing it to their colleagues around the organisation. In this way they will be seen to be leaders in organisational thinking.

Once you are at Mach 2 help your team to join you there – they will be keen to take up the challenge. When that's done – congratulations! You've got to your destination. But the journey isn't really over, because to stay at Mach 2 you have to keep using its principles to get better and better day-by-day and to take your team with you. This way work becomes an inspiring place to be, and your development and growth will enhance your personal and family life as well.

CHAPTER 5 KEY POINTS

- Moving to Mach 2 is relatively easy if you have got to Mach 1.
- Key outcomes required by the new world of work are:

1. Prioritisation – the ability to prioritise what you do based on its benefit to the organisation and not just your role requirements
2. Collaboration – the ability to not only know others in teams you have to work with but to know what they do
3. Organisational awareness – being aware of the context of what is happening in the organisation and not just the formal structures.
4. Proactive change – the ability to identify opportunities for change and implement them and not just support change initiated by others.

Use the Mach 2 pyramid to develop your skills and knowledge in the area of:
- Your own specialist or functional activity
- Knowing how organisations work well
- What happens operationally around you?
- What the strategic organisational objectives are
- What's going on in the market and environment?

Then focus on:

Being an entrepreneurial leader to:

1. Put total focus on delivering what the customer wants
2. Optimise rather than minimise risk
3. Improve by being constantly creative and innovative
4. Take personal responsibility for results
5. Keep things simple
6. Inspire people around you with a clear vision

Support the organisation's entrepreneurial co-ordination system by:

1. Leveraging and understanding the whole organisation
2. Being an ambassador
3. Acting with values and working in collaboration
4. Integrating and aligning activity

Using the Mach 2 imperatives that integrate the above day-to-day:
- Leveraging and supporting the whole organisation
- Delivering world-class customer service
- Being a world-class leader and influencer

Then think about and start to plan how you can get your team to join you at Mach 2.

CHAPTER 5 KEY ACTIONS FOR YOU TO DO NOW

1. How can you improve your team's performance on:

   1. Prioritisation?

   2. Collaboration?

   3. Organisational awareness?

   4. Proactive change?

2. Identify possible steps to improve and implement.

3. How good are you at delivering entrepreneurial leadership? Identify your shortfalls and three ways to help you improve.

4. Develop three critical actions for how you as an entrepreneurial leader could improve the way you support the organisation by:

   1. Leveraging and understanding the whole organisation

   2. Being an ambassador

   3. Acting with values and working in collaboration

   4. Integrating and aligning activity.

References

1. *Engage for Success: Enhancing performance through employee engagement.* MacLeod & Clarke, Department of Innovation and Skills, London, July 2009

2. *Driving Breakthrough Performance in the New Work Environment:* Corporate Executive Board, 2013

3. *UBS: Towards the Integrated Firm,* Lal, Nohrai, Knoop, Harvard Business School, May 15 2006

4. *Driving Public Entrepreneurship*: Accenture, 2011

5. *Complexity: The Human Paradox and how to address it.* The Simplicity Partnership, London

6. *Driving Employee Performance and Retention Through Engagement,* Corporate Executive Board, 2004,

7. *Driving Breakthrough Performance in the New Work Environment:* Corporate Executive Board, 2013

8. *Greece nets two prestigious European Business Awards,* RSM Press Release, 12 June 2013

9. *Action-Centre Leadership*, J.E. Adair: McGraw-Hill, London, 1973

10. *Driving Breakthrough Performance in the New Work Environment:* Corporate Executive Board, 2013

Moving to Mach 2 for teams and organisations: how to align everyone's effort into what matters and delivers success

Moving to Mach 2 for teams and organisations: how to align everyone's effort into what matters and delivers success

In Chapter 5 we looked at how the individual leader could go up to Mach 2, by ensuring that they and their team's maximised effort is focused on the critical deliverables the organisation needs. If you haven't read Chapter 5 you need to do so now as the organisation's Mach 2 system can only work and its objectives be met if you understand what the individual Mach 2 leaders should be doing. Only when you know this can you start building a system to spread and embed these actions where every leader in the organisation is doing the same.

> 'There are three essentials to leadership: humility, clarity and courage.'
> Chan Master Fuchan Yuan

Even more than moving to Mach 1 from basic leadership, moving from Mach 1 to Mach 2 is about the organisation making sure that everyone is clear on its vision, values, strategy, objectives and critical deliverables. This enables the prioritisation and collaboration that the new world of work demands. But even if people are working hard doing their own individual work, Mach 2 demands that there is a significant change in the way people work to maximise the organisation's performance. Previous chapters set out how to boost collaborative activity across the organisation to meet the demands of the new world of work.

You think you have challenges!

Sometimes organisations get to Mach 2 because the enormous challenges they face can only be dealt with by implementing its priorities. Few of us in Europe appreciate the challenges faced in the developing world. The people of Myanmar face civil strife, tsunami, earthquake, floods and disease, and the Myanmar Red Cross provides disaster relief, disaster preparedness education, first aid, healthcare and education, water and sanitation, and works to reconnect families broken by disasters.

> This requires a level of responsive, dedicated and courageous leadership in the harshest of conditions that most in the corporate world have little concept of. Through this dedication and courage they achieve a level of **Mach 2** leadership that I found both inspiring and humbling; they taught me just as much as I taught them. Those in the corporate world should never assume they have a monopoly on effective leadership – they could learn much from others.
>
> That's why £1 ($1.5, €1.2) from every copy of this book will go to the Red Cross – leadership is about doing the right thing.

The key elements that the organisation needs to develop, foster and embed **Mach 2** are:

1. Prioritisation – the ability to prioritise what employees do based on its benefit to the organisation and not just your role requirements
2. Collaboration – the ability for employees to not only know others across the organisation they work with but to know what they actually do
3. Organisational awareness – being aware of the context of what is happening in the organisation and not just the formal structures.
4. Proactive change – the ability to identify opportunities for change and implement them and not just support change initiated by others.

If this behaviour is not set out as a clear objective by the organisation it will make it difficult for even those motivated leaders who are at **Mach 1** to get to **Mach 2**. They need to know this information to ensure their efforts, and those of their team, are focused on the things that maximise organisational performance.

There is significant room for improvement here. Taking the general data from the CEB[1], the research shows that 45% of employees do not prioritise what they do by organisational need, but prioritise instead on completing their own individual work, which means that even if the organisation must have certain tasks done to achieve its objectives, 45% of employees won't do these tasks if they don't have them as part of their job responsibilities. The figures below confirm that 80% of employees are at low collaboration levels, and half of these – maybe 40% of total employees – are at low individual task performance levels as well, and so adding little value to the organisation.

High individual task performance	40%	17%
Low individual task performance	40%	3%
	Low collaboration	High collaboration

Mach 1 should move those with low task performance up into high task performance, but for the movement from low collaboration to high collaboration to succeed requires

Mach 2 leadership. The challenge for the organisation is that this has to be facilitated and driven by the organisation to deliver the significant potential benefits. Hoping that individual line managers will achieve this by chance is a vain hope.

These are the percentage figures[1] for what value high collaborators add to the organisation:

- 63% transfer great ideas from one part of the organisation to another
- 71% improve procedures or processes based on ideas from others
- 78% transfer skills/knowledge effectively to co-workers
- 72% provide useful new ideas for products/services or improvements to processes for others
- 81% improve working methods, techniques or tools for others.

The maximum rating for low performance collaborators in any of these areas is 22%, so again there is much scope for improvement, but which a few simple initiatives can deliver. However, this requires individuals to understand the day-to-day reality of their organisational context. Some people are better at this than others and it requires time for them to assimilate and understand. This again strongly suggests a need for organisational co-ordination.

A further challenge is that the key interactions that drive collaboration are not all within the individual teams. The data below shows[1] that, of collaborative activities that have a positive impact on the organisation, over 37% are driven by collaboration with others outside the employee's team, both internal and external. While the line manager will drive collaboration within the team, the organisation must be the driver and facilitator of collaboration outside the team.

IMPACT ON ENTERPRISE CONTRIBUTION

- Immediate team up to +34%
- Manager up to +29%
- Co-workers in business unit +17%
- Co-workers outside own business unit +5%
- External (vendors, partners, professional associations, alumni) + 4%

The last figure of 24% for external will be a surprise to many, but in the new world of work with its significant outsourcing and need for external perspectives, this is increasingly important. However, only 17%[1] of workers say they work effectively with individuals outside the organisation; this creates an opportunity for the organisation to play a role in improving this.

So the work by individual leaders to move from Mach 1 to Mach 2 depends on the organisation having a system for this critical information to reach them and the critical behaviour developed. Without it, it will be guesswork – and this lack of alignment is a central reason why most organisations fail to become world class or beat their competitors. It is critical to understand that the move from Mach 1 to Mach 2 involves reviewing all the components of the Mach 1 system set up for the organisation in Chapter 4, and upgrading those to ensure they include the Mach 2 elements set out here as well.

'Men build too many walls and not enough bridges'

Sir Isaac Newton (1643–1727), British astronomer, physicist, mathematician, one of the most influential scientists of all time

To reach Mach 2, there are two objectives for the organisation, assuming a significant percentage of leaders are operating at Mach 1:

1. To ensure that the organisation's development systems, both on and off the job, make clear what the individual leaders need to do (as set out in Chapter 5), and give them the skills and knowledge to do it using the Mach 1 system.

2. To upgrade the Mach 1 system to Mach 2 across the organisation by adding these additional Mach 2 elements to create an '*aligned community of effort and collaboration*' of aligned, networked, entrepreneurial leaders to deliver what maximises the organisation's performance and then by spreading and embedding Mach 2 performance day-to-day.

There will be many benefits if this can be achieved. The upgrade from Mach 1 to Mach 2 is often seen by both leaders and employees across the organisation as an opportunity to become more involved and contribute more to the organisation and its customers. They will willingly adopt it because it helps them understand in more detail than ever before why and how what they do adds to the bigger picture, how it helps customers and how it benefits the organisation. It helps every employee take ownership and responsibility for his or her actions. And the benefits of Mach 2 apply absolutely as much to the public sector as to the private[2].

This is a direct driver of organisational success where it occurs, but there are also indirect benefits, as we found, in a number of places when implementing Mach 2. For example:

Human Resources

As leaders around the organisation begin to get to Mach 1 level, the number of management and other issues caused by poor leadership reduce significantly. Leaders take on more responsibility for the performance and development of their people rather than expecting the HR function to do much of this for them. This frees up time within HR and allows HR staff to then a) become more entrepreneurial themselves to make their service delivery even better and b) to spend more time supporting leaders around the organisation to be successful on their journey from Mach 1 to Mach 2.

Risk function

The communication cascade for Mach 1, and in particular Mach 2, of the critical elements of the organisation's vision, strategy, values and operational objectives ensure that a) people know exactly what they should be doing and why, and b) what the expected standards of behaviour are, including what is right and what is wrong. This provides a moral compass that enables more effective risk management across the organisation over and above the formal risk systems. This also deals with reputation risk – things you don't want to happen but which aren't illegal – which formal risk systems can't.

Dealing with risk in organisations is a challenge. In some environments what starts as a small problem can very quickly get out of control and turn into a major disaster. Industries including oil and gas, transport, fisheries, healthcare and banking have all experienced how quickly things can go wrong.

Someone, somewhere must be doing something wrong 24 hours a day!

One day in 2003 I had lunch with the chief risk officer of UBS, and what he said about both risk as a challenge, and the mistaken assumption that systems provide the complete solution, was revealing. He said, 'You know, Chris, I know that with many thousands of people in over 100 countries someone somewhere must be doing something wrong all the time. That's statistical fact. My systems and teams are there to spot that small problem and deal with it before it becomes a disaster. However, I would sleep much better at night if I knew how to stop people doing the wrong thing in the first place.' 'Is that possible?' I replied. 'Yes of course it's possible – that's what leadership is about – telling the difference from right and wrong.' So that exchange started a new world of co-operation between our team and the risk team. These lessons feed into the idea of Mach 2 and how it manages risk.

Finance

From the perspective of the finance function, having every leader in the organisation a) seeking to do things that maximise profit and b) minimising things that add to cost, might sound like an implausible heaven. However, with the right information cascade and implementation, that's just what Mach 1 and then Mach 2 can achieve: people constantly looking for opportunities to make more money or save money. And the drive towards collaboration, customer focus and other alignment activity onto critical organisational deliverables, means that any money spent is more likely to be on things that earn a greater ROI than previously. This is why the finance director said, 'This is a no brainer; we should have been doing this for years!'

Marketing/branding

Given that the ultimate focus of Mach 2 is the delivery of world-class customer service, it's not surprising that marketing and branding gain additional benefits. The impact of every leader across the organisation understanding the customer, wanting to optimise customer service, knowing about the brand and seeking to make it better, can be significant. And that impact is vastly increased as they move onto Mach 2. They become ambassadors for the organisation and help to market and promote itself better and in new and different ways.

Reputation as a great place to work

As momentum continues to build, the reputation of the organisation as an employer of choice grows, attracting the best talent to work for it. This then further enhances the quality of both employees and leaders, again ramping up the capability of the organisation to be the best. These are not theoretical concepts but real events, as we will see in the UBS case study in Chapter 7, and which others have seen elsewhere, when Mach 1 and 2 start to work.

So the indirect 'ripple effect' of Mach 2 spreads into many 'corners' that enhance the benefits for the business as whole even more. This then reinforces the effectiveness of the move to Mach 2, creating even more benefits – a virtuous circle of ever-increasing performance that inspires even better performance. How this can be taken even further forward and with greater benefits once Mach 2 is achieved is shown in Chapter 8.

WHAT DOES THE ORGANISATION HAVE TO DO TO GET TO MACH 2?

There are two key actions:

1. Get all leaders up to Mach 2 by developing them as individuals
2. Spread and embed this by having a system across the organisation that enables, supports and enhances Mach 2 working by everyone.

GETTING YOUR LEADERS TO MACH 2

As I advised individual leaders in Chapter 5, this is what you need each of them across the organisation to do to become Mach 2:

Mach 2
skills

Market/environment
knowledge

Strategic business understanding

Operational understanding

Core business/project/financial knowledge

Great functional knowledge

And for entrepreneurial support functions!

Great functional knowledge –

It is essential that all leaders are good at their functional or professional role as the basis to their effectiveness and credibility. They must get all relevant development both on and off the job and assessment to ensure this happens. This should be in place already if you have got to Mach 1.

But as we said, Mach 2 requires leaders to take a wider view and have other skills in addition to Mach 1, to drive more effective prioritisation of work that maximises organisational performance and also enables the better collaboration that is critical to success. Mach 2 must also be used to help support functions in particular to become more entrepreneurial and customer and output-focused.

This is often the weak point in Mach 2 working. It is relatively easy to get front line customer-facing staff to adopt Mach 2, but often more difficult with support functions. And the organisational front line will be frustrated, because they won't be able to get fully to Mach 2 unless the support function is also there. This relates to all types of factors, such as speed of response, customer focus, optimising and not minimising risk, to name a few – but all of which impacts on both performance and collaboration.

These are the other areas the organisation needs to develop to get leaders to Mach 2:

Core organisational knowledge

How good are your leaders at understanding the basics of how any good organisation works and how to make it work better? This includes understanding the principles of finance, project management and the general principles of business. As this helps them understand how any effective organisational 'machine' works, it also helps them ensure what they do works effectively in your organisation. This can, in itself, deliver improved working through better project management, financial management and operational management.

Operational understanding

Too many leaders just do their own job, and are aware of only the things they have to know about the organisation to achieve this. As we have seen in the new world of work this is no longer viable. The highest priority must now be doing what drives organisational success and not just what the individual's job is. This behaviour will block both prioritisation and collaboration and prevent people, and thus the organisation, getting to Mach 2.

Strategic understanding

This is assumed to be present in all organisations. 'Of course everyone knows the organisation's strategy!' How many times have I heard that said by a CEO or senior leaders, only to find that those three or four levels below haven't a clue? It is absolutely essential that all leaders, if not all employees, understand what the organisation is trying to achieve at strategic level. What are the key objectives, the vision, its values?

In the simplest terms – what is the organisation trying to achieve and how? And what are the standards and values we observe when doing it?

If leaders don't know this they cannot possibly make sure that what they and their team does is aligned to what the organisation needs. They must have this knowledge to ensure that they deliver maximum benefit to the organisation. If this is not achieved the organisation will not be able to get to Mach 2: it's that simple. This is not, however, merely having the strategy, objectives and vision/values on your intranet or included in the occasional employee magazine. It's about every line manager discussing it with their team and doing it regularly, to make sure they support and help deliver it.

Market and environmental knowledge

It helps if leaders and staff also understand the market and environment, that is, how your organisation relates to the world around it. This is not just about the environment in the 'green' sense, but all the external factors that might impact upon the organisation: political; regulatory; technological; social; economic; cultural, and others. This helps them understand the external factors that impact on your organisation and where its future opportunities or challenges may come from. It allows them to think about and potentially develop ideas to deal with those.

The key knowledge to enable prioritisation and collaboration

The operational, strategic and market knowledge above is vital to get leaders to Mach 2, and if possible all employees, to understand the wider picture of what goes on in the organisation around them day-to-day, what the objectives and challenges are of those areas they work in, and to appreciate the perspectives of others with whom they have to interact – the critical organisational 'context'. This allows them to get their prioritisation right and be collaborative.

Much of this knowledge, from operational to market and environment, can be very quickly and simply delivered through lunchtime briefings, on development programmes or structured self-study. Individual leaders can also deliver it to their teams at team meetings. That said, where possible, it is always beneficial to develop this understanding where different teams can come together to share their thoughts, ideas and perspectives, as this will speed the development of knowledge and understanding as well as building networks.

Mach 2 skills and knowledge

Finally at the top of the pyramid is the key Mach 2 behaviour that applies the knowledge and understanding being developed day-to-day by focusing it on what the organisation really needs. This behaviour comprises actions that a) focus on maximising the value of what the team does and b) help the overall organisational system work better. We know that this approach works, and works well, as it was implemented at UBS between 2002 and 2006[3], delivering significantly better performance than comparators.

The approach needs to be facilitated and developed across the organisation so that every leader and if possible every employee is following it. These have to be specific objectives to be achieved in the organisational system, spread and embedded by many different means to provide consistency, as we will see later.

These key **Mach 2** skills every leader has to be able to use are:

Entrepreneurial Leadership

Using the skills of the entrepreneur to focus maximum effort on critical organisational objectives. This needs to be developed by introducing the ideas within a learning event, where there is discussion and planning about individuals implementing them on the job, and then developing the organisational culture and systems to support this.

Role model for collaboration and values

Making sure that all leaders encourage respect from others by demonstrating integrity, ethics, humility and other core values. They have to demonstrate a desire to work with others for the common good. They have to lead by example to show that respect, decency, trust and integrity are at the core of being an effective leader. This has to be developed by changing culture where required, with senior leaders proactively setting an example and spreading the message, and contrary behaviour being dealt with where it blocks improvements.

> **Allowing change to be blocked is terminal**
>
> I have seen too many situations where senior leaders say publicly that demonstrating exemplary behaviour is crucial, then take no action when long-serving members of management act contrary to the core principles of the organisation. This demonstrates to the rest of the organisation that a) senior leaders aren't serious about it and b) obstruction of plans to improve the organisation for personal interest will be tolerated and successful if persisted with. This has particularly been the case historically in some public sector organisations, for example in central and local government, where the importance of a process having been completed is often greater than successful outcomes. CEOs will fail if they are unwilling to get rid of people who are ineffective in the 'new world', even if it suggests they have made a bad initial selection or decision[4].

Leadership ambassador

By developing their organisational knowledge, all leaders can act as champions for the wider organisation as well as for their own area. Championing the brand and its strategy effectively, both inside and out, helps spread the word to employees and beyond to potential customers and the local community. This is very simply done. Even by spreading the word verbally in conversation it is possible to communicate to as many people as possible what the organisation stands for and is trying to achieve, and that encourages them to become engaged as employees, customers, local community or brand supporters.

Driving integration and alignment

This is a benefit based on the wider organisational understanding you have developed in your leaders. It encourages them to look for opportunities to align and prioritise their activity better to organisational objectives, to what other leaders and teams do, and to seek opportunities to integrate and drive effectiveness and efficiency where possible. They will always be trying to make the organisation simpler, slicker and more focused where it really matters. For those at the senior levels, this is a key part of strategic leadership, where their role is largely made up of leading, not just their team, but also the organisation as a whole.

All of these areas are a mixture of knowledge and behaviour, and applying that knowledge for the benefit of the organisation. So from the organisational system perspective, the key challenges are to a) get the information across to leaders and teams, and b) get them to act upon it. The former is relatively easy to achieve, as has been suggested, through lunchtime briefings, communication events, team meetings and any situation where people come together regularly; the latter challenge of getting them to do it day-to-day is harder.

Let's look at each in more detail:

ENTREPRENEURIAL LEADERSHIP

This is the application of the behaviour of the entrepreneur to the larger organisation. It is central to getting Mach 2 to work across the organisation; every leader has to apply this behaviour day-to-day. Entrepreneurs have to get things right or they don't survive in the market. They don't have the financial resources to weather problems or recover from errors like larger organisations do. They have to make sure they really focus on what is important, and get it right. There are no second chances. So what are these things?

- Total focus on delivering what the customer wants
- Optimising risk, not minimising it
- Constantly being creative and innovative to get better
- Taking personal responsibility for organisational as well as personal results
- Keeping things simple
- Inspiring people around you with a clear vision to collaborate for success.

The entrepreneur recognises that the customer needs to get what they want, that you have to take risks to succeed, that you always have to strive to be better and beat the competition, and that you have to take responsibility for results.

The challenge with organisations as they grow larger is that as the 'bureaucracy' builds up these things tend to get less important and compliance with the systems more so. As these systems get more complicated they actually obstruct the organisation's ability to deliver its own objectives. This can mean you losing between 10% and 20% of performance[5]. So it's likely that your organisation has lost some of the good entrepreneurial behaviour above, and that individual leaders, by virtue of the way their corporate career may have developed, may never have been told that these entrepreneurial behaviours were vital for success, nor experienced them. Conversely, those who have run their own business successfully will know exactly what this behaviour is and why it is so key to success for any organisation.

If larger organisations can get back to using the entrepreneurial behaviour and skills that their original founders used to create such a success story, they will be re-energised and performance significantly improved. If individual leaders are trying hard to deliver this, but the organisation is not supporting them, not only by words but, for example, by failing to review legacy systems, then eventually they will become disillusioned and stop. The attitude often expressed is: 'If they can't be bothered why should I?'

The challenge for the organisation is not only making leaders aware you want them to act in this way, but also a) supporting them in doing so, and b) identifying and changing any organisational systems, processes and cultures that might obstruct that aim.

So in terms of entrepreneurial leadership, what has to be done to make Mach 2 work across your organisation?

Total focus on delivering what the customer wants

Irrespective of where any leader or indeed employee is in the organisation, even if they are not in day-to-day contact with the end customer, they need to understand who the customer is and what they want. Only that way can the organisation make sure that everyone prioritises and aligns their work to what the end customer needs, and thus improves organisational performance.

How does this add value to the service we give to the customer? This should be the question everyone, employees included, asks before undertaking any action. There should be a clearly visible path from that action to customer benefit; if there isn't then it's of questionable value to the organisation. This is certainly critical for those not directly customer facing. Organisations fail to meet customer needs effectively, or find it challenging to do so, if there is a disconnect between the focus of the customer-facing areas, which are more attuned to their needs, and other areas which focus more on process and less on customers. Both need to focus on customers.

Optimising risk, not minimising it

As organisations get larger, there is an increasing desire to make sure that mistakes don't happen. This is a good thing but it has to be accepted that in life statistically mistakes will happen. These can be minimised, not incidentally by control systems, which only catch mistakes before they become disasters, but by good leaders and engaged staff that care about the organisation and know what needs to be done.

It has to be accepted that to change, to meet customer needs, to get better, to be an effective organisation, risks must be taken. If you minimise risk it stops everyone doing anything, or it makes it so difficult to do anything the organisation grinds to a halt, or its ability to respond to customers, markets or other external changes is severely restricted. This will eventually cause it to fail. Leaders therefore need to take calculated risks and allow their teams to do the same – the sayings 'nothing ventured, nothing gained', and 'who dares wins' are as true in organisations as much as in life.

Constantly being creative and innovative to get better

The reality is that nothing stands still; there is constant change around us, whether that's developments in science, technology, economies, organisations, customers' needs or social attitudes. Some people are not always comfortable with constant change but it is a strong driver within the human mind to seek to better oneself, and to try to do the same for society as a whole where possible. So given that the world is constantly changing around us, it is essential that an organisation changes at least enough to keep up, whether with competitors, the environment or technology.

Individual leaders have to do the same but to a) make them want to do this and b) leverage the full benefits, the organisation has to encourage innovation and creativity and then, when ideas appear, to leverage them effectively.

Again, if this doesn't happen, individual leaders will just not bother a second time. The mindset the organisation has to change is the belief that what was good enough in the past – the way we have always done things round here – is good enough now. This may not be the best way to do things any more. So constructive challenges to legacy systems, processes and attitudes should be encouraged and new ideas seriously considered. This is another aspect of the behaviour required to enable the organisation to operate effectively in the new world of work.

How can the organisation find out what needs changing? This is a frequent question and the answer is simple. All leaders should be made to do this key test:

Ignore how you currently deliver your product or service. Now simply ask how, given the current and anticipated environment, that is, the technology, customer needs, market or situation, costs and other circumstances, it would be best to deliver your service or product. If what delivery approach you think is the best solution for now is not what you are currently doing, then something probably has to change. Decide what and why, and present the case for change.

Innovation and creativity makes a real difference

Simple ideas deliver the best transformations

Many informal settlements have grown up around the city of Durban in South Africa. These house some one million people but they have no effective sanitation. The open pits they use present a significant health risk. These are also poorly lit, making them a safety issue at night especially for women and children. The cost and time it would take to build traditional solutions was too much, so the local council came up with a solution through innovative thinking by their leaders and experts. They fitted out old shipping containers with WC facilities for both men and women, with external hand basins. These were then speedily delivered to site and linked to the municipal sanitation systems. Over 350 containers were placed and installed, providing proper sanitation for over 200,000 people.

This significantly improved the lives of over 82% of the residents in these areas, according to a survey[6] , and also reduced pollution, cut disease and even provided 'grey water' for local food growing. This example illustrates the value of Mach 1 and Mach 2 in enabling seemingly insoluble challenges to be overcome through innovation.

The message that change is an *opportunity,* not a threat, needs to be championed by senior leaders across the organisation. It allows every leader, and hopefully every employee, to be creative and innovative in response. But here again some themes we have seen before hold the key to successfully dealing with change. If you want your people to do things differently, remember that an employee's decision to change will be driven by a mix of rational and emotional elements, most of which individual leaders control. They have to be developed, engaged and supported to make this work and get the wider organisation to Mach 2.

Getting them to change successfully reiterates some of the other success factors we have seen before: a clear vision/destination; a reason to do it; a simple plan; clear communication. It also includes making sure that people have time to do their day-to-day job as well as the changes needed.

So it's interesting that if you take up and implement the ideas set out in this chapter and in Chapter 4, then the organisation has a greater chance of making change work. 'Managing change' will cease to be something special that leaders only need to do on occasion; it will be part of what they do day-to-day. Time-consuming large-change initiatives are likely to become a thing of the past as the organisation keeps up with external changes by frequent adaptation.

Taking personal responsibility for organisational as well personal results

The attitude that 'I am only doing a job and have no responsibility outside my own objectives' is one that traditionally and inevitably caused inefficiency, poor communication and poor alignment in any organisation. However, in the new world of work, as we have seen, this attitude blocks nearly 50% of what individuals need to do to enable organisational success. It is no longer acceptable.

To bring organisational performance up to Mach 2, all individual leaders have to be committed to the wider organisational agenda – its vision, values, strategy and critical objectives – just as much as their own personal objectives. Inherently, when entrepreneurs do this it's *their* organisation, but to get larger organisations to perform well, the same principles apply and it's down to individual leaders at all levels and not just the senior leaders to make this happen. The organisation can give them the tools and information, but is *they* that have to deliver within the support framework the organisation provides.

This is crucial: no team is likely to commit to the organisation's agenda if they see that their team leader isn't. We return yet again to the idea of leading by example, or rather the team following the team leader's example whatever that may be, and the team leader following the example of their leader, and so on up to the CEO.

Keeping things simple

Sadly we manage to make things more complicated than they need to be in organisations: people wanting to impress others with their technical expertise; the desire to minimise risk; the development of legacy system on top of legacy system; everyone wanting a say in decisions, but not wanting the responsibility – these are just a few of the many reasons why.

As has been said, we know that the effect of this is to reduce organisational performance by 10% to 20%[5]. Your individual leaders cannot remove significant complexity from the organisation. They can identify it but in most cases the organisation has action on the identification to remove it. All legacy processes should be reviewed. At its most basic level every additional step in any process increases the time it takes and increases the risk of something going wrong in delivering the outcome. Some steps will be necessary to optimise risk management, but any more than the minimum will reduce efficiency and responsiveness.

This applies to approval processes, meetings, project planning, delegating and virtually everything everyone has to do. The key question that the organisation has to ask itself and get everyone else to ask is: 'If we didn't take this step, would it seriously impact on our ability to deliver or make the risk too high?' If the answer is no, then the system or process needs changing!

Inspiring people across the organisation with a clear vision

People need a direction, otherwise it's like driving round and round in circles with no destination – frustrating and confusing. People like a vision or some form of end destination – for themselves, for their team and for the organisation. It gives meaning to why they do things, which engages them with the agenda.

We also know that if individuals are clear about the organisation's vision, and how they fit into it, their effort is up to 32.6% higher[7] than where they are not. They also need step-by-step targets to help them visualise the journey to that destination, and see that it's possible to achieve it. The organisation needs to make sure this happens, buy supporting line managers to deliver this.

Resonance is key. This means that what the organisation says in its communications, either directly or via individual leaders, must resonate both rationally and emotionally with your people. You will recall in Chapter 2 we saw that people's decision to give high performance is 57% rational but 43% emotional as well. So you have to find something that locks into that latter 43% that is often missed in communications – some form of inspiration.

Where possible the organisation as a whole needs to get across the key messages to all leaders and employees, and then individual leaders need to pass that on to their teams in a relevant and tailored form as well. Thus the individual hears the same message about what's important from their boss as well as from the organisation.

This must be communicated to all employees both directly and through their individual leaders. They then need to help their teams understand how they fit into the team vision or operational targets and how to align that to the organisational one. It's quite simple for line managers at team meetings and for senior leaders at larger events to communicate the organisational vision and other key information.

CREATING THE ORGANISATIONAL SYSTEM FOR MACH 2

The Mach 1, and now Mach 2, activity of leaders and employees across the organisation now needs to be harnessed to align it to critical deliverables. In Chapter 4 we looked at the organisational system needed to achieve Mach 1 and the relevant components in the organisational jigsaw. To get to Mach 2 the system needs to be fine-tuned to make sure it delivers exactly what is required.

In Chapter 5 we saw that only 20% of employees[1] are good at driving up the level of collaboration across the organisation to do this. If we could increase this to 50% that would boost profitability by 4%, and if everyone were doing it, the increase would be 12%. So the organisation requires a system to get the less effective 80% to prioritise the organisational objectives of collaboration and alignment. The line managers can only do so much on their own.

It is unlikely that most organisational systems are providing good data for moving this forward. Many surveys reveal a gap between the view the organisation takes via its performance management and other systems, and what is key to success. The evidence for this can be found in the gap between those who are seen as high performers and those who are contributing to organisational success through collaboration, or the fact that people are too often promoted on the basis of performance and not potential. In fact up to 71% of high performers might not have the potential to be effective at the next level if promoted[8].

Furthermore, the CEB 2012 data[1] shows that the 67% of employees who get the highest performance scores are not organisational contributors. That means a significant percentage of those who are rated by the organisation's appraisals are defined as high performers but don't collaborate effectively, which is vital. Therefore, the message to the organisation is to make sure that your systems are checked so that you are measuring what you really need to be measuring; otherwise your chances of success are significantly reduced.

Once you are confident that your system is looking at the right factors then the development of a top-to-bottom system to deliver Mach 2 can proceed. What you are aiming for is shown below.

Entrepreneurial overview is vital

What leaders do lower down the organisation has to be aligned by those above them to the organisation's strategy and critical deliverables. As the graphic shows, each level of leadership plays a role in making this work: those at operational level are focused in delivery and inspiration; those at middle management levels on co-ordinating an organisational approach and supporting its implementation; and the senior leaders are setting the direction and example. This is not a new system, but the one that what was described in Mach 1. The difference is simply the introduction of the Mach 2 elements into that system, and in particular the entrepreneurial.

It isn't just about people being told by their boss what to do for the entrepreneurial element to be successful, however. There are many other influences on those leaders, and indeed employees, from other sources. To get Mach 2 working right across the organisation, those at the top, that is, the CEO and senior leaders, need to consider all the influences on people which could either reinforce the messages the organisation needs to get across, or detract from them.

And these influences are what the employee or leader hears from everywhere, not what the team driving implementation says, and in addition you believe your own perspective, not others'. There are many influences on employees to make them behave in a certain way, and not just their boss:

In most organisations people get signals about what is important and what needs to be done from:

- *The CEO and senior leaders* – what do they say; how do they act?
- *Those who are likely to be the next senior leaders* – what do they say; how do they act?
- *The individual's boss* – what do they say; how do they act?
- *What they get paid or promoted for* – what are my current objectives and what am I assessed on?
- *How the organisation is structured* – how easy or difficult does the structure of teams, departments, procedures and systems make it to do my job, and the Mach 1 and 2 activities?
- *What the external, and internal, brand says is important* – what are we promising our customers and what is the organisation promising to employees?
- *What internal communication systems are saying* – does what I am being told align with what others are saying is important and what I need to do? Are all the internal messages consistent? Am I getting all the information I need, for example, what is the strategy and what are our key objectives for the organisation this year?
- *What they are being measured on* – what information is being collected and reviewed about what I do as an individual and what we do as a team?

These are just a few – add in peer pressure or influence from colleagues or feedback from customers, and the average employee is getting many signals from many sources.

Lack of message alignment hinders performance

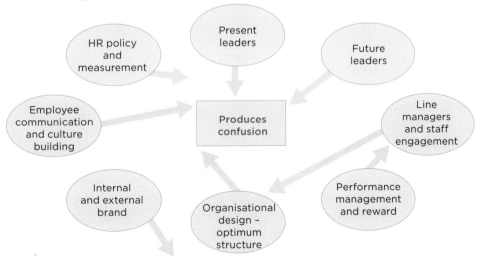

The reality of most organisations is that, like the diagram above, not all of them send consistent messages about what they really want the employee to do and how they want them to behave. The employees, or leaders, lower down the organisation therefore get confused about how they should behave and what should be given the highest priority.

Some may find this argument strange, but if employees aren't sure about what's important they will either just do what their boss says or make assumptions about what senior leaders want as well. This happens in any number of situations, from organisations running normally, to those where major problems or disasters have occurred. This has been a factor in the 2008 financial crisis, the Gulf of Mexico oil spill, the Bhopal disaster in 1984 that killed over 4000 and injured over 500,000 and other disasters going even further back in history.

To get Mach 2 right, these different influences must be aligned to be consistent in their message, and the messages must be clear and simple as well. Getting to Mach 2 becomes much easier then, because it is totally clear to every leader and employee what the organisation thinks is important and should be done, as below:

That's from the employee or other leaders' perspective, but, as we saw in the previous chapter, there are also many other factors that need to be involved in aligning employee effort onto what matters. The complexity of all this means that the chances of it all coming together and Mach 2 happening by chance across the organisation are pretty much nil. It has to be planned, implemented and supported by the organisation.

Taking the core system approach introduced in Chapter 5 to tell individual leaders what the organisation is likely to be doing around them on Mach 2, and how to align to that for their own benefit, let's look at what has to be in place. This also has an impact on the wider system jigsaw set out for Mach 1. With the Mach 1 elements such as the 'performance and potential pipeline' in place, and the actions at each level, the Mach 2 actions and behaviour now have to be integrated into that system. This should be relatively simple, as Mach 1 will have made leaders and employees highly motivated and interested in what the organisation is trying to do. Introducing Mach 2 should then feed their desire for more information, personal responsibility and opportunity to contribute to organisational success.

As a reminder, these are some of the wider elements from Mach 1 that need to be reviewed to introduce and support the Mach 2 requirements (as already seen on page 139).

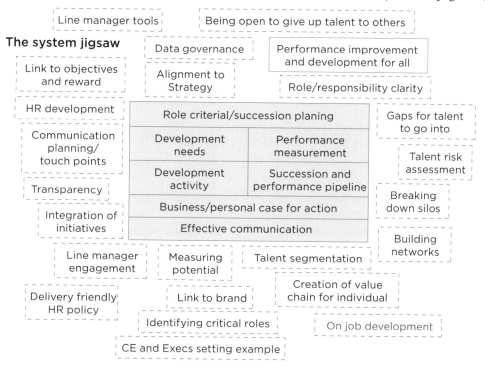

The system jigsaw

MAKING THE COMPLEX SIMPLE

In all of this you can see that the critical success factor, despite a complex system/process in the organisation, is likely to be ensuring that:

1. the messages to all leaders and staff about what they need to do, why and how, have to be utterly simple and memorable: this delivers prioritisation

2. everything else in the system is supporting and aligning this end, not obstructing it: this delivers collaboration.

If we revisit the key imperatives set out for the organisation in Chapter 5 that individual leaders are advised to use to get to Mach 2, it can be seen that these should be the common approach for the organisation to deliver Mach 2 objectives, but extended to all leaders. They are simple ideas that pull together all of the Mach 2 ideas and behaviour into three memorable imperatives for day-to-day working.

This approach of three key imperatives worked well in helping leaders at UBS take up the Mach 2 challenge successfully. These can be simply developed by the organisation using the opportunities available through all the elements of the organisational system in the previous graphic and individual leaders with their teams.

The three key Mach 2 imperatives are:

Understand and leverage the whole organisation through collaboration

This pulls together the key elements of the Mach 2 pyramid on page 155, and all the elements of partnership working and collaboration. So if all leaders and indeed all employees understand all about the organisation at operational, strategic and market/ environment level, this means that they can better leverage it for the organisation, the teams and the customer's benefit. They can also see where they can help others leverage their capability for benefit elsewhere in the organisation. This will naturally help the organisation to break down silos and work in collaboration.

Then they must work in partnership with those people in the other parts of the organisation to create an aligned system that focuses better on what needs to be delivered than it previously did. This poses the interesting question about whom you should collaborate with. It is interesting that the breadth of the collaboration that adds value is much wider than most leaders predict.

These are the impacts[1] that different groups have on the organisational contribution.

- Immediate team colleagues up to +34%
- Line managers up to +29%
- Co-workers in business unit +17%
- Co-workers outside own business unit +5%
- External (vendors, partners, professional associations, alumni) +24%

The line manager and team are predictable, but the value of an external perspective at +24% shows just how much value it can bring. Many organisations now have a significant number of suppliers for what previously would have been internally-delivered services. Yet despite this, only[1] 17% of employees say they work effectively with individuals outside the organisation, creating another important opportunity for line managers to help improve. As has been said earlier, this is now even more critical for the organisation in the new world of work.

Deliver world-class service to the customer

This is the critical driver for all of the areas included in Mach 2, if not the reason for developing Mach 2 itself. No matter what level someone is at in the organisation, they must understand what the end customer wants, the way they think and align their activities to support that, even if they aren't delivering directly to the customer.

One of the key reasons that organisations never reach their full potential is that probably less than 20% of staff really interact with, understand or put significant effort into giving the customer what they want. The other 80% may be working away, but as they don't fully understand the customer, it makes life difficult for the 20% that do, because they are not getting the most appropriate support. If the 80% understood the customer and what needed to happen day-to-day, then the 20% would have much more effective support. The organisation would focus its resources better on the customer, which would improve service, make more money and improve the brand.

Be a world-class leader

We know from earlier chapters that Mach 1 takes leaders to the point where their people are maximising their effort for them. All the actions in this chapter, if implemented, will get them to Mach 2 performance, by aligning that Mach 1 effort on to maximising organisational benefit as well as delivering their own team objectives.

So the organisation's first challenge is to get all leaders to continue delivering the actions that got them to Mach 1 day-to-day, but then to add the Mach 2 actions and behaviour. This is the organisation's leadership challenge and why the system is needed. If you can achieve this, your organisation will be delivering at a level that could put you in the top 5% of leadership in organisations, with the associated benefits mentioned earlier starting to be delivered.

By making sure every leader remembers these three Mach 2 imperatives and acting on them in everything they do, day-to-day – in other words assessing how every action they take supports one or other of these – then they will, step by step, get used to this thinking. Mach 2 will then become a natural way of working for them. But this will only happen if the wider organisational system and culture supports this change. If it does not they will simply stop doing it.

PRACTICAL ORGANISATIONAL SUPPORT

As I have said, to make Mach 2 a reality, the organisation needs to bring leaders up to Mach 1 and be aware of Mach 2, then help them develop Mach 2 working as individuals and support them in this. Chapter 7 sets out how this was developed within UBS, where Mach 2 was implemented successfully in a number of areas. It charts that journey and explains some of the practical steps taken to make it work. The case study looks at the key headline initiatives that were put in place, and the chronology, and will provide a framework to guide implementation in your organisation. But here is a summary of what an organisation needs to have in place to maximise its ability to achieve Mach 2.

1. Agreed clear and inspiring organisational vision, strategy, objectives and values – setting out what the organisation's goals were to allow effective prioritisation

2. Effective and organisation-wide performance management – including 360° appraisal

3. Critical roles in organisation identified

4. Succession plans put in place

5. Development programmes to develop successors and others to Mach 1 then Mach 2, first senior leaders, then all leaders, then everyone

6. Identification and development of those with high potential

7. Creation of a mutually supportive, collaborative culture through mentoring, coaching and partnership working

8. Communication via multiple channels of vision, strategy, objectives and values through regular communication events at all levels that brought people from different areas and environments together

9. Use of simple messages to spread and embed key actions required

10. Alignment of organisational systems to support the above

11. Co-ordination across organisation of client support for major clients

12. Development of internal brand to align to external brand

13. Encouragement of new ideas and innovation at both operational and strategic levels

14. Creation of an innovation group to support development of new ideas and initiatives

15. Development of entrepreneurial mindset in support functions as well as front line

16. Creation of strong corporate, business and team spirit across organisation

17. All leaders, especially senior leaders, leading by example

18. Everyone thinking 'one organisation working together aligned to the customer' not 'do my job and look after myself'

19. Creation of systems to measure positive effects of change, especially financial

20. Feedback sought from clients/customers on general service standards, then into appraisals where possible

21. Contribution by customers to development of senior leaders.

These are some of the key initiatives or actions that were successful[9] at UBS[3] and which have been used elsewhere successfully and all contribute to Mach 2 being achieved. This may seem complex and long term, and to some degree it is. So the likelihood of people being confused and the momentum being lost may seem high.

However, this was all implemented over a number of years, and only the key information was communicated. This was done repeatedly using a small number of very simple messages that everyone could remember about what they needed to do. This was linked to an inspiring vision of the future in which everyone could see the personal and business benefits. They also saw it was achievable through simple, practical steps. They didn't need to know about the complex details, they just had to concentrate on getting to Mach 1 and then Mach 2.

MAKING THE MACH 2 CHANGE EFFECTIVE

So to get people to move to Mach 2 they will have to change what they do as individuals, and the organisation as a community and system will have to do the same – to become that aligned community of effort and collaboration. This will need to be planned and driven from a central point in the organisation, albeit with input from stakeholders, to ensure that it is consistent, of the right quality, integrated and aligned with what the organisation really needs.

A change management team will be needed to run the organisational elements, and this team should have direct access to the CEO and senior management who will be the 'face' of change. The change must not be seen as an HR initiative, because some in the organisation could ignore it. It must be seen as a business or organisational performance-driven initiative, critical to the future and beneficial for both organisation and individuals.

Thus change management must be of a sufficient quality to allow this. Some organisations view change as part of their day-to-day existence and driven by fast-moving markets or demanding customers; others are not used to change historically and find it very difficult. To help those trying to achieve Mach 2, especially those in the latter group, here are some suggestions that I have found useful in implementing Mach 2 over the years. These are based on the vast number of studies of what makes change go well in organisations, and in particular two studies more than ten years apart. One study looked at what makes change work well, and the other at what makes change unsuccessful. Both were revealing, and interestingly, the results are mirror images of each other: the reasons for change failing in one study are primarily the lack of the things that make change succeed in the other.

Making change work

Boston Consulting developed the DICE[10] model (duration, integrity, commitment and effort) and reviewed over a thousand change initiatives. The four key success factors they discovered were:

1. Regular progress reviews: minimum every two weeks on larger projects; six weeks on smaller

2. Those leading the implementation must be the best people in the organisation, and not just those with spare time

3. Those working on the implementation must recognise the need for change and be fully committed to making it work

4. Those implementing it must have the bandwidth to do both the change and any other roles they are required to do.

Unsuccessful change

An interesting study in HBR[11] in 2011 found that the key reasons for change failing were:

1. People not accepting the reality of the situation

2. Lack of management commitment to the change

3. Too many other initiatives distracting from the change

4. Staff that didn't care anyway

5. Loss of momentum over time to complete the change once the initiative had started

6. Either implementing the change or doing business as usual, but not being able to do both.

Bringing the two together and using my experience of change initiatives to make Mach 1 and 2 possible, key success factors are:

1. High profile launch, and keep up the momentum for at least 18 months

2. Confront reality – people leading change and indeed everyone must see the benefit

3. Commitment – those leading change must be determined it will succeed

4. The best – those leading change must be the best in the organisation and good at influencing others

5. Keeping it simple and focused – minimise the number of initiatives and focus on what really matters

6. Reviews – to be focused on outcomes, frequent and include change sceptics as well as champions

7. Change versus business as usual – people leading the change need to have bandwidth to both implement the change and maintain business as usual; they can't do two jobs at once so someone needs to cover part of their day-to-day role.

Not everyone will sign up for the change at once, but there should be enough to create sufficient momentum to bring others on board if the change is run as suggested. There will then be a constant increase in those engaged and who have delivered change as time passes.

As has been suggested, the change to Mach 1 and then Mach 2 can be immense, but with a high chance of success if the very practical and simple steps at operational level are done effectively. It will also reduce the need for large-scale change in the future, as constant change will be occurring day-to-day. In some ways Mach 2 ensures the organisation never needs to have another specific change initiative again as it is always keeping up with where it needs to be. And that should inspire everyone!

CHAPTER 6 KEY POINTS

Getting to Mach 2 is not that difficult if the organisation is at Mach 1 – people will want to get even better.

- It requires a review of everything used for Mach 1 and feeding in the principles, requirements and imperatives of Mach 2 to go up a gear.
- The emphasis of Mach 2 is much more on spreading and embedding it across the organisation and ensuring that everything aligns to it.
- It's about enabling and supporting all leaders in their teams to get to Mach 2 while aligning them to the organisation's agenda – prioritisation and collaboration – and delivering it.
- It has to be led by example by the most senior leaders and key influencers, and facilitated by HR.
- Support functions must be just as entrepreneurial as customer-facing ones.
- It turns people's thinking from 'me' to 'us' and creates one inspired and aligned organisation focused on the customer.
- It's about 'people' and 'outcomes' and not 'process' and 'data', and about 'excellence' not 'just doing the job'.
- It's about being a place where people *want* to work, not a place where people *have* to work.
- Every leader has to:
  - Prioritise by organisational benefit and collaborate for success
  - Understand and leverage the whole organisation
  - Deliver, or support the delivery of, world-class customer service
  - Be a world-class leader
  - Watch out for their de-railers or dark side.

CHAPTER 6 KEY ACTIONS FOR YOU TO DO NOW

1. Do your organisation's senior leaders understand and agree on the organisational and personal benefits of achieving Mach 2? If not, create a compelling case.

2. Does your organisation have a strategy to systematically develop Mach 2 in all of its leaders? If not, develop one.

3. Do your non-customer facing areas have a clear strategy to use Mach 2 to develop their ability to support customer focus? If not, each should develop one.

References

1. *Driving Breakthrough Performance in the New Work Environment:* Corporate Executive Board, 2013

2. *Driving Public Entrepreneurship:* Accenture 2011

3. *UBS: Towards the Integrated Firm,* Lal, Nohrai, Knoop, Harvard Business School, May 15 2006

4. *Why CEOs fail,* Fortune Magazine, Charan & Colvin June 21 1999, p 69-82 and *Victims of their own success,* S. Berglas in *The perils of accentuating the positive* R. Kaiser (Ed.): Hogan Press, 2009 (p77-96)

5. *Complexity: The Human Paradox and how to address it.* The Simplicity Partnership, London.

6. *Innovations in Public Governance,* Success Stories from Winners of the 2013 United Nations Public Service Awards, United Nations Department of Economic and Social Affairs, New York, 2013

7. Employee Engagement Framework and Survey: Corporate Leadership Council, 2004 (p93)

8. Realising the full potential of rising talent, Corporate Executive Board 2005, p29

9. You'll find more information on my website at www.chrisroebuck.net

10. *The hard side of change management,* Sirkin, Keenan & Jackson: Harvard Business Review, October 2005 (p109-118)

11. *Accelerating corporate transformations (Don't lose your nerve!),* Robert H. Miles: Harvard Business Review, January 2010 (p69-75)

7

UBS: A 'real world' example
of Mach 1 and Mach 2
delivering individual and
organisational success

UBS: A 'real world' example of Mach 1 and Mach 2 delivering individual and organisational success

Having looked at the journey through Mach 1 to Mach 2 for both individual leaders and organisations, now is a good time to pull all of this together to see what happened when a real organisation in the real world went on that journey. Before that it's worth explaining why case studies can bring real value. People often dismiss case studies as being irrelevant to them, saying things like:

1. I work in a different sector or type of business
2. The case is in the past not the present
3. The problems we have aren't exactly the same as I have
4. After this happened longer term things went wrong
5. I'm not at strategic leadership level so I can't use any of this.

In reality, case studies have relevance to everyone in some way, shape or form, and so they have significant value. Why? Because organisations are organisations, they have to deliver certain outcomes with limited resources and they use people to deliver products or services to other people. In this respect there is always the potential for any case study, if you have an open mind, to give you ideas that may be of value to yourself or your organisation.

If the case study is from a different sector from your own organisation, the specific implementation of actions may not be possible, but the core principles are still valid. The fact that it's in the past is a fact – all case studies are in the past – but organisations and people still tend to respond in the same way to certain actions.

Many people see symptoms of problems in their organisations and identify those as the problems, but miss the underlying cause. In a very many cases the underlying problem is the fact that leadership is not as good as it should be, and the impact of this is reflected widely around the organisation.

Case studies reflect changes over a period in time, that performance improved, and that this route to success is still valid. For example, Kodak was a leading edge and inspiring organisation in many ways. The fact that it subsequently became inflexible and had financial problems doesn't detract from the excellence of some of their earlier activities.

No matter where you are in the organisation you can always learn from the experience of others – that's why having a mentor is so good – and case studies let you see the successes and failures of others so that you can learn from them without having to go through the experience, and in the case of failure, the pain. In every case study you are likely to find something that is both relevant and transferable.

This case study is based on UBS, the global bank, from 2002 to 2006. It reflects how success can be delivered in a very wide set of environments. Within UBS were and are a number of very different businesses that have both transactional, that is price-based, and relationship-based interactions with customers. The centres of the businesses operate in US, Europe and Asia, and the different businesses have both customer facing and support function staff across the globe. Thus under the umbrella of UBS are a wide range of different experiences, cultures, perspectives and organisational imperatives that reflect many varied working situations. This is similar to many global organisations.

UBS BACKGROUND

Key points (as at 31/12/2004)

1. 67,424 employees
2. International bank with offices in over 50 countries
3. Main hubs in New York, London, Zurich, Asia
4. Five different business divisions, four of them global
5. Each division with several sub-divisions doing very varied work
6. Transactional and relationship-based business models and cultures.

UBS CASE STUDY

Aligning a complex global organisation to a new strategy and culture to deliver world-class customer service using Mach 1 and Mach 2 leadership

Irrespective of the problems in the financial services sector from 2008, the ability to improve the performance of people via leadership in UBS between 2002 and 2006 has proven the value of good leadership activity to organisational performance and bottom line benefits.

UBS was created from a series of global mergers and acquisitions in the late 1990s and early 2000s. This gave the bank substantial potential to develop into a top global institution by leveraging the skills and experience of all the constituent organisations. Given the many cultures and groups in the bank by 2002, the corporate objective was clear: to create 'One UBS' to enable seamless delivery of a full range of world-class services to customers globally, and maximise profit by so doing. This was aimed at attracting high value customers to the bank and at the same time enabling them to use as many services as possible across the world from wealth management and investment banks to asset management for both their personal and professional needs.

Alignment, consistency and world-class quality had to be delivered in everything the business did. To create 'One UBS', the top 500 leaders of the bank had to be aligned to the new organisational strategy, to make their own business area world class, that is, Mach 1, and to build a new local culture. They would then work in partnership with colleagues to do the same for the whole group via Mach 2 leadership. This would be delivered simultaneously in five different divisions through 64,000 people across 50 countries. So the supporting leadership activity also had to meet a world-class benchmark: in effect that of Mach 2 leadership. Although I had not developed the terms 'Mach 1' and 'Mach 2' leadership at this point, this was the leadership and performance level aimed for and achieved.

Essentially this is what any organisation has to do for both its client or customer base and its staff, but as the scale, complexity, geographic and cultural spread increases the difficulty increases and the chances of success decrease. In the case of UBS, failure was not an option, given the critical business need to deliver competitive advantage and create a world-class global bank. In reality this potential could not be achieved without aligned world-class leadership activity taking the constituent parts of the bank, and then the bank as a whole through Mach 1 to Mach 2.

To be successfully implemented, the desire and capability within the senior management cadre to move into a new world and a new way of thinking had to be found. The existing complex and unaligned legacy HR system was not capable of doing this, the leadership development was not sufficiently effective and the focus was on narrow operational objectives.

The new leadership strategy had to be focused on maximising business benefits, developing capability, enhancing motivation, now Mach 1 – then aligning effort and building networks that focused on what really delivered benefit to the bank – and not just the delivery of a range of products, now Mach 2. The value chain had to be created by starting from the customers' needs and thus the business need, and working back to quick and simple interventions that, when aligned and integrated, would deliver the required outcomes effectively.

So in 2002, driven by the traditional financial services desire to minimise support function costs, maximise business focus and keep it simple, the UBS Leadership Academy was established. At this stage the HR function within the corporate centre did not have the skills to deliver a change project of this type. So to ensure successful world-class delivery of Mach 1 and Mach 2, the team was specially recruited from the best internal and external experts available.

This small team reported not to HR but to Peter Wuffli, the CEO. This direct link gave it the instant business credibility that an HR-based team might not have had. The team's objective was to deliver leadership and performance development and support to top management groups so they could improve their performance and that of their business: Mach 1; and then leverage this to enhance the performance of the whole bank to maximise the bottom line: Mach 2.

The core Leadership Academy team was initially a group of just six people, two in the US and four in Europe, all with substantial experience of organisational change and development, and all capable of interacting at the highest level within the organisation. This level of gravitas was vital to ensure that the first impressions of business leaders were positive, which would allow the team the opportunity to get sufficient face-to-face contact with the divisional CEOs, top management and teams to create an effective working relationship.

However, they had no mandate from the CEO to demand that any part of the company implement the plans they developed. They had to gain their commitment by setting out a clear business case and assure staff that agreeing to implement any plans would lead to real change and not just words.

Having considered a range of options with the CEO for the strategy and implementation, it was decided that the most effective was likely to be a combination of development, assessment and support to key groups plus, unusually for an HR team, targeted communication activity to support and embed the implementation. This would all be publicly led by example by the Group Executive Board (GEB) headed by the CEO and then facilitated by the Leadership Academy.

For Mach 1 the key requirement was to have the right people in the right place at the right time with the right skills and motivation. So the critical new components required were:

1. A consistent global performance management system for everyone, available online

2. The identification of key roles in the organisation to enable risk minimisation through succession plans

3. The identification of individuals to fill those roles through accurate performance and potential measurement

4. The development of those people through a small suite of business-focused development experiences

5. The creation of a leadership network and community.

All the above were designed to deliver the alignment of the leadership group to the new strategy and culture to achieve the UBS vision for 2010. So this was no short-term plan, but a long-term strategy. Once enough people had achieved Mach 1 then this would be expanded and taken up a gear to Mach 2 by driving aligned collaboration across the bank.

   All of the initiatives had to be acceptable to all the different business divisions which, driven by their differing business models, adopted substantially varied approaches to development and decision-making. Essentially this was primarily driven by transactional behaviour if the business was based on product, price and speed of delivery, or relationship-based behaviour if the business was driven by client relationships, quality and length of relationship. Thus the relationship-based clients would be more amenable to taking time out to explore, develop and try out options, whereas the transactional-based clients wanted a more defined and simple option that delivered benefit very quickly.

The initiatives had to bring benefits for each individual division as well as to the rest of the bank to gain their buy-in, but the anticipated speed of delivery reflected the transactional versus relationship cultures. This cultural landscape was also overlaid by national cultures of either the location or the key stakeholder personally, which impacted on the strategies used to achieve approval and implementation. The ability to tailor to local needs yet retain a consistent global approach would be critical.

The existing development landscape was a patchwork of unaligned legacy initiatives created mainly by reactive delivery of HR product in turn driven by *ad hoc* requests from different business areas or individuals. Needless to say, this was not conducive to the co-ordination required to deliver what was, in effect, Mach 1 and Mach 2 across the organisation.

But pure leadership development activity was not enough to achieve Mach 1 effort across the bank; the communication element was also essential to deliver the change. The requirements of the strategy decided by the CEO and GEB were fed into all aspects of the implementation using key messages. Through all the activity, for example mentoring, coaching, assessment, development programmes and communication/networking/strategy events, these messages were used consistently to confirm what was required in terms of both delivery and behaviour. This also underpinned the establishment of a 'moral compass' for the organisation. Furthermore it was also reflected in the use of the same branding strategy both internally and externally, 'UBS – You and Us' that was used from 2003 to 2010.

After a considerable amount of work the global performance management system was initiated in 2002 as the first key step together with the identification of the key roles in the organisation. At the same time the first development programmes run at group level were created. Called the Global Leadership Experiences (GLE), these did not focus on the traditional functional areas but on key organisational requirements for Mach 1 and Mach 2, as reflected by the objectives set by the GEB. These were:

1. Understanding and aligning the whole organisation (GLE1)
2. Excellent customer service (GLE2)

3.   World-class leadership (GLE3)

To keep the focus on critical deliverables only these three programmes were delivered. It was decided that it was viable to introduce Mach 1 and Mach 2 type concepts at the same time for senior leaders when brought together from across the globe for mutual development and to initiate collaboration. This speeded up the process by giving those attending a plan for both.

The programme faculty was selected from the higher levels of senior management, ensuring that the content and discussion was completely business-focused and they co-delivered with top-level external speakers on a 75/25 ratio of internal to external.

The team supported the senior management, teaching on programmes in their development as 'presenters' to deliver presentation content well, and 'facilitators' to get a group to discuss key issues and challenges, and then develop ideas to implement to deliver success. They had to run and facilitate a discussion session as part of their contribution at least as long in duration to the presentation they held. This ensured high interaction levels and improved their own skills in working with groups that many then leveraged in their own business areas. All the content of the programmes focused everyone on the business drivers and actions of Mach 1 and Mach 2.

Participants were invited to attend by nomination from the CEO of their business division, and then formally invited by the group CEO to ensure that attendance was seen as a reward and something to aspire to. They were specifically drawn from different parts of the organisation and locations, creating real working partnerships that subsequently delivered new initiatives, solved problems and added to the bottom line.

To turn Mach 1 and especially Mach 2 into reality and prove its value, an academy innovation group facilitated the development of new business initiatives suggested during brainstorming on the programmes. When appropriate, the team also delivered strategic consultancy or facilitation support for top management teams, for example during strategy development days, to further embed the key objectives and help improve their performance.

New mentoring programmes were also a key component in the transition. Unusually, these started at the top of UBS and cascaded down, rather than starting at lower levels. The GEB (12 top leaders) mentored some of the Group Managing Board (60 leaders) and these in turn mentored some of the bank's key position holders (140 leaders). This was done across the business to enhance not only performance but also strategic understanding and spread and embed the principles of Mach 1 and Mach 2. Feedback from participants indicated that within four months of starting, the programme met the expectations of the vast majority of mentees, and 65% identified a specific personal or business benefit, which resulted directly from the programme.

As more of the strategy rolled out into 2003, the Leadership Institute team expanded, but only the highest quality candidates who would deliver world-class work and maintain the team brand were recruited.

Another key element in the success was a new assessment system to identify future leaders – another group to take up the ideas of Mach 1 and Mach 2 and to champion them across the organisation as well as using them themselves.

The first step was to identify those who had performed well over the past two years, linked to the performance data from their appraisals. Then a set of criteria was developed to identify those with potential. This had to be capable of being used reasonably accurately by a line manager within twenty minutes. After working with a number of global experts, five criteria were identified and fed into a number of simple behavioural questions for line managers to use. This set of questions was then used consistently across the bank, enabling the identification of those demonstrating high potential in addition to the already identified high performance. These are the criteria covered in Chapter 4 on page 136.

Those identified and prioritised by their business were then classified into two groups based on experience. The most experienced, the Advanced Career Group, were then developed via a new single global high potential programme, the Advanced Leadership Experience (ALE). This reflected the key senior management programme themes: understanding the organisation, excellent client service, and excellent leadership. Pre-course self–assessment and the delivery of a business-focused project that solved a real business issue supported this.

Post-course support consisted of coaching from a line manager and having a senior mentor from another part of the business. Fifty per cent of those on the programme were promoted or took on additional responsibilities within six months. During this time the principles of Mach 1 and Mach 2 were again discussed and implemented as part of the process.

The Early Career Group was developed by the individual business divisions' own programmes that mirrored the content of ALE but with a higher divisional rather than group content. This enabled an integrated system of mutually supportive development programmes covering the individuals over a five to six year period of their careers, each of which would build on the previous one and develop it for the next programme. In this way a clear development value chain was created for both individual and organisation that any employee could enter at any point if their performance and potential indicated that they would benefit.

Each year two major communication and alignment events were organised: a strategic leadership conference (SLC) for the top 500, and an annual strategic forum (ASF) for the top 80. These events acted as vital leverage and included discussion, debate, planning, networking, cross-business area motivational and team-building activities. These again were all focused on the new way of doing things, regularly discussing and developing ways in which Mach 1 and Mach 2 ideas could drive better customer service and make the bank more profitable. Creating an aligned community of effort and collaboration was indeed achieved although at that time I didn't think of it in those terms.

Very substantial time and resources were employed to ensure the impact of Mach 1 and Mach 2 thinking and implementation, for example in 2005, UBS ran one of the largest corporate leadership events ever held. The top 500 from across the globe came to Montreux in Switzerland to meet, spend two days planning the delivery of the corporate objectives of the bank, to network and develop mutual trust: and to consolidate relationships and build more across senior leadership. On the third day they were taken high up into the Swiss Alps for a cross-business teams competition across multiple team tasks over a large area of the mountainside. The sight of the CEO of a global investment bank trying to build a coracle out of plastic sheets and piping to row over a lake was an inspiration for all. The event ended with a display of Swiss alphorns and flag wavers, then dinner in a marquee on the mountainside with an inspiring speech by the CEO followed by fireworks. The objective of the event was get the top 500 thinking and acting as one group and inspired by such memorable events to go back and inspire their teams.

One thing that was restricting the adoption of Mach 1 and then Mach 2, and primarily the performance and development of the high potential group, was the skills of line managers to develop this group on the job. There were a number of line managers that did not view such activity as their day-to-day responsibility, contrary to Mach 1 principles. To address this problem, CEO Peter Wuffli made a strong statement at the 2005 SLC in Montreux: 'I want to make it clear that you, as line managers, are the key identifiers, developers, motivators and retainers of talent in the bank. HR is only there to support you in this. This is a responsibility you cannot abrogate.'

This was part of an engagement strategy to instil in line managers both the desire and capability to take on this role, and thus make at least Mach 1 happen more widely. This worked to improve capability and change line managers' cost-benefit analysis of spending time becoming good leaders. It was achieved by identifying lever points that would encourage a change in line manager behaviour, including:

1. Sending agreed messages down the line to encourage the change from Group CEO, division CEOs and line managers

2. Proactive HR support with tools and templates that made implementation quick, simple and effective

3. Stronger weighting of development in the appraisal and other influencing levers.

4. This reinforced the internal use of the external branding 'You and Us', as applied to *you*, the employee and *us*, the rest of UBS.

Thus from the individual's perspective every contact from the organisation encouraged and motivated them to change behaviour in a specific way – to get to Mach 1 and then onto Mach 2 performance. This consistent experience was vital to align firstly the senior management and then all leaders to the new strategy and culture.

By 2005 it became clear that the top 500 had started to deliver the new strategy and cultural change. Most had approached Mach 1 and a good percentage were getting to

Mach 2. Below that level the leadership activity was the responsibility of individual business divisions. There were still patches that missed the chance to leverage world-class Mach 1 and Mach 2 activity across the whole organisation, which meant that those entering the top 500 group had substantially different development experiences up to that point and were not aligned to the new way of thinking.

The Leadership Institute then worked with the business division, HR teams and top management to identify gaps and see where world-class activity could be leveraged from one area to another, ensure alignment with business objectives and create new global network groups, for example on innovation and client service. This showed that collaboration was to everyone's benefit, thus also spreading both Mach 1 and Mach 2 type activity in a natural and organic way to where it was needed, and indeed welcomed. That then demonstrated the benefits, further encouraging more people to look for opportunities to collaborate.

This was an effective way to deliver a consistent Mach 1 and Mach 2 process across the whole organisation, develop more people more effectively, align their effort to business objectives and to do so at minimal cost. This also brought more alignment across HR sub-functions, for example using development, compensation, benefits and recognition in an integrated way to maximise the performance of key individuals.

It was also clear from analysis that to deliver maximum bottom line benefit, everyone in the organisation had to be developed to the full and not just the high potential group and senior management. Line managers were encouraged to develop everyone on a day-to-day basis – a critical part of Mach 1.

It became clear that many line managers, even if they had the desire to develop their people, did not have the capability to do it, so a core leadership and management skills programme was instituted. This linked to existing offerings by business divisions to cover at least the Mach 1 elements at lower levels. The key component was the ability to have effective discussions about the organisation's strategy, the individual's performance and the development between line manager and employee, and then the delivery of agreed plans. These are some of the key Mach 1 elements set out in Chapter 2.

The UBS Leadership Institute had created a benchmark centre of excellence driven by business need that delivered simple and effective solutions quickly. It used a world-class global team that gained initial credibility and then subsequently worked in the closest possible partnership with both HR and the business to achieve a common aim – maximising the performance of the group.

This strategic alignment, leadership and performance initiative was a great success. The significant improvements in the bank's profitability, brand value and other measures are set out here:

Changes 2002 – 2004*

Operating profit	+235%
Basic earnings per share	+266%
Return on equity	+286%
Market capitalisation	+130%
Headcount (total employees)	−3%
Distribution per share (pay out to shareholders)	+50%

(*Source: UBS documents via HBS UBS Towards the Integrated Firm)

Other example changes:

Increase in brand value +51% 2004 – 2007 (Interbrand Top 100 brand rankings)

Increase in Human Capital Return on Investment ({profit + wages costs/wage costs}) 2002 – start of 2007 +24% (UBS Corporate Social Responsibility Report 2007)

Rising from seventh to fourth place in global investment banking fees from 2002 to 2003, an increase of 33% (Bloomberg 1/3/2004 reference Freeman & Co, New York data)

Top Global Private Bank 2003 – 2007 (Euromoney)

Euromoney Awards for Excellence 2003 – World's Best Bank (Euromoney)

Investment Dealers' Digest 2003 – Bank of the Year (IDD)

Best Company for Leaders Europe 2005 and in the top ten in 2007 (Hewitt)

These are just a selection but the bank also achieved improved rankings and many first places in specific areas of financial activity over the years 2002 – 2006.

What UBS achieved is now a Harvard Business School case study[1]: *UBS: Towards the Integrated Firm.*

UBS – THE RESURGENCE

In the run up to the financial crisis, and despite the fact that the vast majority of UBS employees observed the firm's principles of excellence, responsible relationships and high ethical standards developed through the work set out in the case study, a handful of employees did not. The way the bank was structured at the time also meant that the behaviour of a few individuals had serious consequences and counteracted the integrity and professional work done by the vast majority. Furthermore, there were some strategic decisions taken at that time that turned out to have been based on erroneous assumptions related to risk ratings, revenues and incomplete communication and understanding. Thus, even despite UBS's achievements between 2002 and 2006 the firm, like its competitors, suffered during the financial crisis. This demonstrates the importance of **everyone** being held to the values of an organisation, not only by their leaders but also by their peers and others.

By 2014, and under the leadership of Sergio P. Ermotti, UBS had strengthened its position significantly and regained its momentum. In 2013, the firm implemented a global initiative to strengthen its risk culture, building on its strategic pillars of capital strength, efficiency and effectiveness, and risk management – and its principles of excellence, client focus and sustainable performance. The firm began a programme to raise awareness and embed the highest standards of behaviour demanded from its employees at every level. Reflecting the importance of this, it incorporated assessment of an individual's adherence to these standards of behaviour in its performance measurement and compensation framework. These high standards of behaviour and principles align to, and focus on, key elements I have suggested are critical to success through people.

UBS put these principles and standards of behaviour into action in key areas via its strategy:

- Focusing its efforts on areas in which the bank excels and high growth regions and markets

- Further reducing risks – now the strongest capitalised bank in its peer group

- Accelerating a group-wide efficiency programme to deliver cost savings

- Investing in initiatives to support growth and improved client service across all businesses.

This combination of a clear strategy combined with engaged and focused staff – Mach 1 and Mach 2 leadership – will potentially see UBS reinvigorated and resume its position as one of the pre-eminent global banks.

WIDER PERSPECTIVES FROM THE UBS CASE

The overall strategy and key components to drive Mach 1 and Mach 2 used at UBS are still as valid and relevant today for any organisation as they were in 2006, maybe even more so, given the alignment, performance and efficiency the tough economic climate demands and the need to position leadership for the future. The key to success, survival and future growth is ensuring that all leaders maximise their own and their team's performance (Mach 1), then get the whole organisation to work as an aligned and motivated team (Mach 2).

This success can be replicated by any organisation with the foresight and determination to be the best by using the strategies set out in this book. The true value of the UBS experience did not become apparent to me until a few years later when I had worked with other organisations. I saw that what UBS achieved was a road map for success in aligning effort onto critical deliverables, and more recently the way we had built an aligned community of effort and collaboration.

Elements of this approach have been successfully used in organisations as diverse as the UK National Health Service, the Red Cross, top international law firms, those running transport systems, international banks, logistics providers, and many others across the world from the US and Europe to India, China and Asia. It worked at UBS and it works elsewhere for one simple reason: it inspires people because it allows them to achieve what they really want from their job while delivering what the organisation and its customers need to the highest quality levels – a genuine aligned community of effort and collaboration.

KEY LESSONS FROM THE UBS CASE STUDY

- Even if you get the CEO's support for Mach 2 that doesn't mean everyone will come on board – everyone needs a reason to engage. Mach 2 must be seen as a strategic objective driven by the senior leaders.

- Response to Mach 1 and Mach 2 is driven by the current culture, which is in turn often driven by whether the business is transaction or relationship based – you need to create a compelling new culture for all to aspire to.

- For the transactional people – if you can't convey the key benefits of what you propose in less than three minutes don't bother going to the meeting.

- Always align the benefits of Mach 1 and Mach 2 to your organisation's key deliverables and stress the need for collaboration from everyone. This is key for HR if involved in 'facilitating' the delivery.

- Beware the 'not made here' resistance to even good ideas; rebrand if required. Get people to think it was their idea in the first place.

- Use every available opportunity to get the same consistent, simple message across about what people have to do and why – and do so relentlessly.

- Commitment is demonstrated by actions not words. People get selective amnesia about what they agreed to in meetings – hold them to account.

- For some people, emotional factors, for example peer pressure or the fear of being let out of the 'club', can work better than presenting logical business benefits. Remember the balance of emotion and logic.

- With global implementation there are more cultural differences than you think; they may be small, but they can be very annoying to others. Get people to talk and understand each other better. Again collaboration is key.

- Never miss a chance to get people from one part of the organisation to meet people from another, discuss what they are trying to achieve, how they can help each other, get better and inspire others.

- You are trying to build an aligned community of effort and collaboration at all levels and across the organisation – in other words truly build 'one organisation'.

CHAPTER 7 KEY ACTIONS FOR YOU TO DO NOW

1. Review the actions taken in the case study and see how many of them your organisation has taken

2. List any that could be done quickly and easily in the future

3. What are the key lessons from the case study you and your organisation can learn?

Reference

1. *UBS: Towards the Integrated Firm,* Lal, Nohrai, Knoop, Harvard Business School, May 15 2006

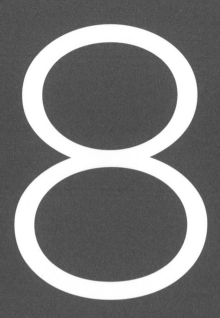

8

Mach 2 – the holistic catalyst
for success in the 21st century
– the alignment of effort and
collaboration

8

Mach 2 – the holistic catalyst
for success in the 21st century
– the alignment of effort and
collaboration

ALIGNED COMMUNITIES OF EFFORT AND COLLABORATION

Over the years it has become clear to me that an organisation is never really one organisation; it's always made up of a number of parts. But sometimes these parts don't understand or effectively work or communicate with each other. In the worst cases they actually obstruct each other's work.

> 'The ultimate measure of a man is not where he stands in moments of comfort but where he stands at times of challenge and controversy.'
> Martin Luther King (1929-1968), US pastor and civil rights activist

As we know, not many people in an organisation are truly aligned to the organisation's strategy, their customers, or the critical areas of optimising risk, maximising efficiency, maintaining effective cost control or building the brand. Yes, they do their jobs as best they can and as they are told, but that doesn't mean there is any significant focus on those critical areas.

Until the barriers across organisations are broken down, and the silo 'I'm just doing my job' mindset that currently exists is replaced with an *'aligned community of effort and collaboration'* mindset, then customers, employees, shareholders where they exist, leaders or other stakeholders will not get the potential value from working together as they could.

There are organisations around the world where employees are involved and motivated to deliver high levels of performance, because they are co-owners of the organisation. This is not just the preserve of small co-operatives but a few larger organisations also work in this way.

John Lewis – mutual effort and collaboration

A UK example is the department store, supermarket chain and online shopping outlet John Lewis, which employs 85,000 people and is owned by its staff, who are all known as partners. Every staff member gets a bonus at the end of the year depending on the firm's performance and there are limits on the difference between senior executive and staff pay. John Lewis consistently performs as well as its traditional commercial shareholder-owned competitors and is renowned for its excellent customer service and well-qualified staff. All John Lewis employees have a stake in the organisation so everyone gives their best. There is evidence that increasing employee involvement in ownership does encourage better performance from higher staff effort, and that in difficult economic circumstances this is better than normal shareholder-owned competitors. This is due to employees putting in more effort to help 'their' organisation succeed[1].

Many organisations and leaders fail to recognise that getting maximum performance from individuals, teams and organisations is as much about emotion as it is about logic. By denying this obvious fact, which they themselves know to be true from their own experience, they significantly limit how well their people will perform. This is particularly true during tough economic times.

The potential improved effort is there, but lost!

Most people want to give their best at work. In July 2012 the Hay Group released a study[2] that showed 72% of workers want to give maximum effort at work, but 33% globally, rising to 42% in Europe and Middle East, claimed to be unable to deliver excellence due to 'significant barriers' put in place by the organisations themselves. So organisations are often unknowingly obstructing the delivery of their own objectives by not being entrepreneurial enough to optimise performance.

In the previous chapter, the UBS case study showed that it is possible to achieve this maximum performance and cover areas critical to organisational success as well as do your job. In this final chapter I want to look at how using Mach 1 and Mach 2 can help people achieve this wider success as well as allowing them to focus on their job. The power of the idea of the aligned community of effort and collaboration is that it deals with the challenges of the new world of work in slimmed-down organisations by helping people to understand the wider context and not just their own job, and that it is part of their job to do this.

So the individual will understand the organisation's strategy, what other teams and departments do, what the customer wants, the wider requirements of cost efficiency and risk management and other key contextual information. This then allows them to focus effort on not only their own job but also that additional up to 50% collaborative effort now required. Thus getting to Mach 2 means that everyone, and not just a specialist few, will understand their organisation's most critical agendas to a sufficient depth to be able to support them. In other words, they are *aligned communities of effort and collaboration* in practice.

MACH 2 **AND ORGANISATIONAL STRATEGY**

As we have seen a key element of Mach 2 is to make sure that everyone in your organisation: a) is aware of your strategy; b) knows how they contribute to it; and c) understands what they need to do to achieve that. It is impossible to envisage a scenario where any organisation could maximise its effectiveness without all those involved being aware of this information.

In the simplest terms Mach 1 and Mach 2 ensure that the only effort that gets applied in the organisation is that which delivers the organisation's strategy. There are no wasted resources, no wasted time, no confusion, and full clarity to allow maximum return on investment. Furthermore, if things ever do go wrong, armed with the knowledge of the organisation's desired destination, those involved can quickly adapt plans to enable a change of operational action to one that still meets the strategic objective. And they can do this without having to wait a long time for clarification on what they should do from those higher up.

This responsiveness through understanding the bigger picture has significant benefits in other areas too:

MACH 2 **AND INNOVATION AND CREATIVITY**

A key part of both Mach 1 and Mach 2 is encouraging leaders and employees across the organisation to come up with ideas to improve the organisation and its performance. This is in contrast to many organisations where – even if not overtly discouraged – too much innovation and creativity by those below them is seen by some senior leaders as a distraction which gets in the way of the smooth running of the organisation. 'You are here to do as you are told and I am here to do the thinking' might not be explicitly stated, but this is the message that organisations often send out.

Remember the best boss list, that showed how encouraging and listening to ideas from others can encourage performance improvements, and particularly if implemented, over and above those delivered by the idea itself? As we know, the ability to be innovative and creative is the secret to any organisation keeping up with the changes that occur inevitably and naturally around it. Mach 1 and Mach 2 encourage leaders to proactively 'give permission' for people to come up with new ideas to help the organisation and its customers, by creating an environment where positive change is seen as part of the day-to-day, and not some special project that needs a dedicated approach which then uses up additional resources through the traditional 'project management office.'

Furthermore, the ability to innovate and create on an ongoing basis also minimises the likelihood that the organisation falls so far behind its competitors, so adrift from customer wishes or the market that it needs to programme major change to catch up.

It is more likely that the Mach 2 organisation will be leading the agenda, with others following in its wake, potentially disrupting current market practice or identifying as yet untouched market opportunities. This behaviour also supports the understanding of the wider context – looking for opportunities to innovate and improve requires a wider perspective – and this then creates further opportunities for collaboration which in turn leads to more opportunities for innovation.

MACH 2 AND CHANGE

Mach 2 allows for change to be a successful part of day-to-day activity through collaboration, understanding of the context and the wider organisation, and constant innovation and improvement. Moreover, if – as above – Mach 2 encourages the proactive identification of change opportunities, rather than waiting for them to be pointed out by others, it facilitates the rapid initiation and adoption of change when and where it is required. This in turn increases the speed of response and ability to adapt to requirements of markets, customers and technology.

It also means that there is less need for the type of large-scale change initiatives designed to help an organisation 'catch up' after a period of maintaining the *status quo*. These often fail to deliver their full potential and distract the organisation from its critical day-to-day deliverables.

When an organisation is out of sync with the world within which it needs to operate, change is required. The greater the gap has become, the more significant and disruptive the change will have to be to recover the situation. So by making constant small changes happen to keep the organisation aligned with the outside world, Mach 2 minimises the potential widening of the gap between what the organisation is doing and the world it's operating in. This in turn either removes the need for large change initiatives, or at least minimises them, and if they have to happen, makes them less painful for all involved.

This is because the collaborative culture that Mach 2 creates means that if such initiatives are required, the willingness to work together and the networks to facilitate this are already likely to be in place, so the implementation will be faster and more effective.

MACH 2 AND FINANCE – MAXIMISING EFFICIENCY/COST CONTROL

As Mach 1 moves towards Mach 2, adapting the behaviour developed in the previous sections means that it can then be very simply applied to seeking out further opportunities to make the organisation more efficient and cost effective. In the previous section it was very much about looking for new ways of doing things, but this mindset can equally be used to look at how to make the current legacy systems and processes better and more cost efficient. Within this, it is very simple to extend the question from: 'how could we do this better?' to: 'how could we do this better and save money?'

The Mach 2 mindset positively encourages this approach. After all, the best cost-efficiencies are often those identified by the people doing the job rather than the frequently used fixed percentage across-the-board budget cuts, that often harm the organisation more than they benefit it.

So from the perspective of the finance director, benefits from Mach 1 and Mach 2 are significant. This includes making sure that:

1. The return for the organisation on the wages paid out is maximised
2. Cost efficiency is maximised in all areas
3. The chance of people doing the wrong thing and running up costs is minimised
4. Alignment to organisational objectives is likely to maximise bottom line
5. Collaboration is more efficient and cheaper than silo operation.

This then frees up time for those in the finance function to concentrate on developing their ability to add even more value to the organisation, for example by using leading edge techniques to plan the future and support business development, rather than be chasing up parts of the organisation to conform to basic financial management.

The finance director as a leader also gains value from Mach 1 and Mach 2. This role requires good leadership just as much as any senior management role. Thus the finance director needs to take up Mach 1 and Mach 2 as an individual leader and also within his or her role as a strategic leader. Using Mach 1 and Mach 2 will allow them and the team to maximise their performance, understand the customer and align to the organisation's strategy.

Often the professional training undertaken by many finance professionals includes little or no focus on the 'people' factors in driving organisational bottom line or outcomes. Mach 1 and Mach 2 provide a powerful opportunity for finance functions to become more proactive and effective while improving their own employees' motivation and capability.

This will then naturally ensure that both new and existing finance systems can be structured to maximise this objective, rather than the traditional approach of making the organisation conform to what the finance function wants. This brings better understanding in turn between the finance function and the rest of the organisation. Hence everyone benefits and other functions are encouraged to support the finance department's absolutely critical requirements.

MACH 2 **AND CUSTOMER SERVICE**

'Happy employees mean happy customers' is a phrase often quoted but rarely acted upon in terms of making employees literally happy to maximise the quality of customer service. We know that most employees are not really inspired by their organisations[3]. There is also the problem mentioned earlier that in most organisations only the customer-facing staff really understand the customers, so therefore they are the only group who can align their actions to support or deliver better customer service.

As we have seen, Mach 1 is likely to maximise the effort of all employees. Thus for those already servicing the customers it is likely to give them additional knowledge and greater motivation to make their customer service even better. Remember the possibility that with Mach 1 you could get up to 30% more effort from up to 65% of your people[4]. That will have a significant effect on the quality of customer service delivered. On top of this, Mach 2 encourages innovation and creativity together with cost efficiency and effectiveness. So customer-facing staff are not only working harder, they will also be looking for ways to make the system better and to find new ways of working better themselves.

This combination of your staff's enthusiasm for the current customer service delivery and their seeking new ways to make it even better will be transmitted to customers. This paves the way for a potential deepening of the relationship, increased customer loyalty and additional services or products being requested. There is an example from the world of retail banking where increases in the levels of effort generated increases in customer satisfaction, which led to a 6% increase in sales of additional services for every 1.0 standard deviation increase in engagement[5].

Making knowledge of the customer and their needs a key element for every employee, and not just those who are customer facing, brings big rewards. With this new awareness, activities that might have used resources but which did not focus on customer benefit can now be realigned to do so. This focus on customer service as part of what the organisation must deliver is all driven by collaboration. Once everyone understands the context of their own work and is also collaborating with others, the 'supporting' systems and culture of the whole organisation are aligned to be customer focused. The support the customer-facing staff receives is therefore not just in general compliance with the organisation's systems, but is aligned to help them deliver even better customer service.

MACH 2 AND MARKETING/BRAND

This naturally leads onto the area of marketing and brand development. If you are able to get to the point where customer service is being maximised by the customer-facing staff and other staff know what the customers want and support those staff in delivering it, you will inevitably have very happy customers. Thus all the work that the marketing function has to deliver will be easier. Inspired staff will help create inspired customers.

The way that happens is the same rational and subsequently emotional journey for both. You will recall we covered the employees' perspective by looking at Maslow's Hierarchy of Needs model[6], where deeper engagement between organisation and employees develops when the organisation enables them to meet their personal development needs – self actualisation – and their esteem needs.

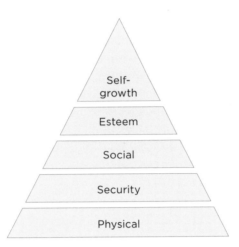

Interestingly there is a commonly used branding model, Lane Keller's CBBE model, which shows the same deepening emotional relationship, but this time between customer and organisation.

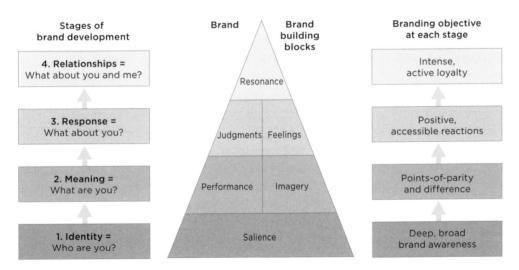

Here the brand building blocks include 'feeling' and 'resonance', with 'positive accessible reactions' leading to 'intense active loyalty'. This is exactly what is happening with employees inside the organisation as suggested by Maslow[6]. Thus engaged staff are simply your internal customers who need to engage your external customers.

So from the marketing perspective Mach 1 and Mach 2 both assert that employees are just as much customers as external customers are. Employees need to believe in the brand as much as external customers do, and for them to engage external customers, as the branding model sets out, they must first be engaged themselves by Mach 1 and Mach 2.

By the time the organisation reaches Mach 2, as a minimum it will have got all the organisation's leaders starting to function as external ambassadors as well as internal ones. With further progress all your employees will be doing the same. From the marketing and brand building perspective, the power of every employee being a potential brand ambassador is extremely exciting and innovative.

If everyone in the marketing function reaches Mach 2, it will enable them to understand the wider organisation better and thus make the interaction between marketing and other functions more effective. Those senior leaders within marketing will also be able to enhance their strategic leadership role across the organisation through Mach 2.

MACH 2 AND DIVERSITY

Diversity is often misunderstood and therefore badly presented by those trying to develop it. It is too often focused on getting more individuals from a certain 'group' into organisations and quickly becomes associated with quotas, tokenism and 'political correctness'. This causes pushback from the 'front end', where those doing the delivery see it as a distraction from their real work. It is also often seen as an imposition from the organisational centre for "PR" rather than 'real' delivery driven reasons.

In reality, diversity is a critical driver of great performance and Mach 2 helps to make it so. The real power of diversity is 'diversity of thought'. In other words, having people in the organisation or team who think in different ways and thus bring different perceptions to the challenges the team or organisation face. This diversity of thought means you get more and potentially better ideas to consider and thus more chance of finding the optimum solution.

Diversity of thought depends on having people from a wide a variety of backgrounds, experiences and cultures, which not only enables diversity of thought to flourish but also that in itself helps everyone become more open minded and prepared to take a flexible viewpoint. This then propels Mach 2 actions, such as being entrepreneurial, even further.

Diversity also ensures that your people reflect the demographic of your customers or end users, thus enhancing the ability to not only deliver the best service but also to understand your customers' needs better in the future. If your organisation does not develop 'diversity of thought' and gets locked into 'group think' then failure is the inevitable result.

MACH 2 AND INTEGRATION/MERGERS AND ACQUISITIONS

The Mach 2 ability to facilitate change also naturally applies to integration of previously independent organisational units and also mergers and acquisitions (M&A). Internal integration and the alignment of different business units on different levels will be identified and achieved more quickly if the culture and day-to-day behaviour set out in the previous section – collaboration, wider understanding and constant improvement – are already in place.

With M&A activity it is more likely that the high-performing Mach 2 organisation will be the one doing the acquiring rather than being acquired, but in any event the Mach 2 culture will facilitate speedy and effective integration here as well. There is significant evidence that over 80% of M&As fail to deliver their expected potential, primarily due to the human and cultural elements.

Mach 2 minimises that possibility of failure by having a culture and staff that are attuned to change, keen to improve, willing to build networks and collaborate for the common good, and constantly seek improvements. So even in the M&A environment where this may exist only in one organisation, this culture is likely to quickly win over those in the other organisation from a number of perspectives, including the business case, personal benefits and being a great place to work.

Even if neither organisation has a pre-existing Mach 2 approach, then Mach 2 can be used as a 'new' and common culture to develop across both organisations, and this will be more acceptable than the imposition of one culture on another. Thus Mach 2 also serves as an inspiring vision of the future in any M&A environment, with the power to bring together all parties in common purpose by creating our aligned community of effort and collaboration. So in the bigger picture achieving Mach 2 is the secret to M&A success.

MACH 2 **AND HR**

Of all the support functions in the organisation, HR has the most critical role in facilitating and supporting the achievement of Mach 1 and Mach 2. This is because many of the elements critical to achieving this are delivered or influenced by the HR function. Furthermore, HR has potentially the most to gain both as a function and for the individuals involved.

The successful delivery of Mach 1 and 2 across the organisation will require HR to go through the same journey itself, preferably before it helps guide everyone else on that same journey. This will require a change in much of the way HR thinks about itself, its knowledge and skills and its relationship with the rest of the organisation and the external customers.

The system that enables the achievement of Mach 1 initially – and then Mach 2 – will have to be designed primarily by HR in partnership with senior leaders and all other stakeholders, in order to produce a viable strategic imperative, rather than just an HR-driven initiative. It must be both credible as an achievable plan and gain commitment for implementation from everyone.

HR must build consensus amongst all stakeholders for implementation and to have sufficient credibility with senior leaders to help them set the example for that implementation.

At no time must the HR function be seen to be leading the move to Mach 1 and Mach 2 or the organisation will draw the conclusion that this is not a strategic organisational imperative. So although HR will be doing a significant amount of the implementation planning and support, that implementation must be seen to be driven by senior leaders who will be inspiring line mangers at all levels, who in turn must inspire their teams to move to Mach 1 and Mach 2. HR cannot possibly make any organisation achieve Mach 1 and Mach 2 on its own.

There is insufficient space in this book to cover the critical steps that HR functions have to take in making the journey to Mach 1 and Mach 2 possible, save to say that as with other functions and indeed the whole organisation, everything HR does and how it does it, must be aligned to the organisation's strategy of maximising customer focus and doing so in a simple practical way. The key elements are:

1. Working with senior leaders to develop 'the way forward'
2. Facilitating the move of line managers at all levels to Mach 1
3. Developing the capability and desire of everyone to move to Mach 1
4. Enabling line managers to build on Mach 1 to get to Mach 2
5. Helping them do the same for their people
6. Linking this all through to the end customer.

Why HR is critical

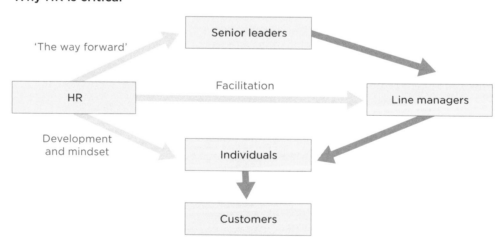

If Mach 1 has traction it will start to reduce the time HR spends in dealing with problems caused by ineffective management or leadership within the organisation, as Mach 1 will reduce the likelihood of these occurring through poor leadership. This in turn will allow HR more time to focus on supporting the movement to Mach 2.

If successful, the HR function will have taken the organisation to the leading edge of potential performance and thus into an elite group of organisations. This will bring benefits to all involved at both a personal and professional level and – as I have personally experienced – will be inspirational.

MACH 1 AND MACH 2 AND RISK AND LEGAL

Mach 1 and 2 can make a real difference to the legal and risk functions. The movement from an organisation full of people unclear about the risk environment, unsure of what exactly to do and unsure of how to do it within any value framework, is likely to produce a number of potential examples of people doing things they should not. As mentioned in Chapter 1, my view, and supported by CEB/WSJ[7] research from December 2013, is that the critical area of risk for most organisations is middle management. This is where the operational decisions that initiate potential disasters are made. This is primarily because the communications filtering down from senior management often miss out the key caveats required around the delivery of the objectives.

For example, if the objective is to make more money, the caveats are that it must be done within the risk framework and customer service values and to develop sustainability. This is confirmed by the CEB/WSJ data that shows increasing levels of risk being shown by leaders as you move down the organisation. The effects of this can be seen in any number of corporate disasters or failures, from the 2008 financial crisis to the 2010 BP Deepwater Horizon oil spill in the Gulf of Mexico.

Mach 1 and Mach 2 initially help clarify the risk framework that the organisation wishes to use by clarifying strategy, objectives and values/behaviour. Once staff know clearly where the organisation wants to go, what they have to do, what's right and what's wrong in terms of behaviour, then the chances of an individual 'stepping over the line' reduce. Furthermore, as everyone else uses the same values, behaviour and framework, then the chances are that if there are any problems, the individual's colleagues will recognise there is a problem and either bring him or her back within the agreed framework or raise the alarm.

This is particularly important with reputational risk, which in many cases is the most dangerous challenge for those organisations not engaged in safety-critical activities. The use of Mach 2 to optimise organisational risk and not minimise it within a clear framework also gives the potential for risk to be more accurately assessed at operational level and more visible. The benefit for the risk function staff is that it's not just them managing risk alone but that everyone on every level is actively managing risk within an agreed framework day-to-day. This leads to much more effective real-time risk management and this risk management is then more business focused, that is, it allows the organisation to function very effectively rather than take a lowest-risk approach that restricts everything or any change unless cleared by a long, drawn-out and complex approval system.

Getting the risk function staff to Mach 2 helps them understand how the business works and thus enables them to design risk systems and operate them in a way that is truly organisationally friendly and customer focused. A customer-focused risk function is currently the exception to the rule. This is also good news for the legal function. Better risk management means fewer mistakes and better organisational knowledge of the critical legal issues through Mach 1 and Mach 2 that will make things run more effectively and efficiently.

MACH 1 AND MACH 2, THE CEO AND SENIOR LEADERS

In a world where CEOs and senior leader are expected to deliver results quickly, where there is increasing change and complexity and increasing expectations of leaders from employees driven by improved education, communication and social mobility, the leader's task is evermore challenging. We have seen that the slimming down of organisations has resulted in a new world of work where many employees are at their physical limits, with 55%[8] saying they don't have enough time to do the work they have to do. Resorting to pressure and coercion, as we have seen, is counterproductive in the long term; your leaders have to take willing followers with them and not herd organisational slaves.

If CEOs and senior leaders want these people to do more to improve organisational performance, then a new way of working is the only possibility. It cannot happen the way things are at present. The senior leaders' challenge to get leaders lower down the organisation to be more effective, inspiring and customer focused, and then to align them to what the organisation really needs to happen, is even more challenging.

But Mach 1 and Mach 2 present senior leadership teams with a way to approach this challenge that is simple, practical, inspiring for everyone and is known to work in the real business world. The strategic, financial and operational figures for the benefits of Mach 1 and Mach 2 speak for themselves.

In a world of confusion, complexity and sometimes an unclear future, people in organisations, and indeed in life, need an inspiring vision and a way to get there. By offering this to employees via Mach 1 and Mach 2, organisations provide the opportunity for those employees to become inspired with what their organisation needs and for them to respond accordingly. It is above all creating an aligned community of effort and collaboration that is what every CEO wants and needs to make their organisation the best.

From the CEO's perspective, this is key. The creation of this 'common purpose', the culture that everyone is working in partnership, heading in the same direction and supporting each other to achieve the common goal, is why Mach 1 and Mach 2 should be their holy grail. As Mach 1 and Mach 2 build the aligned community of effort and collaboration, any work that the 55% are doing that is not fully aligned to critical organisational outcomes is identified and removed. Consequently they are enabled and inspired to give more effort than they thought possible – remember that extra 30% effort from 60% of the staff – and they work better together with the collaboration that drives higher profitability.

It's not about being nice to everyone or removing internal competition. There is still competitiveness in the organisation, as there should be, but the frequently seen desire to be the best to the detriment of others gives way to the desire to just be the best and to help others be the same. This is fundamental to the success of Mach 1 and 2 and a marker of world-class organisations and teams. Everyone wants to be the best, but they also want their colleagues to be the best alongside them; they recognise that working with the best in collaboration is better than just you being the best surrounded by people who aren't willing or capable of helping you or working with you. The 'silos of excellence' ethos is no route to organisational success.

Common purpose and collaboration is always more powerful than individual focus, provided the skills of individuals are leveraged for the group effectively. Mach 1 and Mach 2 put this culture in place and the inevitable result is better performance, better bottom line, happier employees, happier customers, happier senior leaders and happier shareholders where they are present.

This is one of the key differences between many teams in civilian organisations and the military, where common purpose, collaboration and indeed mutual trust is part of the culture, where the objective is to make the whole team the best by working together and not just having a few great individuals surrounded by others who can't compete. That's a group of people, not a team.

Even in organisations where much of the work is done on an individual basis, for example in investment banks, the principle of the team taking precedence over the individual is key. With that view the organisation will, in the most basic terms, do better, and make more money, than if individuals just focus on themselves.

If you don't think that creating common purpose is key to organisational success then, to be blunt, you can never be a good CEO, or indeed a true leader, as that is exactly what leadership is about. The sting in the tail is that common purpose through Mach 1 and Mach 2 can only be delivered if honesty, humility and integrity are present to build trust and genuine mutual respect. And that trust and respect has to be earned.

An occasional 'look in the mirror' is good for senior leaders, as is good honest upward feedback, as we will see from *Undercover Boss* on the next page. It's also useful to identify and think about your own potential derailers. You don't need a black mask and cloak to tell yourself the dark side might be coming out. If you see people running for cover as you walk round your organisation, it's a hint that it might just be starting to show!

- The 6 most important words: I admit I made a mistake
- The 5 most important words: I am proud of you
- The 4 most important words: What do you think?
- The 3 most important words: Please would you?
- The 2 most important words: Thank you
- The single most important word: We
- The least important word: I

I have tried to make this book as simple and practical as possible so readers can use its contents to make a difference for themselves and their organisations. As a CEO or senior leader, you often see the world through the filter of figures and reports from the levels of management between you and the front line. This gives you a factually accurate but probably contextually distorted picture.

You need to know what's going on out there

In the Channel 4 television series Undercover Boss a CEO goes disguised for a week into their own organisation as a 'front line' employee to tackle a number of different roles. The series has covered over 160 organisations globally from public, private and not-for-profit sectors and all types of organisations from transport to healthcare and from small chains of pet supply stores to global courier companies. It therefore covers a wide spectrum of CEOs and their organisations. And there are other versions of the programme in the US, Canada and Australia that add further weight.

This may not be a statistically significant sample but the hour-long episodes of CEOs coming face-to-face with the reality of front-line working in their organisations in real time is both inspiring and salutary. I reviewed most of the episodes for Channel 4[9] and have charted the common experiences of the CEOs globally. From my point of view, there are some highly significant revelations:

1. Many corporate leaders have never been anywhere near their front line in their careers

2. The reality is that working on the front line is tough and not well paid in many cases

3. People sometimes have to do boring jobs but at least the organisation can show it cares by optimising work conditions

4. Organisations have hard working, loyal and dedicated staff: some even regularly put in their own time unpaid but never get recognised

5. Those at the front line understand the customer and how the company operates locally better than those in the boardroom; not everywhere or everyone is the same

6. Key messages from the top often fail to get to the bottom and great ideas and identification of problems from the bottom often fail to get to the top

7. Once employees start to feel the organisation doesn't care about them or listen to them, they soon stop caring about the organisation or its customers

8. Organisations have great people who need better support. It must show it cares more about its people as this could transform the organisation's performance because excellence and inspiration is infectious

9. Spending time on the front line reinvigorated and inspired the CEOs, who all went back to do much more after the programme to make the organisation better for the sake of both staff and overall performance by dealing with the issues above

10. CEOs must never forget that the figures they see in reports relate to real people with real lives and real families. In almost every programme the revelations from an employee about personal challenges and tragedies they had overcome while continuing to work with little or no time off made CEOs describe themselves as 'humbled', 'speechless', 'emotional', or similar words.

Leading by example means getting out there; getting hands-on; being genuine and treating people as equals. I have worked with several CEOs who allocated a certain amount of time each week to visit specific locations unannounced where they would chat to workers and talk about how things were going and how they could change things for the better. That demonstrated genuine concern, did wonders for the reputation of the CEO and increased engagement with the organisation's agenda. If, as a CEO, you only take one thing from this book, then this is one action that will make a difference.

From the CEO perspective, and from my own experience, it's crucial to get everyone quickly onto the same agenda. So if every leader in your organisation reads this book and completes it by the same date, and then implements its message, think how powerful that would be. I have seen it done with my previous book[10].

MACH 1 AND MACH 2 FOR ALL LEADERS – THE SPIRIT AND DUTY OF LEADERSHIP

This leads on to the more challenging side of leadership at any level for you as an individual. Mach 1 and Mach 2 leadership must have within them an element of duty and service to drive that culture of success. This is absolutely implicit in Mach 1 and Mach 2.

So to some degree there are the 'mechanics' of leadership – the steps in the process that have to be taken, for example

> 'Management is doing things right; leadership is doing the right things.'
> Peter Drucker (1909–2005), Austrian-born American management thinker[11]

briefing a team, assessing a problem, giving feedback on performance, as set out in the toolkit in Chapter 3. Then there is the 'spirit' of leadership, which is the way you deliver the mechanics and the underpinning values that drive your behaviour, for example respecting others, working for the common good, having integrity, fairness, belief in those around you and a desire to help everyone become the best they can be.

If you only ever use the mechanics, then Mach 1 and Mach 2 will never come, as the spirit underpins everything on the best boss list that propels satisfactory performance to super performance.

Many enjoy the privileges of power from leadership, but failing to deliver on the spirit of leadership is a key reason why people often have no respect for their leaders and would put in little or no extra effort to help them. Unless you are prepared to use this spirit of leadership you can never be a true leader, and will never reach Mach 1 or Mach 2.

Serve to lead

The Royal Military Academy Sandhurst, which trains officers for the British Army has as its motto 'Serve to Lead'. This seems confusing at first but it simply means that to lead people well and to win their trust and loyalty, you have to put them before yourself. You might be in charge, you might be making decisions, you might be more important, but unless there is the bond of trust between you and your people you will never get to Mach 1 or Mach 2, simply because they won't know if you care about them or not. You have to put yourself out to make sure your people are getting what they need to do their job and be inspired, and not just use them as a springboard for your own ambitions. As we have seen, the simple demonstration that you do care can increase their effort by 26%, but caring is about showing you care for them as much as for yourself[12].

Time out for humility

The idea of duty and service is taken to some degree by a whole country! As covered earlier I was asked to go to Myanmar by the President of the Myanmar Red Cross Society to talk to his staff about Mach 1 and Mach 2, so that they could optimise their performance to deliver the best for those in need. Seeing what they have to do and the challenges of disease, disaster and human strife they have to deal with in their day-to-day working life was in itself an exercise in humility for me, and one I will never forget.

But on the trip I also discovered an interesting perspective on humility and service in Myanmar, which I think clearly shows the value of junior leaders being engaged in some form of service work during their careers. All young boys between 10 and 16 in Myanmar have to spend a time, probably at least a few months, in a monastery learning about the contemplative and community-based world of the Buddhist monks. More girls are doing this as well.

During this time they have to abide by all the rules and do the community work the monks do. This means living off the gifts of food from the local people that they have had to seek out, and working in the community in some way. Some will stay until they are 20 and then become ordained, others can return to non-religious life after a while. However, they can, provided they have observed certain conditions, return to the monastic life a number of times throughout their life. This experience seems to build a degree of calm, humility, thoughtfulness, sense of duty and common purpose in all the leaders I met in Myanmar, to the extent that it is never acceptable to lose your temper there. A similar time out from the normal organisational or school world is something that I think would perhaps benefit many leaders and organisations around the world.

As the world faces ever greater challenges from increasing population and reducing resources, the role of leaders, not only at national level, but in organisations as well, is to get people to work together to meet these 21st century challenges, and I believe, the only way to move forward. A dog-eat-dog or winner-takes-all approach to dealing with these challenges will only lead to disaster for individuals, teams, organisations and nations. This is one of the key lessons that Nelson Mandela has left the world with – that collaboration, not conflict, is the way forward.

At the most personal level, remember that your people spend more of their waking time with you than they do with their families, and that the decisions you make will not only affect them but also those families. That is also your responsibility. So when you think about making decisions, whether to tell the truth or a half truth, to work hard to support your people or not bother, to be a true leader or a self-interested boss, then think about what's right and what's wrong, and what you would like your children, partner or parents to think about the decisions you made in that position.

You, as a leader, can literally change people's lives, and those of their families, for better or for worse. That is a great responsibility and if you can use Mach 1 and Mach 2 to change them for the better then you are a leader and you should be proud of yourself. Just a genuine 'thank you' from one of your people says not just two but a thousand words about your leadership. The words of Lao Tzu in the sixth century BCE provide a fitting finale, reminding us that good leadership has essentially remained the same for the past 2,500 years:

'A leader is best when people rarely know he exists; not so good when people serve and acclaim him; worst when they despise him, Fail to honour people they fail to honour you. But of good leader, who talks little, when his work is done, his aim fulfilled, they will all say, 'We did this ourselves.'

Lao Tzu (604BCE – 531BCE), Chinese philosopher and poet

So if you always try to be a leader for the common good, as well as simply a good leader, you will get to Mach 2. Good luck on your journey.

CHAPTER 8 – KEY POINTS

Organisations are never one organisation; they need to be made one to get to Mach 2, but often the 'system' gets in the way of individuals, leaders or the organisation reaching it. Mach 2 not only directly helps the organisation by maximising performance and the leaders involved, but it also has additional benefits that then enable to organisation to be even better through:

- Aligning to the organisational strategy
- Making innovation and change part of day-to-day working
- Seeking good financial management and cost efficiency
- Maximising the quality of service to clients and customers
- Enabling more effective marketing and brand development
- Helping HR become more effective and HR in turn helping the organisation become even better
- Making effective risk management part of everyone's day-to-day activity
- Working to manage risk more effectively and develop a clear moral compass
- Driving effective change and making M&A more successful
- Keeping an eye out for derailers
- Enabling the CEO and other senior leaders to look for opportunities to take the organisation further for the benefit of all, in the knowledge that the inspired Mach 2 people they lead support them
- People are dedicated to supporting the leader who demonstrates and inspires in them the qualities of trust, loyalty and hard work.

CHAPTER 8 KEY ACTIONS FOR YOU TO DO NOW

1. List the areas of your organisation where, given the contents of Chapter 8, additional benefits of Mach 2 could accrue.

2. How could these be actioned and achieved?

3. How could you most effectively ensure that the achievement of Mach 2 and its benefits in one part of the organisation are spread and embedded elsewhere?

4. How could your people be helped to understand duty and service better?

References

1. *Does employee ownership confer long-term resilience?*, Lauder, Bhalla, Chordia, Jha: Cass Business School, January 2014

2. *Depressed employee engagement stunts global business performance*: Hay Group, July 2012

3. *Driving performance and retention through employee engagement*: Corporate Leadership Council, 2004

4. *Engage for Success: Enhancing performance through employee engagement*, MacLeod & Clarke: Department of Innovation and Skills, London, July 2009

5. *Test of a service product chain model in the retail banking sector*, Gelade & Young: Journal of Occupational and Organisational Psychology No. 78, 2005 (p1-22)

6. *A theory of human motivation*, A.H. Maslow: Psychological Review No. 50(4), 1943 (p370–96)

7. You can find more information on my website at: chrisroebuck.co/files/2014/02/Companies-need-to-be-more-aware-of-risk.pdf

8. *Driving Breakthrough Performance in the New Work Environment*: Corporate Executive Board, 2013

9. *Undercover Boss* TV programme: Studio Lambert, from 2009

10. *Effective Leadership*, Chris Roebuck: Marshall Editions, 1999

11. *Essential Drucker: Management, the Individual and Society*: Harvard Business School, 2001

12. *Employee Engagement Framework and Survey*: Corporate Leadership Council, 2004 (p109)